the
boy
who
said
nothing

'Hard-hitting, moving and informative,
The Boy Who Said Nothing is a deeply personal story
that tackles an incredibly difficult subject matter'
– Nick Owens, Head of News, *Sunday Mirror* and *Sunday People*

'Regardless of how much hate was evident within the war, the
human spirit was stronger. Captured beautifully through the eyes
of a young boy, the boy who said nothing'
– Amra Mujkanović, Remembering Srebrenica partnerships officer

Mirsad Solaković is from Bosnia, a little town called Kozarac.
When the war broke out in 1992 he fled out of the Trnopolje
death camp with his family – mum, dad, brother, sister – and
they all came to England and settled in Birmingham; he was only
thirteen years old at the time. His creative writing shows the
power of arts to heal war trauma and has helped him overcome
such barriers as PTSD, while giving readers some idea of what
today's wave of refugees fleeing brutality will have to endure
even when free – as just one example, Mirsad was tortured
and tormented by one of his school teachers. The author of a
well-received volume of poetry, he has spoken on various media
broadcasts including Sky News, World News, BBC News, BBC
Breakfast and BBC Radio News.

Cass Pennant is a writer, historian and filmmaker who lives in
Surrey. He is the author of nine published books, five of which
have been UK Top Ten bestsellers in the sport, biography and
crime genres. He is also the eponymous hero of the British
feature film *Cass* (August 2008), based on his bestselling
autobiography about his turbulent life and character, constantly
strengthened through adversity.

MIRSAD SOLAKOVIĆ

with Cass Pennant

the
boy
who
said
nothing

A child's story of
fleeing conflict

JOHN BLAKE

Published by John Blake Publishing,
2.25, The Plaza,
535 Kings Road,
Chelsea Harbour
London SW10 0SZ

www.johnblakebooks.com

www.facebook.com/johnblakebooks ▪
twitter.com/jblakebooks ▪

First published in paperback in 2018

ISBN: 978-1-78606-903-0

The right of Mirsad Solaković and Cass Pennant to be identified as the authors
of this work has been asserted by them in accordance with the Copyright, Designs
and Patents Act 1988.

Papers used by John Blake Publishing are natural, recyclable products made from
wood grown in sustainable forests. The manufacturing processes conform to the
environmental regulations of the country of origin.

Every attempt has been made to contact the relevant copyright-holders,
but some were unobtainable. We would be grateful if the appropriate people
could contact us.

John Blake Publishing is an imprint of Bonnier Publishing
www.bonnierpublishing.com

Contents

Acknowledgements

Special thanks to those people who inspired my thoughts and emotions during the writing process. Thank you for the wise words and encouragement: from one word, we have developed the chapters and the book was born.

My sister Meliha Hadzović and my brother Jasmin Solaković, always my guiding angels who stood by my shoulders to help me to tell my story. I guess the war experience has given us many talents, the best one is born out of your love to care about the others. Unfortunately, some of us didn't make it, may they rest in peace: Osman Solaković, Hasim Solaković, Nijaz Solaković, Junuz Jakupović, Atif Jakupović, Fikret Hodžić, Džemal Hodžić, Mirsad Hodžić, but they will always live in our hearts and form part of our souls.

Granddad taught me all about life and he will always be my shadow, in the background watching over me and guiding my footsteps in this world, only one Ramo Solak, a true

Northerner with a smile. My dad Mehemed is my solid rock, and I have always followed his orders for the best results. 'Son, you follow my orders and you will have everything and your dreams will come true.' At times, it was hard to believe and trust, but in the end he was right. Mum is a silent soldier who saved the silent boy. After the war, the fight was bigger than during the war. Mum, your silence gave me the courage to go on and help others who were silenced in the same way and made me the man that I am today with my own children.

My close and immediate Bosnian family and my dear friends who supported me within the Bosnian community, in particular big Mirsad Balić, who I've known since I was a young boy and with whom I forged a lifelong bond of friendship. Also within the UK I am thankful I have made friendships with some special people I have had the honour and pleasure to know; there are too many to name individually but those people who are my friends know who I mean. I'd also like to dedicate my gratitude and thanks to my former students and teachers, plus those professionals I worked and studied with at Moseley School, Small Heath School, Coventry University and Birmingham School of Acting, plus, of course, the now sadly closed Birmingham Sports Centre.

I'd also like to thank the following dear friends like Luke Brown, Luke Smitherd, Joe Egan and Greg Hobbs, without whose support and friendship my life would not have been as full as it has been.

Most of all, I'd like to express my gratitude for Cass Pennant's patience and dedication in getting this book over the line. With immense gratitude we would both like to thank Mary Tobin for providing us with her editing services, and also to thank publisher John Blake along with Toby Buchan and his team for the belief that there is a lot for all of us to learn from this book.

Special thanks to my daughter Jasmina Solaković, who's a little sweetheart.

Finally, thank you to my beloved wife Lejla Solaković, who always made sure that the story is my own.

Some names and identifying details have been changed to protect the privacy of individuals.

Prologue

Before this whole nightmare began, my childhood was like a fairy tale, with long peaceful summers in idyllic countryside full of greenery, open fields and beautiful fruit trees. Families worked together, harvesting everything that they grew on their land, and the whole village felt like one big, extended family. Farmers lived and worked in harmony with their neighbours, helping and supporting each other. The men protected the village, as well as trading their goods for anything they could, while the women carried out most of the hard jobs, including physical jobs on the farm, with the help of their kids.

Our town, Kozarac, was part of the former Yugoslavia, presided over by the great dictator Marshal Tito. It consisted of six socialist republics – Slovenia, Croatia, Serbia, Montenegro, Bosnia and Herzegovina, and Macedonia – and the two Autonomous Provinces of Vojvodina and Kosovo. Living under the socialist republic regime was like belonging to a religion – you would do everything for the people, communities and the prosperity of Yugoslavia, sharing its values and all of your wealth.

History tells us that many wars have started from the middle of Europe. Every fifty years it seems we fight different wars and face different invaders. In 1914, Archduke Franz Ferdinand was assassinated in Sarajevo, one of the catalysts for the First World War. The Axis powers invaded during the Second World War, then this bitter inter-ethnic war began the break-up of Yugoslavia in the late 1980s. It feels like there are a lot of angry people living in this part of Europe, yet people are also warm and welcoming.

Nobody ever believed that the war would rage between people who lived together in small communities. The powerful Communist system under Marshal Tito had taught us to love, support and care for each other. It was that strong that I never knew what religion I was – I thought we were all the same.

Yugoslavia was becoming a superpower, with its industry booming and tourism developing, and its natural resources were exported worldwide, creating wealth and prosperity. Tito often visited and encouraged small communities, companies and factories. They were making their own cars, motorbikes, planes and weapons. In no time at all, it became the third most powerful and resourceful army in post-war Europe, with powerful munitions and a large army. Military service was compulsory and it took one year to complete.

We lived in Bosnia, which we believed was the most beautiful Republic of Yugoslavia, where people were the warmest and most kind, with the best-looking women in Europe. We were surrounded by the beautiful green Kozara Mountains, where we used to ski in winter and long fields stretched out all the way to Ribnjak, huge fish reservoirs, where we would swim in the summer. The Adriatic Sea and coast was a world-famous holiday destination. Bosnia was ethnically mixed, and everybody lived together happily: Serbs, Croats, Bosnians, Jews, Roma, Rimo-Catholics, Grko-Catholics, and Ukrainians. The education system in Yugoslavia had a very good reputation, so students came from all over the world, predominantly from Syria and Africa, and after their studies they would get jobs and settle down here. Before the war, seventeen different nationalities lived in Kozarac in peace and harmony. There was huge respect and tolerance among all the different people, and they celebrated each other's differences. It was a place of freedom, love and care.

As in any country, people had friends and enemies. The big football clubs, like Hajduk Split, FK Željezničar (Željo), Crvena Zvezda (Red Star Belgrade) and FK Partizan, had their fanatic supporters, who were quite often rivals. One of the most well-known gangsters in Eastern Europe called Željko 'Arkan' Ražnatović was an influential recruiter of football hooligan clans. These guys were involved in all sorts of criminal activities, from drugs, prostitution and robbery to extortion and money laundering. Arkan was the most feared man in the region and the mere mention of his name would frighten off other gangsters. He was married to a superstar pop singer called Ceca (Svetlana Ražnatović). During the war, Arkan formed a paramilitary group from his football hooligan clan called the Red Tigers. They were barbaric, and they committed crimes against humanity on civilians, including women and children. His reputation for brutality was such that when people heard that Arkan and his men were coming, they would often kill themselves so as not to fall into the hands of those butchers. During the war, they robbed everyone and sent all the money back to Serbia.

When the break-up of Yugoslavia started, they had a problem with the Northerners – how do we break them? They knew historically Northerners never feared anyone. In this war their strategy was to make Northerners fall out with each other and divide them. This was the biggest loss that the Bosnians suffered during the war and it had a huge impact on how the war was shaped in Bosnia. Fikret Abdić, known as 'Babo', meaning 'Daddy', who came from the heart of Northern Bosnia (Krajina), was one of the most influential politicians and businessmen in Bosnia. He formed his Agrokomerc group, then later joined a Bosnian National political party (Stranka Demokratske Akcije) and separated himself from the rest of the Northerners and joined the Serbs to fight the Muslims. The best candidate to go and break the Northerners was Arkan. He was one of the very few Serbs trusted by the Serbian party leader Slobodan Milošević, who was later indicted for war crimes. Arkan's paramilitaries landed in the North West of Bosnia, but they could never have predicted how tough these guys were, even though they were not properly armed due to the UN embargo on selling arms at that time. One of the biggest challenges was who would arm the angry Northerners.

Serb masterminds Radovan Karadžić, known as 'The Beast of Bosnia', President Slobodan Milošević and the 'Butcher of Bosnia' Ratko Mladić, the head of the Bosnian Serb army, gave the orders to flatten the whole of Northern Krajina and to kill anybody male from the age of sixteen to sixty. But the shelling could not scare the Northerners, the troops could not kill all the Northerners, and even the murderous Arkan could not achieve his goal in Krajina.

The Serbs came up with an even more inhumane strategy and set up concentration camps all across Northern Krajina, where people were beaten on a daily basis, starved to death, butchered and brutally killed. Even then, they struggled to get any information from the hard-as-rock Northerners.

But fear surrounded the mountains of Kozara, North West of Bosnia, and the beautiful little town of Kozarac. This is Northern Krajina: These are Northerners, fearless people, who fought all the battles holding the borders of the North West of Bosnia. They fought against the Romans, the Ottoman Empire, the Austro-Hungarian Empire, Second World War Germans and this war, the break-up of Yugoslavia. The hard gate to break, they always gave their hearts, their souls and their lives for their country to live in prosperity and peace. They would give you their word of honour in order to deliver their promise, even if it meant giving up their lives; they would never bring shame on their families. Northerners were taught from a young age to fight their own battles and never make a promise that they couldn't deliver. The young people had to learn to live with fear, but never to show it.

It is true that Northerners fought against each other: brother against brother, cousin against cousin, the whole family against another family, only because one decided to go on one side and one decided to go on the other. One side fighting alongside Serbs and another side fighting everybody: Serbs and Northerners. There was so much bloodshed. The worst mistake made by the Northerners was to fight against themselves. Eventually, the true Northerners would win through and scare off Arkan's paramilitaries. When the Northerners were united again, together with the Bosnian Croats, they started clearing all the Serbs from Krajina and from Bihać to Banja Luka until the Americans and NATO stopped the war, because they knew the Northerners would finish the war in Bosnia and clear all the Serbs from there. People say that was the only time that all the Northerner soldiers were crying like children, because they could not come home and take the land back from Serbs.

Places like Bosanski Novi, Kozarska Dubica, Prijedor, Ljubija, Kozarac and Banja Luka stayed in the hands of the Serbs and became the Republika Srpska, the Republic of Serbia. The country is now divided into two entities: the Federacija, the Federation of Bosnia and Herzegovina, which holds 51 per cent of the country belonging to Croats and Muslims, and Republika Srpska, which makes up the remaining 49 per cent. My birthplace was Prijedor, my family lived in and around Kozarac, is a small town at the foot of the Kozara Mountains in North Western Bosnia and Herzegovina, which fell into the Republic of Serbia.

I always used to ask my dad: 'Why do they call us "Angry Northerners"?'

'It's because we live for the word of honour – anybody that is trying to break us away from our cultural norms we turn on them,' he said. 'We are not angry but we stand up for what is right and wrong.'

Old people would always describe Northerners as big and strong people; they are not necessarily all big and strong, but they do have very strong willpower and honour, and are determined in anything they do. Over the next few years, that honour and strength would be tested to their limits.

1

True Northerners
with a Smile:
The Solak Clan

I was born in Kozarac, a small town of Balići, on 29 September 1978, into a large extended family, who were well known and respected in the area. My dad, Mehemed Solaković, was a well-connected businessman and a trader. He dealt in everything from motorbikes and cars to farm machinery, and worked all over Europe, from Sicily to Slovenia and throughout Yugoslavia. Like most women in the area, my mum Zumra worked on the farm while my dad was away. She was one of the toughest women around, the blisters and big veins on her hands evidence of how hard she worked. I had an older sister, Meliha, and later, a younger brother, Jasmin.

All the children in the village would start work on the farm from a very young age, learning the trade and helping their families. The village was full of hard-working and good-hearted people; they were grafters, working from early morning to late at night.

Many people liked my dad, as he always had a smile on

his face and they respected his dignity. He helped everyone he could and never let anybody down. Any issues anybody had in the village, my dad would help resolve them; he seemed to have the town under his control. Everyone would help each other in the town and all our family members had different businesses, which meant everyone was protected.

If there was any little quarrel or argument in the town, our name would be whispered: 'He is from a Solak family, don't mess with them!'

Solak was a nickname given to one of our uncles who lived in Banja Luka, who was the toughest man in the town. His real name was Sefer Solaković, but everyone called him Sefo Solak. He was also known as John Wayne because he always wore a cowboy hat. He was the best bare-knuckle fighter and he would fight ten people at a time. When he walked into a pub, all the tough guys would walk out. He used to carry a briefcase, and the kids in the village were always happy to see him, as he used to pull sweets out of it for them, even though it was rumoured that he carried guns in it.

Sometimes it was good belonging to this clan of a family, as we were always protected, but it was also a doubled-edge sword, as people would attack you, just to break down that toughness and respect the Solak family had. They were known as quiet people, but if you messed with them, they would show you their bad side. They had an old saying for Northerners: 'When they are good, they are good as gold, but when they are bad, they are worse than the enemy'. Northerners are described as good-hearted people and when you come to their house, they give you their best spoon, plate, chair and table, but quite often they will snap and a big argument can blow up from the smallest things that other people wouldn't even notice.

My dad was busy working when I was growing up, so I did not see him much and spent most of my time with my granddad, Ramo Solaković. It was my granddad who instilled my Northerner values and work ethic in me. He made sure all the chores and little jobs around the farm were completed. I went everywhere with him and saw exactly how he operated. Like all the family, Granddad was a real tough guy. I remember one time when we went to the forest to get some wood. The stamped wood was free to everyone, but Granddad was also taking the best wood and hiding it on the trailer under the pile of wood he was allowed to take. We had just filled the trailer when the forest security man turned up, pointed a gun at Granddad and ordered him to unload it all, so he could check the wood he was taking away.

Granddad was a quiet man, but no one pushed him around; he pointed to the trailer with his axe and said, 'You do it.'

The man eyed my granddad, who looked fearsome despite the smile on his face, and said, 'Drive away.'

I used to love going to the pub with Granddad; he always bought people drinks and I would get a glass of Coke. He drove us there on his motorcycle and I would sit in front, pretending that I was controlling the bike.

My granddad was raised without his father in a very poor family, and he had worked like a slave in a mill for rich people just for shelter and food. He moved around from one city to another, looking for work and opportunities for a better life. I remember him telling me that he first saw my grandmother on a bridge over a stream by the mill where he worked. She was from a rich family, and when her brothers saw her talking to him, they sent her home and told her not to come back. Then they threw my granddad off the bridge to scare him, and warned him to stay away or he would disappear overnight. He was a fearless person, and took no notice of that threat; instead, he threw the brothers off the bridge as revenge. The family married my grandmother off to some rich guy in the village who had been seeing her secretly. Granddad was constantly warned to stay away from her but he never listened to anybody.

After a year, Granddad went to the rich man and asked him to call his wife, so he could ask her who she loved the most. He taunted the man: 'If you can't do that, you're not a man.'

When my grandmother saw Granddad, she started crying and just pointed at him. The rich man told her to pack her bags and go. She went with Granddad and they lived very happily together. She gave birth to eight children, two of whom sadly died. My grandmother was a tiny creature who worked on the farm and raised all the children herself, while Granddad became the most powerful man in the small village of twenty houses. My grandmother is still alive and well at the age of ninety-two. Sadly, my granddad passed away three years ago when he was ninety.

I learned so many things from my granddad, many of which would help and guide me when things became so bad later on, but one thing in particular that stood out was his toughness and what it means to be a true Northerner. He told me, 'When you look at your opponent, give him the silent treatment; always stare at his eyes and you must punch him first to shock him. The rest of the job is easy.' He always used the boxer

Mike Tyson as an example: 'Look what he does in the ring at the beginning of his fight. People fear him and he is not that big, but he tears people apart in the ring. If you get attacked by a group of people, rule number one is: do not show them fear. Look for the loudest guy – most of the time he is the leader – knock him out first and the rest of them are easy. Some will try, but the rest of them will run off.'

As he was talking he was clenching his fist and telling me which knuckle breaks the teeth. I absorbed everything he said. At that time my granddad was sixty-three years old.

One day, we went to the local shop, where the men would have a beer or two. There was a football pitch in front of the shop, where all the local guys would play in the late afternoon. For some reason, one young guy started goading my granddad, calling out his name, Ramo, and swearing at him. Everything stopped, even the guys playing football. I was sitting on the sand, and Granddad was standing right next to me. As tough as my granddad was, he was very quiet and hard to provoke. Unexpectedly, this guy landed the first punch on my granddad and knocked him out cold. I was tapping him on the head with my little hands to see if he was all right. 'I'm OK, son,' he said softly. He got up and walked up to the guy, apologising, then, all of a sudden, he threw sand right in the guy's face. The guy stumbled and Granddad jumped on him. He was like an unleashed beast, pounding this young guy, who was double his size, with his strong farming hands. In the end, people had to tell my granddad to stop. I saw this guy the following week walking past our farm, and his face looked like a pumpkin. He never even looked at my granddad again. The village was talking about that fight for months afterwards.

Another day, I was playing outside with my friend Mirsad Balić. We were hiding behind the big hedge in front of my house and messing about, using a sling to throw stones at people passing by on their bicycles, horse and cart, etc. All of a sudden, we heard a horse galloping towards us and some shouting and swearing; before we knew it, the horse had jumped over the hedge, landing almost right on top of us. The cart was stuck in a ditch and two big guys were beating up our cousin Osman Solaković. We were frightened as he was already bleeding. I ran to Granddad's house, where he was sleeping, and shouted, 'Granddad, run! Some guys are beating up Osman.'

He ran outside, jumped on their cart and started punching one of the guys, while the other one was hitting him with a shovel. So Granddad shouted at the horse, which jumped up on its hind legs and pulled the cart, making the two guys fall off. Granddad landed on them and taught them a lesson. My friend and I were shouting, 'Come on, Granddad!', as we knew he would finish them off. The commotion brought all the villagers out to see what had happened.

My cousin Osman worked on our farm, and he was one of the first guys to be part of the Territorial Army to stop Arkan's paramilitaries coming in and killing people savagely and indiscriminately. Osman was a hero to us, never giving them the slightest hint that we feared them, and he was constantly reassuring us and telling us that the Serbs were cowards, who could only kill civilians, women and children. He was like a commando or Robin Hood character coming out of woods with his lads fighting Serbs, then during the night he would return to the mountains of Kozara. Nobody would dare go in search of him, unless they had a whole battalion of an army with them – which was how they caught his unit in the end.

There were many other situations when I witnessed my granddad lose his rag and beat people up. One particular time I remember was when we were in a field, collecting hay. This particular land didn't have a road, so you had to cross another farmer's land to get in and out. When we had a full load of hay on the trailer, my dad and Osman were about to start the tractor when four or five men jumped out of nowhere, brandishing farming tools. One of them said, 'Take your load back – you're not going this way.'

My granddad, who was on top of the trailer, told them to let it go a couple of times, but these guys were stubborn. They wouldn't move, and insisted we had to go back. There was a lot of shouting and threats from everywhere, until Granddad jumped off the trailer and called them to come to him. As soon as they saw him stand his ground, clearly ready to fight, they all backed off and walked away. I will never forget that scene, as I learned that day who was the toughest guy in the village.

But perhaps the toughest man in our family was Fikret Hodžić, known as Fikro, a close relative of ours through marriage and a famous bodybuilder. Born in Kozarac on 26 June 1953, he grew up in a little village called Trnjani. Throughout his childhood he got on with everybody and everyone liked him – he always had a smile on his face and he was a loyal Communist. His father Meho Hodžić worked really hard as a blacksmith and they were the best blacksmiths in the region. Like all kids in the village, Fikro worked really hard on the farm helping his family, as well as helping his dad.

At a very young age he learned about the discipline and hard work needed to be a blacksmith, as well as a farmer.

All of our family had massive forearms – which they called Popeye forearms – including me, so I guess I had some of their genes. As a child, Fikro was very good with his hands and started making his own weights from scratch. From bars to plates, he made everything, which is where he developed an interest in bodybuilding. Growing up in a little village, you get recognition very quickly, and in no time he became an inspirational character for all of us kids. When I was ten or eleven, we were so excited whenever we saw Fikro that we wanted to jump on him and hug his huge muscles.

A short person with a wide back and muscles everywhere, he always had a tanned body, and because of his dark skin and black hair people often called him Franco Columbu, after the Italian actor and bodybuilder. All the girls in the village fancied him and always wanted a photo with him, but he only had eyes for his beloved wife Suada, his childhood sweetheart, who supported him in all his hard work.

Fikret was well known all over the former Yugoslavia as he had started competing at such a young age. He was an unbeatable champion, competition after competition, year after year. For fifteen consecutive years, he was number one in Yugoslavia, and nobody could take his title away from him. He had rigorous daily bodybuilding routines that he followed religiously. Also, he had an advantage over other bodybuilders because he made his own equipment, including bench press, shoulder press, lat pull down, leg extension and leg curl machines. He would see the machines in *Flex* magazines and then make the same ones, but he would adapt all the measurements to his own height, so he had more stability while he was using the machine. His theory was: if you are very tall or very short, you have to have specially designed and adapted machines. As he trained harder and his body developed, he won many trophies, and with all of that competition success, his weight machines were in great demand in Serbia, where he was selling them to newly opened gyms.

Bodybuilding had become very popular since the seventies, and, with his machines selling so well, Fikret and Suada decided to set up a bodybuilding club called Partisan in Kozarac; it was one of the first bodybuilding federations that was recognised in Yugoslavia. He trained everybody, young, old, disabled – he gave everyone a chance, there was no discrimination against anyone. This man with the huge smile united all the little villages in Kozarac and Prijedor and brought all the kids together to get involved in sport. We all loved bodybuilding, because of Fikret – he became the Caesar for our sport in Bosnia.

In 1981, at the Mr Universe competition in Cairo, Fikret took third place in the world behind the winner, Arnold Schwarzenegger. This is where the two legends shook hands and became friends. Arnold told Fikret that he was in his best shape ever, which meant the world to him. To get a compliment like that from one of the biggest international bodybuilding champions in the world was a huge honour. Fikret's name was now recognised worldwide and most respected in Yugoslavia. He came home with an enormous trophy and they threw a massive party for him in Kozarac.

Later, after he told us that he had met Arnold Schwarzenegger, whenever we watched any of Arnie's films, we would say, 'We want to get as big as Fikro, so we can meet Arnold Schwarzenegger too.'

He wrote two books, *Body Building For Men* and the follow-up, *Body Building For Women*, which sold really well all across Yugoslavia. From 1983 to 1990, he competed in and won many competitions all over Europe. He was always in top shape and never seemed to have a bad day. Magazines always wanted to use his photographs, and many companies were keen to sponsor him to market their products. Local farms were happy to provide him with the fresh organic chickens, eggs and beef that were part of his strict diet.

Fikret was a great role model and we all wanted to be like him. Whenever he would appear anywhere, we would all run towards him, waving pictures of him that we'd ripped out of magazines, asking him to sign them for us, or shouting our heads off: 'Fikret, Fikret, Fikret, our champion is here!' We wouldn't stop until he said something in his gentle voice: 'Thank you, kids. One day, if you start training, you could get as big as me.'

'Fikret, when can we join your gym?' we always asked.

He would say, 'Whenever you can touch the top of my head with your hand, you can join my gym.'

We would jump around him like excited puppies, but none of us could reach his head yet.

For Fikret and Suada, bodybuilding was a complete way of life. Fikro believed that training outdoors was much better for the lungs, as you can expand your lung capacity further, so therefore you can get more air in your lungs more quickly to feed your body and your muscles.

Suada controlled all aspects of his nutrition. She studied

various diets and cooked all his food, steaming it to get rid of all the oil. He ate up to twelve eggs for breakfast and a whole chicken for dinner. Fikro had a sweet tooth but she would never allow him to eat sweets. One day, we were outside and she gave us all homemade Baklava, and when she went inside the house, Fikro quickly grabbed one and popped it in his mouth. She came out and made him spit out all the cake, shouting, 'Don't you know you've got a competition next week and your body fat should be less than 9 per cent!'

I felt bad for him, but it showed me just how hard and disciplined this sport is.

Training was part of his life, helping others was part of his soul, loving and sharing was part of his heart, and a smile was part of his face.

Fikro would use his amazing strength to help anyone. One freezing winter, during a heavy snowfall, an old man was driving his car with a trailer full of logs and his wheels got stuck in snow and he ended up in a ditch. Fikro's big black Cadillac pulled over behind the car and he got out to help. But, instead of chaining the man's car to his Cadillac, he unhitched the trailer full of logs from the back of the car and started pulling it himself. He rolled up the sleeves of his training top, showing off his Popeye forearms with veins standing out everywhere. All the villagers were enjoying the scene, and all the kids were shouting, 'Come on, Fikro! Push the car out of the snow as well!'

He grabbed the back of the car, lifted it up and placed it back on the road. We were all applauding him and the driver thanked him for his effort. Like a local hero, he always seemed to turn up when he was most needed.

Next to the school we had a social club called Dom, where all the social activities took place. One year, the school had organised a magic show for us, and we were all excited and really looking forward to it. But the school had a surprise for us: they knew that we all loved Fikro and that he got on really well with the children, so they invited him along as a special guest. The magician did all his stunts and entertained us as much as he could, but when Fikret Hodžić appeared on the stage, the real show began.

The magician performed a few tricks with Fikro, and then asked him to take his top off. He pulled a snake out of his bag and asked Fikro if he was scared.

Fikret just smiled. 'Put the snake on my back; I'm not scared.'

The snake was moving its head, its tongue sticking out, and gliding its body on Fikro's silky shining skin. All of us kids were really tense and we didn't say a word. Everyone in the audience was taking photos, and Fikro smiled and turned to different angles and poses so that people could get a good picture of him. Finally, the magician gave him a metal bar, which Fikro placed behind his neck and started bending it in the shape of a snake. We all applauded him and cheered wildly.

That day was one of the best and most memorable events organised by the school. For the next couple of weeks, no one talked about anything else. It is one of my favourite memories of Fikro.

Everyone has a favourite story about Fikro and they are part of our local history, our heritage. We were immensely proud of him, but, looking back, perhaps we didn't realise just how fortunate we were to have such a heroic character living on the other side of the village.

When the war broke out, like many people, Fikret thought that he wouldn't be in any danger; he was a celebrity, a loyal Communist, a sportsman who never got involved in religion and politics. He was wrong, of course: the war doesn't distinguish from good or bad, it simply wipes out the whole population, and for us that day was fast approaching.

2

Innocent Child,
Who Showed Them
No Fear

Sometimes it's hard remembering just how perfect our life was in Kozarac before the war; we were not rich but we had more than enough. We lived in a Communist country so there was not that much to want anyway. There was nothing missing in our lives. Most of the time our parents were busy working on the farm and we took care of ourselves and each other, and the whole village looked out for us.

Looking back now, I would describe our childhood as like a fairy tale. We had everything that perhaps this generation's children cannot even dream about. Nowadays, our kids are surrounded by mobile phones and sophisticated technology that is taking their youth away. We never dreamed of leaving home or leaving our people and our village.

In this part of the country there were Serbs, Croats and Bosnians. We all looked the same, spoke the same language and lived in the same area. But, in the months leading up to the war in 1992, I sensed a change. I began to hear people grumble that the Serbs ran pretty much everything, and that Yugoslavia was not fair and equal anymore.

At this time, my dad didn't seem too concerned, so, as kids, we didn't worry much either, and we carried on with our lives, going to school and playing sport.

I was a good pupil at school. The schools in Bosnia are well disciplined, education is hard and the teachers are strict. Every morning when the teachers entered the classroom you had to stand to attention. One literature teacher, Mr Srećo, was really strict, and you wouldn't step out of line when he walked in. He was a good teacher, but I didn't enjoy his lessons; we always had to study the Serbian writers and poets. I hated the literature and nobody wanted to know about the dead poets.

Mr Srećo used to pick on me, because of my lack of knowledge in literature. We had oral examinations, where the teacher would ask you questions in front of the whole class, and it always made me feel embarrassed and uncomfortable. I thought it was just teachers' bullying tactics. I used to say, 'Sir, I find literature really boring.' All the teachers liked my honesty, and somehow I got away with being a bit cheeky and always got good marks.

My favourite subject at school was physical education and I was best at basketball. Basketball was massive in Yugoslavia, much like football is in the UK. One of the coaches was my hero and I looked up to him as a father figure; because my dad was so busy working, I felt he was never really around. After training he would invite me to have a coffee and a chat with him. He gave me the best advice about everything, but particularly how to be a good sportsman. He used to tell me great stories about when he was young, and I listened to every word, as he made everything sound so exciting. He told me about his military service, and I remember around this time going home from school and telling my mum that I wanted to join the army. My mum said that I was crazy, and that I didn't need to go to the army, as the army would come to us soon enough. The fighting had started in Croatia, which was not far away from our home town, and our parents were obviously more worried than we realised.

At this time, we went to school as normal. I carried on with my basketball coaching and I always did my best; I was very competitive, trying to impress my coach. At school, we joked around as all kids do, teasing and winding each other up, and playing pretend fighting using sticks and all sorts, but I began to notice a bit of tension in the air; everywhere you went, people were talking about the war. Then, one day, my basketball coach started coming to school wearing a uniform and fully armed with a Kalashnikov. One morning in the changing room, as I was getting dressed, I said to the coach, 'Sir, the gun is pointing at me, could you put it away?'

He was smoking in his office; back then it was normal to smoke, but probably not in his office while he was teaching, which probably tells you what kind of person he was. He looked at me and said, 'Who are you scared of?'

'The gun,' I said.

'Are you scared of us Serbs?'

I didn't reply; I just kept quiet, but I was thinking, why would he say that? I knew he wasn't joking as he had a really angry face; I had never seen him like that before.

All the other kids in the changing room froze and pretended

like nothing had happened, but they all got changed in seconds, as the atmosphere was very tense and uncomfortable.

Gradually, we were starting to feel that pressure from occupation and the Territorial Army guarding our little towns and villages from invaders. Our parents used to take turns patrolling the town twenty-four hours a day, together with Serbs and Croats, who were the minorities in our Bosnian village. It was May 1992, and the wise people in the village knew the war was getting closer to us.

Our uncle Hašim Solaković warned my dad, 'The war is almost on our doorstep and it will be a nasty bloody war.'

My dad always thought we would be safe; he used to get angry with his uncle, and tried to explain to him that he had lots of friends and was well respected. He said that we would not be harmed, and it would be the same with the whole village. Their arguments would last for a couple of hours each day, but still my dad would not believe him.

On the TV there was some coverage of the war in Croatia. It was clear that Yugoslavia was breaking apart, but it all seemed a million miles away from our sleepy little town. TV news was about as interesting to me as those literature classes with Mr Srećo. Yet, looking back, I sensed something was changing, just little things. Mum and Dad seemed anxious; you know when your parents are trying to appear normal, so as not to worry you? My dad would give us all lingering looks before he left the house to go to work. Normally, he left with a spring in his step. These days it was like he half-expected not to come back.

'My son,' he said, 'if the dogs of war turn up at our door, you must say nothing, even if your life depends on it. Your silence might distract them, and you might have a better chance of surviving by not showing them fear.'

I listened very carefully, absorbing his every word, my eyes alert with fear. I didn't say a word in reply to my father, but a clear tear rolled down my soft cheek. But I was too embarrassed to wipe it, too scared to cry, to show fear to my dad. It was clear he was no longer so confident the war would not touch our family.

'Do not lose your honour. Do not embarrass your family,' he said, raising his deep voice. 'My life might be in your hands. I do have a few enemies who could use this opportunity to target me during the war.'

At school our teachers started to say that we might finish this academic year in May instead of July, just for safety reasons. It didn't make much sense to us, but we were only kids and of course we would be happy if the summer holidays began early, not knowing what was around the corner.

Something strange happened during the last couple of days of school before the war broke out. A lot of kids started acting out war scenes – it was like a game but we obviously sensed something bad was about to happen. I remember my school friends Siniša and Saša Baltić looking out of the window at the minaret of a mosque and saying, 'Do you think if we had a bazooka we could take that minaret down?'

We all crouched on our knees, pretended that we had a bazooka on our shoulders and fired. Then we made the noise of an explosion. Siniša and Saša's granddad had helped to build that mosque, and then at the end the Serbs destroyed it. It almost felt that the Serbs knew more about the war than us and what was about to happen.

I remember my last day in school, the teachers had to give us our final grade for the year and my overall pass was A. It was the top grade level five. I ran home so excited to tell my mum and dad, as my dad had promised me a new motorbike if I got the level-five pass. As I reached home, I found my mum working in the garden, and I just managed to say, 'Mum, I've got the level-five passes for this year!' when the siren went off to signify the war had started. My mum grabbed me and ran into the house to get her belongings. People started panicking and running up and down the street, not knowing what to do or where to go. I had never seen my parents more worried and concerned.

What will happen now? Who will go against whom and why?

What we had once seen as a TV report of war in Croatia was now happening for real in Bosnia: we were in the Serbian-dominated part of Bosnia, not a good place to be. We started to hear about villages being attacked and non-Serbs being kicked out. People were dying. At one point, we ran to our Serbian neighbour, Dušanka, to hide, and she said she would save us all. We stayed in her garage briefly, but people had become paranoid about who they could trust now and soon started panicking, saying that we should not have stayed with her, that she would get us all killed. Eventually, we all went back to our homes hoping for the best.

My dad stopped going to work; he was too well known and it was too dangerous to go out. In the end, he didn't have to – they came to us. One day, some men burst into our house and took all our money and everything they could carry, even the TV. We had watched the war unfold on it, now it even claimed the TV itself. Anything they couldn't carry, they smashed. They weren't soldiers, they were just thugs in uniforms.

But it wasn't enough for them to rob us, because then it happened, the event that would change my life forever.

Suddenly, all the looting and destruction stopped as their officer arrived – it was my basketball coach, but even now I can't mention his name for my own safety. They dragged my dad outside in front of the huge hedge, and I could hear them talking to him: 'Hey, Mr Big Shot, not so big now, are you, eh? Look at you now, you filthy Turk, you are nothing! All your money, your business and your house are now ours. I bet with all that money you ripped off from the honest Serbs you've been supplying guns to the Muslim guys, eh? You filthy Turk!'

My dad just kept quiet.

I thought I knew fear – how stupid I was! Fear up until that point had been about whether I would lose some stupid basketball match. This was a different ballgame. They took me outside to where my dad was. He was on his knees, his head hung low, surrounded by these drunken thugs, pointing their guns at him and laughing.

'Don't say anything, son,' he whispered to me. He was scared, of course, but somehow he was still strong; there was no panic in him. He knew not to provoke them.

My coach said to me, 'My Ustaše little Turk friend, your dad will be watching when I kill you – he will be our audience.' (The Ustaše – pronounced *oostahshay* – were a fascist terrorist organisation founded on Croatian nationalism in 1929.)

He turned to my dad. 'I bet you want to call out to your boy, eh? I bet you supplied weapons to the rebels. If you tell us everything, we'll let your boy go ... or would you like to see him scattered over your fields? You'll be ploughing him for months.'

And so I stood in what I thought was to be my execution spot with my family's life in my hands, while they were hitting my dad and questioning him, trying to make him look at me. He just kept his head down – he knew that if he looked at me his heart would have broken. I wanted to call out to him, to make it stop; but I somehow knew that would just make it harder for him and for me. So there we were with each other's life in our hands. Oh yes, I knew fear that day and it seemed to go on forever. That was the longest day of my life.

All of a sudden, I saw my cousin Sandra Solaković; she was only fifteen at the time but she was brave. She said to the soldiers, 'He's only a little boy – what has he done wrong? Let him go!'

I was concerned about her, as we'd heard that some of the soldiers had raped girls. I motioned to her with my head to go away, then her mother, my aunt, came out and brought her back inside the house.

Nobody could help me. I'd wet myself by now, but still stood like a soldier in front of the officer in complete silence, scared, embarrassed, all sorts of things going through my head: fear, death, honour, will my dad disown me, will I die, will they kill me?

They stripped me naked behind the bushes and started hitting me. My dad was in front of me with his head still down and my mum could hear the noises as they beat me, screams that I tried to hide. She was crying out, 'Take my life instead! He has done nothing wrong – he is just a little boy.'

Next, they forced me through the hedge in my bare feet to look for weapons, and I stumbled on to my cousin's army belt. When I didn't find anything, they got even angrier and said, 'There must be munitions and guns here for the soldiers – we know your dad supplied them.'

As I went further down that hedge, I found an army knife, which one of the soldiers quickly grabbed off me. I thought he was going to stab me to death. Instead, he cut a cross deep into the skin on my forearm, just missing my vein, and then he drew another cross on my chest in blood. Strangely, I didn't feel any pain at the time as my brain was just focusing and concentrating on survival. I kept quiet; even my tears were drying up. My mum was so distraught she had an epileptic fit, and she has suffered with epilepsy ever since, even now, twenty-five years later. My dad was under huge pressure and fear was inevitable, but he still pretended that he was fearless.

It is very hard to explain that day. For them it was like a game and we were at their mercy. Angry men wearing Serb Militia police uniforms told my dad to give them a plum drink called Šljivovica, a very strong spirit, and, as they got drunk, they couldn't stop laughing. They were hitting me with their truncheons, and the more they drank, the harder they beat me. By now, I was just hoping for a quick death. All sorts of things went through my head: when will this stop? Is my mum OK? Why is my dad not helping me – what kind of chicken is he? All of this started because of him. He is the toughest man in the town – maybe he'll jump out at the soldiers, grab their weapons and kill them to free his son, like they do in films. Where are those fearless Northerners who used to run the town? It felt like everybody went underground and I was alone, left in the hands of evil invaders.

I had never seen my dad more quiet, his head hung down, hoping they would not kill his little boy. All sorts of things must have been going through his head too: the powerful man he was, what he used to do and the people he used to know.

Then one of the soldiers put two grenades into my trembling hands. I didn't even know what they were or how you activated them. In my mind, the whole world stopped – the life of my family and village was literally in my hands. I remembered my dad's words: 'Do not show them fear.' But how does a young boy not show fear when he is holding two bombs? I had only ever played with toy guns, now I had real grenades in my little skinny hands, my palms sweating. My whole body began to shake – it was like a tornado deep inside me.

My old sports teacher addressed us again. He said to my dad, 'Call out to your boy.'

My dad said nothing.

'Call to him.'

My dad said nothing.

'Ask your son if his arms are aching.'

My dad said nothing …

Then he turned to me: 'What kind of father is this who lets his son die?'

I said nothing.

'Go on, call your father for help!'

I said nothing.

'Like this … "Oh, Dad, please help me."'

I said nothing …

It seemed to go on and on, the pointless questions followed

by our silence. The muscles in my arms were burning now; it was agony. Then just when I thought I couldn't hold out any longer, he came over and put the pins back in the grenades. 'Get him out of my sight.'

Then he said to me: 'I bet you want to hit me now.'

'No, sir.'

'Didn't I train you to be a fighter? Let me tell you something: I know you hate me now, but if you do nothing, in years to come you will hate yourself.'

He was staring at me. I was so scared, too scared to hit him.

As he was leaving, he said chillingly, 'One day, we'll meet again.'

The following day, once the shock and adrenalin had worn off, I felt the pain of the beating, my skinny body covered in bruises, but this was only the start of our ordeal.

Over the next few months, fighting for survival became an everyday thing. It was like a game of death: if you got through the day without a bullet in your head, you would be a winner.

We would lose many family members over the next few years, and, sadly, our uncle Hašim was one of the first victims, as he was involved in politics. A few days after the soldiers came to our house, he disappeared. Then somebody from the village came and told us that they had found him in the bushes. My dad and uncles drove the tractor to get him and brought him to our house on a trailer. That was the first time in my life that I had seen a dead body. I thought he was alive when I climbed on the trailer and I saw his legs and head, but his stomach was completely blown away. My dad shouted at me to get down. I jumped off and ran in the house, shaken and confused, not knowing what was going on. Our dear relative and childhood bodybuilder hero Fikret Hodžić was also murdered in the early days of the war, but we would not hear the full story of what had happened to him until much later.

Our own lives were also in danger. A few days later, another Serbian unit came to our village and the surrounding villages, rounded up all the non-Serbs and took us to a concentration camp. You wouldn't believe where they imprisoned us. Yes, in my school: Osnovna Škola Bratstvo Trnopolje.

3

From School to Death Camp

My school was no longer a school but a concentration camp for anybody non-Serb they considered an enemy. This once beautiful country had been turned into a living hell. In my school, the lesson now was how to stay alive. We were starved and beaten on a daily basis. There were many people there, mostly Bosniaks but also some Croats. One day as I was going to the toilet, which was outside in the open with no sanitation, one of the guards spotted me and took me straight into the interview room where they questioned people and beat them up. It was my old sports teacher again, who was now a concentration camp guard.

From outside, I had heard people screaming as they were being beaten, and now inside this little room full of fear I could see it was full of blood, the white walls smeared with red, and it smelled of death, like rotting animals. It was a dark room, with a little rotten window, and hazy with cigarette smoke. Ironically, it had once been a first-aid room attached to a little medical centre when we were at the school, but now it helped no one. Hundreds of people went through that room and most of them didn't come out alive.

I was really shaken and frightened; I was only thirteen and this was the second time that they were interrogating me and threatening to kill me – the least I could expect was a good beating, but, if that was all they did to me, I would be happy with that.

As I was alone this time, they were hoping I would tell them something about my dad. I still had the bruises from the first beating outside my house. They tortured me again to make sure I told them everything, but of course I didn't say anything. It lasted for a couple of hours but it felt like I was there all day. I was told later that I was the only child who went there and that I was lucky to come out alive. One old man told me that I was lucky that I was interviewed in the morning and the soldiers were not drunk, as if I had been taken into that room during the evening I would probably have been killed.

Most of the Serbian soldiers who were torturing people in that interview room had come straight from the front line, where they might have lost a relative, a father, brother or cousin, or a friend. They were very angry and that was their way of getting revenge and dealing with their loss: beating innocent civilians to death: cowards, soldiers with no hearts, beating up an innocent child.

All the time I had this recurring nightmare. I hated sleeping because I relived the hell over and over.

I will never forget that morning – very quiet, misty, the mysterious sounds of people whispering hanging in the air, threatening to betray them. They wanted to disappear; to be airlifted above all the problems to peace. Here I was, in my own school where I was taught how to become a good honourable citizen of this world, fighting for my life. Already questioned and tortured twice, I was too scared to wait for my third questioning, as in most cases people didn't come back alive.

As I walked shakily out of the interview room I saw my dad selling cigarettes. He later told me that they had given him the whole pack and if he didn't sell them by the end of the day they would kill him. My dad was a businessman, but he had never done business like this before; his life depended on selling the cigarettes. Apparently some people turned on him and said, 'Are you going to be a money grabber in this hellhole?'

But he sold the cigarettes and he survived. Later on, people understood why he had to do it.

All we could hope for now was to keep our heads down and not upset anyone so we would survive. We no longer knew the rules but we had to try to play by them anyway.

My parents were so tense, especially my mother. When I looked at her, she had aged so quickly that new wrinkles seemed to be appearing on her face every day. She had all three of us children under her arm, Meliha, Jasmin, who was only three at the time, and myself, but I was the one that they wanted so badly. She could never understand why; she was risking everything to save me, even her own life. My dad was always with us, most of the time with his head down, but it was no longer my father who could save me, but my mother.

At night, we were squeezed into a room on top of the Dome; the building where we used to watch theatre, magicians and stand-up comedians had become a place of horror, torture and killing of innocent women and children. I was scrunched up in a little corner like a ball behind my mum's back. That was the only bit of heat that I got during the long cold nights, as the wall behind me was freezing cold. We had a blanket that covered some parts of my body and some of my mother. My younger brother Jasmin was next to me, completely muted. I didn't realise at the time that even babies sense the fear and keep completely silent. My mother pretended that I was not there, and the blanket was disguising my existence. My grandmothers were on either side of me to cover any remaining sight of me. Breathing was the biggest challenge, as I had no air, squashed from all sides as I was shielded by my family like a little chicken. At this point, we did not trust anybody, as everyone was fighting for his own survival.

We were expecting to be killed where we slept, probably burned alive or maybe they would throw in a few hand grenades to finish us all off. In this dark, fear-filled room, all you could hear were ghosts talking with one another in a barely audible whisper. Anything we said echoed downstairs, where the camp guards were.

Everything had fallen on me, a thirteen-year-old boy, just because they suspected my dad of supplying munitions. My mum was so scared; her little boy had no human rights in his own school, he had been targeted. I could hear people in that room whispering, 'The boy has done this and that, and we are not part of that.'

Perhaps they were scared I would grass them up for something, get them all executed, but I didn't know anything.

The worst thing for me was the toilet; I suffered with diarrhoea as I hardly ate anything. My mum would stretch a little piece of bread between us three children, just enough to stop our stomachs rumbling. When I was desperate to go to the toilet, she would not let me out in case the soldiers spotted me again. She told me to use a bag, instead of going to the toilet. People started complaining about my mum's actions, but she was good at keeping quiet and would do anything to keep me safe. That became the norm, but as people worked out that Mum was too frightened to let me out to the toilet, she became even more scared that someone might grass her up. All she was trying to do was save her son.

What does a little boy know about the war? Does he know how to hate? How would he know how to discriminate? How can he hurt anyone? What has he done so wrong to be interrogated by camp guards and fully armed soldiers? All he knows in his heart is that he has given a promise to his father: a vow of silence. Nobody in that room understood the importance of the boy's silence, nor that it could save all of their lives. Not even the boy himself knew that, but he knew what it meant to be a true Northerner: the key is not to show fear and never to be scared of death.

Using a bag instead of going to the toilet became a normal occurrence, as the soldiers started to come in more frequently, taking the young girls out late at night for questioning, and I was so scared that the girls would say where I was. The screaming voices of young girls being raped still echoes in my ears, as their voices were still undeveloped and shallow. I sometimes wonder if the actions of those drunken soldiers were part of the punishment for the girls for not telling them where I was hidden. Other girls were petrified, waiting their turn, for what now seemed inevitable.

Some of the camp guards were the teachers who had taught us in that very school, yet they couldn't do anything. I later heard that some of the rapists had been teachers themselves. How could that happen? What made those people commit such atrocities? Where was their humanity? Did someone make them do that, or was it their own choice? These questions have always preyed on my mind, especially now I have a child of my own – I know I could never do that to someone's child.

One day, a soldier burst in, very angry and kicking people with his heavy boot, saying, 'I lost my best friend on a battlefield – you guys will get it tonight.'

The more volatile the soldiers became, the more we stuck together; we stopped falling out with each other, and started helping each other instead. We would all huddle together so when we got a beating at least the kids would be missed out, and it was harder for the soldiers to walk on top of us, as when they were drunk they would often tumble over and fall on us. That was one of the soldiers' biggest fears – that, if they fell over, someone might pull their gun off them and kill them with it.

One day, this particular soldier flew in like a tornado, kicking the door off its hinges; my mum put me in a big bag, that's how scared she was. That was a terrible night and in the morning, soldiers were taking men out to help with burials. At the end most of the guys would be killed to destroy the evidence.

There were only sad moments in that Dome; there was no hope for happiness.

* * *

One sunny morning, for the first time, I heard the birds singing, and my grandmother said, 'The birds will bring us good news.'

Suddenly, the soldiers started shouting, 'Everybody out!'

We were scared to come out, as quite often they would just start firing a machine gun to terrorise us. Who would come out first? We were grouped together like naughty children who didn't do their homework, but this was nothing so trivial. Gradually, people started walking down the stairs, and we were made to stand in long queues. Soldiers would take out the men and send them to the other side of the camp, although they didn't bother elderly men.

Then my dad's turn came. His head was down and one of the soldiers shouted, 'Where the fuck do you think you're going, motherfucker?'

As he raised his head, another soldier recognised him and said, 'This man is ill – let him go.'

My dad had had a heart operation before I was born and everybody knew that. Even today, he doesn't know who saved him, but it was probably someone that he got out of trouble in the past.

We didn't know where they were taking us and we were too afraid to ask. It was the longest queue that I have ever seen in my life.

We had been cut off from the world and there was no communication with anyone outside the camp. The outside world didn't have a clue what was happening with us. Nobody knew that the concentration camps even existed in Bosnia until British journalist Ed Vulliamy discovered them in the summer of 1992. Over 100,000 Bosnians were killed during the war in Bosnia from 1992 to 1995, including civilians, women and children. I guess we were lucky to survive.

On that day, we were ethnically cleansed and expelled from Kozarac to Gracanica in the North East. We were taken to the train station in Trnopolje, a couple of hundred metres from the concentration camp. Although we were traumatised, horrified and didn't know how many of us they would kill, we still had some hope for survival; we were just hoping for the best. As we had not been given any food for the last couple of weeks, hunger was taking over and we hoped we were going somewhere better, where at least the children would be fed.

They started loading people on to a train they used for animals. The wagons were small and full of animal waste but none of us complained. As people were walking in, they would whisper to each other, 'They will kill us all!'

Some people even suggested we should try to jump out when the train set off, but we soon realised the doors were locked from the outside. The wagons were dark, with no air, and we were crammed on top of each other like sardines.

My little brother Jasmin was crying and he had diarrhoea. A woman next to my mother started complaining about the smell. That was the only time that I heard my usually calm mum snap: 'My child is frightened and he is three years old.'

When the train stopped at a station in a different town, I heard soldiers shouting, 'Bloody *Balije* – we should kill them all, don't take them anywhere.' (*Balije* is a word used for Bosnian Muslims and it is the most offensive word to use to describe a particular race of people.)

The wagon doors opened and we thought they were going to start firing at us, as the soldiers were fully armed. Instead, they threw us a bag and one of the soldiers said in a deep, threatening voice, 'Make sure this bag is full of money, if you want to go any further alive.'

People didn't know what to do at first but then they started to produce the money they had hidden, stitched into secret pockets of their clothes so that the soldiers wouldn't find it. I must admit that money came in handy, as our grandmother had done the same. Eventually, they collected what we hoped was enough money to get us past this station. The soldier peered in again, looked at the bag, grabbed it off an elderly lady and shut the door, saying, 'You are lucky this time around.'

We breathed a sigh of relief, thinking, that's it, we got through this, but what's next?

There were three more stops and the procedure was exactly the same. But each time it was more tense, as the soldiers at the different train stops were getting more drunk as the night wore on, and shouting their heads off, demanding more money. But of course with each station, our family members had less and less money to give.

I will never forget that day. Our last stop was on top of a bridge, and the soldiers started shouting, 'Hurry up, get out!'

We were jumping off the wagons like kids leaping into water. Elderly people in wheelchairs who couldn't walk were being pushed off the bridge by their family members. That was the most horrific picture that stuck in my head and it will live with me for the rest of my life. I heard women screaming, as they had to push their parents off the bridge. Both my grandmothers who were in their late sixties jumped off the wagons like they had springs in their legs – we just wanted to get off that bridge as quickly as possible when the soldiers started shooting and shouting at us to move. In front of us, all I could see was a dark tunnel with no light. I thought, this is it, this is where we are all going to die.

The tunnel was pitch-black, you couldn't even see your own hand in front of you. We started running through the tunnel, falling on top of each other, losing our family members and our belongings as we fled. We lost contact with both of our grandparents that day and it took us two weeks to find them. It felt like this tunnel had no end. We were sweaty, exhausted and hungry, running for our lives. All of a sudden, some elderly people in front of us started shouting, 'Nobody come out – they might fire at us on the way out!' At the same time, we were looking behind us, scared that the soldiers might run us over with tanks. We slowed down, catching our breath and looking for our beloved family. I will never forget how tightly my mum's sweaty firm hand gripped mine, pulling me along the tunnel with my sister, while my dad was carrying my younger brother.

Then we stopped, everything stopped; there was an eerie absolute silence.

All of a sudden, the soldiers started calling out, 'Come out! Don't be afraid – this is our side! You are on our territory, you are safe now.'

But we didn't believe them – they couldn't persuade us to come out.

So the soldiers came into the tunnel to get us, holding the kids by their hands and saying gently, 'It's OK, now you will be OK. Nobody will die.'

We were still petrified; then we heard some people saying, 'Look at the uniforms – these are Bosnian soldiers.'

Then we started crying, but they were tears of happiness and relief that somehow we had got through all of this and survived with our most precious family.

Not all of us made it, sadly, but most of us did.

This part of Doboj was still controlled by the Bosnian army, and as we started walking towards the villages, the local people were standing outside their houses holding cheese pies, bread, water and fruit for us. We were like hungry children coming from school. I was so thirsty that when a woman gave me a bottle of water I drank it all at once, two litres of water in one gulp! The woman looked at me amazed and said, 'Do you want more?'

My mum said, 'That is enough – we must go now.'

The villagers organised for tractors with carts to help the elderly people who couldn't walk any further.

As we were walking, we felt like we were reborn. I felt in my heart that there was a light switch and someone had just switched it on!

Our walking turned into marching through our motherland, our freedom regained. I could never explain that overwhelming feeling, as I was too young to think what's next, but all I remember was that light switch in my heart and I started loving and caring about people again.

I still found it hard to understand why my dad couldn't protect me, but he had lived through enough traumas to understand fear, and my mum went through so much pain that I wanted to love and care for them both again.

From then on, I kept my pain and sorrow deep inside me and it became the dark side of me, but I learned to hide it with a smile. Words were not necessary and I didn't bother saying anything to anybody anymore. I would need the strength of that smile for there were many more dark times ahead.

4

They Looked at Us
Like We Were Aliens

Walking through the hills of Gracanica, northeast of Bosnia, took us far away from Kozarac, but not far away from my sorrow and pain. That was still deep in me like a fire in winter, slowly burning.

Eventually, we arrived at the secondary school where we were staying. The walls were covered in pictures of Marshal Tito and inspirational quotes from the good old days when Yugoslavia was alive and prosperous. No one could believe what this country had become.

We were huddled in a small sports hall, cramped on top of each other, with very little light. As I sat down next to my mum and dad, devoid of hope, my shoulders slumped forward, trying to guess our fate. I didn't want to disturb them, to ask what they thought would happen next. Instead, I retreated into my own world, deep in my own thoughts and emotions. I began to think, all of this is a trick – they will take us one by one and kill us. What else was I to think about? I was only thirteen, traumatised, shivering cold and hungry.

All night, I was scrunched up like a little ball, my stomach rumbling like there was an earthquake inside me. I was so hungry, but I wouldn't ask my mum for food or water, as I knew she didn't have any. No one asked for food, as they were too scared. No one gave us any information about what was going on, and even though they had told us that they were our army and we didn't need to worry about anything, we had lived through a lot and had learned not to trust anyone. Just being put in another school was enough to make us panic after the concentration camp in Trnopolje. At night we didn't sleep. Nobody guarded us, which made it worse. We thought all of this was a set-up; that soldiers would come in the middle of the night and massacre us all. Stripped of any hope, we were just praying that nobody would turn up.

I will never forget the early morning at the beginning of June when the Bosnian soldiers walked into the school hall with the local villagers, and they looked at us like we were aliens. We were hesitant to say anything, but they were too busy talking among themselves about who they were taking to speak to us anyway. Nothing made any sense, nothing added up, where were we going now? Would these people take us to secret locations and execute us? At first all the formalities reminded us of the concentration camp in Trnopolje. We had no choice yet again, but to follow their instructions and orders.

Families started leaving with other families and soon, our turn came. We were transported by tractors again; it was a bumpy ride but we soon arrived at a house on top of the hill. We were put to live with families that were near each other. They gave us a warm welcome and they were really nice people. The guy who lived in that house had the same name as my dad and his dad had the same name as my granddad: Mehemed and Ramo.

At this point, we were literally starving, but we didn't ask for food. The first thing the woman said to us was: 'We haven't got enough food for our own families, let alone to feed you, but we will share what we have.'

She gave me a piece of warm bread; it was very small, probably the size of a Mars bar, but it was so delicious that I licked all my fingers, like I was eating my favourite chocolate. At that time you could only dream about having chocolate.

Soon, I was introduced to the young boy who lived at the house. He was very naughty and always got me into trouble. He would break things and blame me, and eat all the food and say that I ate it. I never complained to anyone or said a word about it, but my mum and dad knew there was something wrong. So, one day my dad followed us to where we were playing and he saw this young boy pissing on me. That was a regular thing that the kid did to me, as well as kicking and punching me every day. I was full of bruises, but I loved the pain. My dad told his mother what the boy had done, but she still blamed me for stealing all the food. My parents were in a really awkward position – they knew that I wasn't taking the food, but they were too scared to make a fuss, as they thought we could be kicked out of the house.

My dad complained to the eldest member of the family, Ramo, the boy's grandfather, who lived in a separate house. He knew that his grandson got up to no good and suggested that I stay over at his house most of the time to avoid getting into conflict with the boy. As I have already said, Ramo was also my granddad's name, and I was very obedient there, as he reminded me of my own granddad. I followed his orders and we got on like a house on fire. I quickly realised I was being fed much better there, and so I offered to do all the household chores in return for regular meals. I used to cut the wood for the stove on which he cooked and which kept the house warm at night. When he saw what a good worker I was, Ramo would hire me out to other people to do all sorts of farming jobs around the village.

I will never forget those hot summer days walking through beautiful peaceful countryside and dense forest; all you could hear was the birds singing and children playing. It was like a fairy tale, like being back in Kozarac before this nightmare began. We would set off early in the morning, walking for at least an hour, to cut the wheat with a sickle. It was hard, physical work, and the farmers were in the fields from morning to evening. It was so hot that you could fry an egg in the pan on that heath, but no one complained, because we were fed well, and I was always given a piece of bread to take home.

My dad couldn't work as he had had a heart operation and he couldn't bear that heat. Mum had to look after my younger brother so therefore I was stuck on my own again with complete strangers. All the farming skills that I had picked up from my granddad came in handy, and I worked like a machine. The farmers were amazed at my strength and work ethic.

Soon, the word spread around the village about the kind of worker I was and then everybody started hiring me. With just one week of work on the farm, I was able to provide the entire household with a bag of wheat, which we then took to the mill to turn into flour. We had enough flour to make the bread and pies that we lived on. The hardest jobs I did were collecting the hay on a steep hill no tractor or even a horse could reach. I had to make a bundle of hay on a blanket made out of tent material and then tie it on my little back and carry it down the hill. From a distance you couldn't even see me, just a massive bundle of hay sliding down that hill.

I would start early in the morning and finish late at night. The worst thing was if I slipped down the hill and hit my head on an anthill, as all the ants would get into my hair and nibble my sweaty skin. At that point, I would call it a day and run under cold water to rid myself of the ants. There was no running water, and the only place to have a shower was outside at the back of the house. We would fill the plastic barrel with cold water in the morning, so, as the day grew hotter, the water would warm up. In the evening, we would put a hosepipe on top and feed it through to have a shower. It was a fast and effective way to refresh ourselves after a long exhausting day at the farm.

I could see that my parents felt sorry for me, but they could not have stopped me working, as we needed the food. The work didn't get any easier and the days didn't get any shorter. The best thing that came out of it was that I was able to provide food for the two households and I didn't have to communicate with anybody – I was just working.

Soon, my dad decided that we would be better off finding somewhere new to stay, as I was getting exhausted with working, and the family we were staying with started hinting that enough was enough: they had helped us as much as they could and it was time for us to look elsewhere. They also knew that we would struggle in the winter, as there would be no farming and there would not be enough food for everyone. All of the people from Kozarac started to find themselves in the same situation, and it was time to move on again.

5

Journey Deeper into Hell

We had been relatively comfortable on the farm and didn't really want to move, but we didn't have much choice, and so my dad started to organise a lorry for all of us. He had to collect the cash for the transport as quickly as possible, and that was his biggest challenge as people didn't have much money. It was expensive as the two drivers would be smuggling us through the mountains, avoiding the military points – they pocketed a lot of money from people like us. Dad had raised only half of the money but had a full lorry of people. The only solution was to take a lot more people until we reached the price for the transport. By the time we had enough money, we were squashed in like sardines, all standing up. But there was no going back – it was time to move on and this was the only way.

My dad sat with the drivers in the cabin and we were in the trailer, and, oh God, it was so hot! Within five minutes, we were sweating buckets, but no one would get off in case they lost their spot. We could not leave until it was dark, so we were roasting in the lorry for six hours.

Finally, when it was dark, we set off on the long bumpy drive. Bosnia is 70 per cent covered in hills and forest, and the only way to escape was the route through the forest. The biggest challenge was the landmines and booby traps that killed a lot of people. It was hot and uncomfortable but the drivers never stopped or asked how we were. All we could see through the cabin's tiny window was our dad gesturing to us, trying to check if we were all right. We were driven like cargo without knowing where we were going or how we were going to get there. Although we couldn't see anything, we could feel the steep hill, as the lorry was weaving its way through the deep dense forest. Then, just when we reached the top of the hill, we had a puncture. Strangely, after we stopped, the drivers and my dad stayed in the cabin for ages, so we didn't know what was going on. When they finally got out, they said, 'Everybody needs to be quiet. Get off the lorry.'

We were scared at first but Dad reassured us that they just needed to change the tyre. He explained we were very close to the military base, and if they discovered us there, we would be taken away by the soldiers. No one made a sound.

The screws on the wheels had seized and wouldn't come off, so my dad helped as he had mechanical knowledge from maintaining the farm equipment. He used the oil from the engine cap to grease the thread of the screw. It took them a couple of hours and, by the time they had fixed it, it was early morning. As we could only travel at night, we were trapped again with nowhere to go, just waiting for further instructions. What made it worse was that the drivers always stood away from us, talking on their walkie-talkies, one standing at one side of us and one on the other, as if they were guarding us. It felt like we were prisoners again.

One thing that I learned in the war was never to trust anyone, which became the rule and my survival mechanism. We heard many stories of people being sold to paramilitary rebel groups for just a handful of gold. Now we were in the same situation, those stories played heavily on our minds. All you could hear was people whispering to each other, so the kids couldn't hear them, but we strained to hear every word, even the gruesome details of how they cut off people's fingers, torsos, even heads.

It was a cold misty morning and you couldn't see very far so we wrapped ourselves around each other, embracing and holding each other's hands to create heat. We were like kids – one minute we loved each other and the next we hated each other, depending on the situation that we were in. If we were all in trouble, we would be mellow and soft, but, if things were relatively peaceful, we would start picking on each other – I could never understand that.

Back in the lorry, I was standing up again, along with most of the young and the thin people. The arguments would start when the lorry was going at some speed over the bumpy rocky roads and suddenly we would be thrown to the other side of the trailer, landing on someone's head or lap, or quite often someone's baby. All you could hear were babies crying and people shouting, 'My head!' 'My arm!' 'My baby, you idiot!'

Then the drivers would intervene with a very strong knock on the cabin's little window, telling us to shut up. One time one of them said in a deep harsh voice, 'Do you want me to stop? This is the biggest Chetniks' nest and if I do, they will eat you all alive like wolves, even your babies.'

Whenever you mentioned Chetniks to anyone, their blood would stop flowing and their tongue would freeze. Chetniks are a paramilitary group of nationals that formed during the Second World War to fight the Partisans as well as the Germans. They are known for their brutality, and would butcher people like animals, with no mercy for anyone: women, children and babies. So the bickering soon stopped, and for the next couple of hours we tried to sleep, and all you could hear was people snoring.

The trip became so exhausting that people wanted to jump out of the lorry. We ran out of water, and the toilet was an issue again, as the drivers were too scared to stop anywhere during the night, so the shopping bags came in handy again. People were prepared for it too, as they had more bags than bread in their pockets. Smell was an issue, of course, but by this time the abnormal had become normal. People would just cover their mouths and noses with scarves until the waste was thrown out of the lorry.

It became a survival game, and people started crying and hallucinating. I remember one lady, whose husband was killed during the first attack on Kozarac, had a panic attack, and she was screaming, shouting and crying. I remember her kids more than her, two boys about my age, who were saying, 'Please don't let my mother die!'

This panic attack lasted for a good four to five hours, and in the end she was making so much noise, she had to swap places with my dad in the cabin of the lorry so she couldn't be heard. But this made the boys cry even more. One old lady tried to comfort them, and in a very mellow soft voice, she said, 'Children, if you stop crying, your mum will not die.'

They instantly stopped, but their mother carried on, alternating between loud and quiet, but always crying. That squealing voice stuck in my head and, even now, when anybody cries, I see that woman and her two children.

It became so bad that she was losing consciousness and needed medical help. The drivers now had to take a big gamble and come out of the forest during the day to drop the lady off at the hospital in the city of Konjic. They knew the area well and they had to chance it to save her life. But now we were in danger from shelling and snipers as we were in a town.

Fortunately, this town was under the control of the Croatian army, so we had a good chance of surviving and of that lady getting medical treatment. The lorry was going at real speed now, swerving from one side of the road to the other, and I was being thrown around inside. But I'd had enough of that and I managed to squeeze to the end of the lorry where everything was open, so I had more air and I could get a better grip to hold on to two metal bars.

Suddenly everyone was deathly quiet. I hadn't realised why the lorry was swerving so much until a grenade hit the ground behind the vehicle, narrowly missing my leg, which was dangling outside. The detonation lifted us all from our positions. The lorry was still moving at speed and quickly drove off as my face was covered with the dust of the shell.

I heard my mum's voice shouting, 'Where is my son?'

I couldn't speak, as my mouth was full of smoke and dust

from the shell, and it took a good couple of minutes to clear. Then I saw my mum crying. I stood up to show her I was OK, and then she started crying even more with relief.

The lorry never stopped until we arrived at the hospital in Konjic, and then the drivers ran out to see if anybody was hurt. One of them froze when he saw me, as he thought I was injured, but all I had was a little cut on my hand from falling down when the grenade just missed the lorry. I managed to hide my hand from my mum, so she wouldn't panic.

Meanwhile, the distressed woman was still crying and slipping in and out of consciousness. The decision was made on the spot that she had to stay at the hospital, and as they had no other family, her two young sons had to stay with her.

Our hearts were broken as we could not help them anymore. Some people started protesting and saying they wouldn't go anywhere if she wasn't coming.

The drivers jumped back in the lorry and one of them said, 'OK, you can all stay if you want, but whoever wants to go further, you have a couple of minutes to get back in the lorry. The shelling will get more frequent during the night and I'm not taking any more risks for any of you, enough is enough. The enemy borders are changing every minute and our crossing route through the forest is becoming very challenging, virtually impossible.'

It took us all under a minute to climb back on, so the lorry was full again, but this time people already looked half-dead. We could not stop anymore. I crouched in my ball position again, thinking, this is real chaos. What kind of heartless people would throw a grenade on a lorry full of civilians, women and children? Don't they have any morals? Are they drunk? Do they have their own family? What will they achieve by doing that? I never got any answers, even today, just vivid memories and mental and physical scars.

Now, the lorry was going even faster, cutting through roads and swerving everywhere. We didn't panic anymore, we didn't even care anymore; we were too exhausted to think about anything. We were hungry and trying to process everything that had just happened.

I heard someone say, 'I wish I'd stayed in Gracanica – it would have been much better, even if we had to kill ourselves there. It would have been much better than being left in the hands of these monsters who are controlling the forest!'

Then, suddenly, the lorry stopped and the engine cut out. People started panicking again as the shelling was still intense. We didn't care that much about the shelling when we were moving, but now that we were standing still, it was a different story: the soldiers from the mountains could locate us in minutes. All of a sudden, the drivers jumped out of the lorry, shouting, 'Everybody run! We've run out of fuel.'

People were jumping out of that lorry and running like Linford Christie. When I saw my sixty-six-year-old grandmother jump from that lorry, I thought she would lose both her legs, but she didn't even fall down.

We all hid in the woods until night-time, watching the lorry and hoping a grenade wouldn't fall on it. Then we started worrying that maybe it was a set-up, and they would send their army unit to get us. We were not even sure whose territory we were on: Serbs or Croats. The drivers had a plan to get to the lorry and put in fuel as soon as it was dark so we could carry on. Then they realised if it was Serbian territory they would have got us straight away, so this must be a No Man's Land area, and they were right.

The shelling was even louder during the night, almost like fireworks. Every time there are fireworks in the UK today, it reminds me of the shelling in Kozarac and Konjic.

At last it was night, and the drivers were able to fill the fuel tank. As soon as the engine started, people woke up and ran to the lorry as though they'd heard a fire alarm going off. Within minutes, the lorry was full and we were heading into the dark forest again.

I had blisters on my hands from gripping on to the piece of metal at the back of the lorry like a monkey. But my hands were strong and there was always someone holding on to my legs for balance on that bumpy ride. My hair was so dirty that I could not even run my fingers through it, as standing at the back I collected all the dust. It was the longest and most exhausting trip of my life.

All of a sudden the atmosphere seemed to change, became less tense, and I felt there could be a light at the end of the tunnel. My dad started clapping his hands and said, 'We have reached freedom! We are in Posušje!'

6

Fighting for Food

We had arrived at Posušje, a town in west Herzegovina, controlled mainly by Croats, where we were taken to a refugee camp at another secondary school. As we walked to the school, I saw shops with fruit and groceries for the first time since we left Kozarac. Oh my God, I was so tempted to steal a bunch of grapes, but my mum stopped me, saying there would be a lot of food in this camp. I didn't believe her, but carried on walking anyway, holding her hand.

The school didn't feel like the concentration camp at Trnopolje, as we could get out at any time and we didn't have camp guards shouting at us, but it was cramped, hot and smelly. People were sweaty and dirty, as there were no proper washing facilities and the toilets were in a terrible state. As we followed each other through the masses of people already there, we were trying to get our bearings. We were not registered there or told where to go, and we were still hesitant to say anything or ask anybody how things worked there.

Soon, we discovered the unusual way food was distributed there. Very often, there wasn't enough food for everybody, so they had to throw bread and tins of sardines and corned beef into the crowd and people caught what they could. Some people ended up with nothing, so you often had to fight to keep hold of anything you'd caught. We joined in straight away and started ducking and diving, playing catch for the food. I was good at that and passed the tins to my parents. On the first day I couldn't get bread, but we soon learned the trick to it: I stood on my dad's shoulders, and when the bread was thrown I would jump in the air to catch it, then give it to Dad. He was strong enough to hug it so that no one could snap it out of his arms while we walked back through the crowd to our family in a classroom. Quite often I knocked people out when I landed on them and once even broke someone's arm. Other people started to copy our idea, and one day I collided in the air with another person head to head and I saw stars – I still managed to hang on to the tin of corned beef in my hand, though!

Somehow, we were all fed – not enough, but enough to get us through the day. People exchanged corned beef for sardines or bread, etc. and it always seemed to work. Some days when they didn't have food in tins, they threw pickled vegetables in glass jars! I remember people being knocked out cold by the jars, but all we cared about was getting a jar and making sure it didn't break. It was like kids playing dare games in a playground. In fact, when I think about my entire journey through the war with my family, we were placed in schools and our behaviour was always compared to how kids act in school. We always talk about that when we sit down together as a family and discuss our war experiences.

Soon after we arrived, my grandmother fell ill with heat exhaustion and she passed out. We all panicked as there was no doctor in the school camp, so people tried what they could to help: someone wet a piece of cloth and put it to her lips, while other people were waving pieces of cloth to try and give her some fresh air. The classrooms were dusty and smelly, with no air and no sanitation, which had the biggest effect on the elderly. My dad had to take care of my grandmother and he was always with her, so I went on my own to get food. It was a real challenge. I managed to get bread and one tin of sardines, but then I was beaten up and my food taken away from me.

The next time I teamed up with another guy, who threw me in the air to catch the food, but I landed on a fearsome strong guy, who knocked me out cold. I went back to the classroom with my eye completely closed and no food. My dad started panicking, and although he was angry, you could not take revenge at this place because you couldn't escape, so it would just go in circles.

I came up with a better plan; early in the morning, I climbed on top of the roof so that when the food was thrown I was the first to jump, and from that distance people had enough time to get out of the way so I could land on my feet on the floor. Time and again I jumped from a height of five to six metres. Landing on my feet was the biggest challenge, and while I was getting my balance, the others would jump at me to snatch the food. I then tried putting it under my top while still in the air, but that didn't always work and I was beaten up a couple of times when I landed and the food was taken away. There were so many people that you couldn't even see who was hitting you or who took the food off you – they would pile on top of you, like rugby players fighting for the ball.

Later, we realised that people worked in teams to get the food and we joined them, sharing the spoils. I made friends with a lot of people, as I was the best food hunter, and we came up with our own tactics. It was very cruel, but as we were kids, we got away with it. We were not strong enough to punch people, so we would grip good-size stones in both hands. Then three of us would jump from the roof at the same time, throw the stone in our right hands at anybody underneath and then try to catch the food with the same hand. When we landed, people attacked us, but we hit them with the stone in our left hands. Oh boy, that hurt! People could never work out what we hit them with because we were holding the stones so tightly. They always thought we caught them with our elbows on their heads and we got away. If any of us missed, one of the other two would catch the food. It was a brilliant way of working as a team and feeding our hungry families.

It didn't always work, of course, and we were caught with the stones a couple of times and beaten up. We also ended up with bruises, broken heads and massive headaches from accidentally landing on each other or hitting each other with the stones when we missed people. I guess through the war I learned how to survive different hardships. The world can be a cruel, unfair place to live, and the only ones who make it through are the people who learn how to play the game well.

As we got used to the place and how things worked, we found out that Zarka, one of our neighbours from Kozarac, was in charge of distributing the food. From then on, things became a lot easier; all we had to do was go early in the morning when the food storage opened and we would go through the back way to get our full bags of groceries. At this point we were being spoiled as Zarka would occasionally throw a few bars of chocolate in our bag. We had to earn them by unloading the full lorry of groceries, but for chocolate we would do absolutely anything.

As the weeks passed, this school started to get overcrowded and stealing became an everyday occurrence. Fighting and shouting was the only way to get through the day.

At this point my dad decided it was time to move on again, and this time we hoped it would be our final move to freedom and peace in Croatia. He made some enquiries about the coaches that could take us to Croatia, but they were all expensive and by now people had hardly any money. Somehow, Dad persuaded one coach company that he would pay them half of the money before we set off and the other half when we arrived in Croatia. He told them there were lots of families in Croatia waiting to be reunited with us, and that they would pay the rest of the money when we got there. People must have used the same strategy in the past and it worked. The coach driver believed my dad, that the families in Croatia were desperate to see us coming out of the war alive and they would pay anything just to get us out of that hell.

We were moving on again, full of tears and emotions, as we were not sure where we would end up and if it would be better or worse for us. It also felt as though we were getting further and further away from home. When we were captured in Kozarac, even though we had enemies all around us, at least we were at home, in a place we all knew. Now we were constantly on the move, rootless, unsafe; we felt that nobody wanted us and we didn't belong anywhere. We became hungry, desperate refugees. People saw us as poor, dirty, smelly, even black sheep. Wherever we turned up, they pointed at us, whispering about us: 'Watch them, they will steal, they're hungry.'

'Where are you going?' they asked us.

'What are you doing?'

'Where are you from?'

As soon as we said Bosnia, they would say, 'We haven't got anything for you,' and walk off. Even if we just wanted directions, they would ignore us.

We soon realised that it was some people from the Roma community who had caused a lot of trouble and gave us a bad name for stealing and pickpocketing. The Roma have lived in Bosnia for the last four hundred years, and are actually one of the earliest settlers from India. They look like Indian people and speak a very old Hindu language; when they speak Bosnian, they have a very distinctive twang. Roma people were always on the move in Bosnia even before the war and they called themselves travellers. Now I understand their problems.

7

Auttie Dina to
the Rescue

We were on the move again. The coach arrived for us, and it was a luxury after our transport in the animal wagons and lorry. The last time I had seen a coach like this was when we had our last school trip. We used to have a trip at the end of every school year all across Yugoslavia – it was the best experience ever. Every year we went somewhere different, and as we got older, the destinations were further away and better. I would never compare this experience to our fun school trips but at least our journey from Posušje to Croatia was comfortable.

My dad was in charge again, taking the money off people and counting everybody in. I sat near the window and I must admit I started to feel a little excited as we set off for Croatia, as our Auntie Dina had lived there most of her life, so we hoped we would be welcomed at her place rather than staying at a camp again. I enjoyed looking at the scenery as we travelled, the beautiful lakes of Yugoslavia and the waterfalls in Plitvice. Coincidentally, we had come to Plitvice on a school trip the

59

year before. I remembered the excitement and enthusiasm we all shared, going on a trip with our best mates – Milorad, Siniša and Saša – and our karting experience, smashing our electric cars into each other. Those were some of the best days of my childhood. At the waterfalls, we splashed each other with water to impress the girls, and one in particular, Tamara, who we all fancied. Then it was time to soak the girls, and the usually strict teachers let us mess about and have fun. There was a grin on my face at those happy memories, and my mother noticed and said, 'What are you smiling about?'

'Oh, nothing,' I said. 'We came on a trip here to Plitvice last year – do you remember when you made me Kentucky fried chicken?'

'Of course I did, that was your favourite food whenever you went on a school trip. Now, here is your sandwich.'

I looked at it and I smiled, saying to my mum, 'I am sick of these sardines and corned beef sandwiches. I wish I could have my Kentucky fried chicken.'

'You will,' she said.

I ate my sandwich and fell into a deep sleep.

Suddenly, panic jolted me awake. At first, I thought I was dreaming, until my mum grabbed my head and pushed me underneath her legs. I could hear people saying, 'It's the Croatian army – they want the boys!'

They wanted to conscript young boys into the army, as they were losing soldiers on a daily basis. I was only thirteen but I looked sixteen, and they didn't care about your age as long as you looked big enough and could carry a gun. Through my mum's legs, I could see the soldiers' boots as they walked up and down the coach, looking everywhere and asking the young boys to stand up so they could see their height. My pulse shot up so high that I had to put my hand on my heart to calm myself down. I knew if they took any boys from this coach, their mothers would point me out to the soldiers too. Luckily, they didn't and on this occasion we were all saved.

The driver said we would have a few more of these stops, so we needed to be prepared. Our mothers started crying and saying, 'We are not giving our children to go and fight for anybody!'

My father tried to calm them down, saying they would only take people if they thought they were old enough. But the tension was palpable now, with huge pressure on the parents. As kids, we didn't know that much; how could we understand what it really meant to go and fight on the front line? The army said they would feed us regularly (which of course was tempting), train us for a couple of weeks, and then we would get weapons and go on the front line.

At the next stop, soldiers got on again. I stayed hidden under my mum's legs and covered over with a blanket as they walked up to a very tall kid who had buried his head in his legs. He was very quiet, and I hadn't even noticed him until the soldiers told him to lift his head and stand up.

'Leave him alone, he's only a child. Here are his grades from school,' his mother pleaded, holding him tight. 'Please let him stay! He is my only child. I lost my husband and the rest of the family.'

'Come outside with us with your son,' they said.

She was petrified, screaming, 'As soon as I go out the game is over – they will take him!'

The woman went outside with her son and the soldiers

asked him a few questions: 'What is your date of birth?', 'How old are you?', 'When is your birthday?', 'What year did you finish school?'

The woman got back on alone and never spoke a word for the rest of the trip; she never bothered anybody, but she cried a lot.

The pressure was on me now. My mum and dad's faces dropped and they were sweating: who was next, would they pick on me next?

Another stop and this time the soldiers went straight to the back of the coach and took two young guys out; they never got back on. The coach driver was told to drive off immediately, which he did – he knew not to argue.

From then on, for the last ten hours of the journey I didn't eat, I didn't even go to the toilet; I just became part of that blanket.

All of a sudden the atmosphere changed and people started shouting, 'Croatia, Croatia! We are at Zagreb.'

As the coach pulled into Zagreb, the capital city of Croatia, I sat up again in my seat and felt like I had come back from the dead. My body was like a solid rock – I had sat hidden in the same position for so long, I felt like I was paralysed. I looked out of the window and saw masses of people everywhere. They were not panicking and running away to find shelter from shelling, they were walking casually on the street, talking normally with each other – after what we had experienced, this normality seemed very strange to me.

We were taken to the Zagreb Mosque, a beautiful white building with Islamic architecture and calligraphy on the walls inside the main praying area. It was a very peaceful place, even though it was busy with people milling about everywhere, and for the first time since we left Kozarac, I began to feel some peace and tranquillity. People seemed more civilised, and they came from all over the world to greet us and give us humanitarian aid. There were lots of Arabs and big lorries full of food, which was distributed among us. Most of the Arabs spoke Bosnian, but later on we learned that most of them were Syrians, living in Croatia.

We still didn't speak much with anyone, as we had learned in the concentration camps it was safer that way, but I was happy to see my cousin Almir Solaković there. He had fled the fighting on the front line and was working as a volunteer, helping to unload the food lorries.

Interestingly, even on that first day, we started noticing things around us again – the grass, nature and the buildings. For the first time in months I smelled cooked food and had a real appetite to eat it. I guess over the past few months our only focus had been staying alive and now we could let ourselves relax a little.

This was one of the biggest refugee camps that I have ever seen, and there were reporters, journalists, the Red Cross and many different humanitarian organisations from all over the world, who wanted to know about the war in Bosnia. My dad spoke to them all about the concentration camps, saying, 'The world should know there are concentration camps all across the North West of Bosnia, with hundreds of people being killed on a daily basis and the rest starved to death. These people should be released and given freedom but they have been captured like animals and slaughtered like animals.'

Many families were reunited at the mosque. People's names

were called out over a megaphone, which made me a little uncomfortable as it reminded me of the concentration camp. People would panic if their family members' names were not called out, as it usually meant they had not made it. If you hadn't made it this far, the chances were very slim for survival, although their families still lived in hope of seeing them turn up one day. There were happy tears and sad tears on people's faces and quite often a mixture of the two.

We were only there one day before my Auntie Dina came to pick us up and took us to her home in Zagreb. Her flat was full of our family members when we arrived and we had the most emotional reunion, hugging each other and crying. They could not believe that we had made it; it had taken us three months, but at last we came out alive and that was the most important thing. It was good to be reunited with family again, but it was tinged with sadness too – we were delighted and relieved to see our loved ones safe and well, but we also learned the terrible stories of those who had not survived.

Our granddad Ramo was already in Zagreb; he had been ethnically cleansed before us when he went to take food to the concentration camp. I had missed him a lot, and I was very happy to be reunited with him. Our hug, our love, gave me new strength to carry on. Everything I had learned was from him and because of him. He was proud of my bravery when the others told him what had happened to me, and he said, 'At least we have someone who saved our village, our people, our purpose, our Solak clan.'

I didn't really know what he meant, but then he told me that our cousin Osman Solaković had been killed. I was distraught – I thought my silence had saved him, but he was brutally killed in the Omarska concentration camp. It hit me so hard that for three days I didn't sleep and I think that this was when my first PTSD kicked in.

To lose someone like this feels like part of your heart goes missing and it can never be replaced, no matter what anybody says or does. Osman was someone who grew up on the farm with us and had helped me with all my homework.

'Bring me my Osman back, you cowards! He was a real soldier, a true Northerner, who never feared you cowards, Chetniks!'

I was shouting in my dreams, sweating, and waking everyone up. At this point, they began to realise that there was something wrong with me, that I was traumatised by my experiences. I wanted revenge for Osman, but how? He was already dead and I was only thirteen, a child. No one told me the full horrific story of how my cousin had been killed – I think they were all trying to protect me from more trauma. In fact, it wasn't until I was eighteen that I heard the full details. We had gone to Switzerland and met one of our relatives, who told me how Osman had been killed. At first, I felt proud of his strength and courage, but then I felt my blood run cold. How could someone do that to my true Northerner? They had put salt on his open wounds and vinegar all over his feet, and they made him drink car oil. He said, 'I will never fear you cowards! You never fought like a true soldier, like a true Northerner, and you will never wipe us all out!'

Those words echoed in my head and kept me going throughout my life.

I think I was affected so deeply by loss for a number of reasons, but particularly because I was so young, and the people around me had been such an important part of my childhood and made me who I am. All of a sudden they were not around anymore and I felt like the green apples fallen from the tree. Where is Osman, where is my youth, where are my people who made me who I am today? I felt alone, so alone that I didn't want anyone anymore. I thought I had saved all of those people, but no. I didn't know where to go or who to turn to. All I had was my granddad to give me some answers. But even he didn't have them anymore; he was lost and he could not control his emotions. He said, 'They have killed us all, wiped us out, like we were never there. But you were there and you saw everything and you will remember the history as it was. Never give up your values, hold them and carry on with your life.'

It was a bittersweet time, but at least we were safe now and with people who loved us. Auntie Dina told us she had plenty of food there, which brought a huge smile to my face, but as soon as I saw it was all tins of corned beef and sardines, I felt sick. She was getting donations from the Red Cross and she had stacks of them. I'd had enough of them to last the rest of my life, but I had to eat them for there was nothing else. Occasionally, when my auntie had the ingredients, she would cook us Arabic food, which I loved, especially aubergines. What I really wanted was some grapes – I always loved them, and throughout the war I never had any. I thought I must try and get a job, just so I could buy some grapes. My auntie was married to a Syrian called Aladin; he was a lovely guy and a good uncle. He had a clothing business and I used to help him loading and unloading his stock. He would give me pocket money for helping and I went straight to the outside market to buy grapes. Soon, I became a regular helper with my cousin Mirza and we used to clean my uncle's cars; he had two cars at the time and that was my speciality. He said, 'When Mirsad cleans my cars, they look as if they've just come off a production line.'

The flat next door was empty, and my auntie had asked the government if the refugees could move in there and they agreed. Our family was huge, and there were about twenty of us in two one-bedroom flats next to each other. Our granddad, Ramo, was already there. Both of our grandmothers – Kada, my mum's mother, and Hasnija, my dad's mother – had come with us, along with my Auntie Asima and her daughter, Mersiha. Our grandparents' health was good and we were extremely lucky – quite often elderly people hadn't managed to complete the trip. They kept praying, asking mercy from God to at least save their children.

And we did survive and came to freedom. In Croatia, we felt almost like we were at home as most of our family were with us, apart from our Uncle Ismet and his son Samir, who were still being held at the concentration camp. But it was not our real home and we were away from our regular routines on the farm – working on the land, feeding the animals, working with the tractors, cultivating the land, etc. The old saying was certainly true for us: there is nowhere like home.

More families joined us from Bosnia, and the two little flats were fast running out of space. My dad built an apartment out of a garage for my granddad, so he and my grandmother had their own space, as the kids were making a lot of noise. Dad always had golden hands, and he could make anything; he was well known for his skill in improvising with whatever material he had. We all helped him, including our cousin Almir, who told us more about how he escaped the front line.

Almir had completed his military service with the Yugoslav army, but of course when the war kicked off, he was sent to the front line and had to fight against his own people. His brother Nijaz fought on the opposite Bosnian side, so it was like in a movie, brother against brother. Sadly, Nijaz was killed towards the end of the war in a city called Kupres. Almir had had enough of fighting against his own people and his only option was to run away from the army. He made two attempts but was caught each time and put in solitary confinement, with hardly any food, and he lost a lot of weight. Then he was sent back to the front line. One day, when they were quite close to the Croatian border, he took a chance and managed to escape. He threw away his gun and uniform, and while sneaking through the villages, he took clothes from a line, dressed himself as a civilian and fled to freedom.

Auntie Dina's flat was like a bus stop – everybody met there, including all our friends and family from Kozarac. She turned her home into a public humanitarian centre. People stayed over for a couple of days, a couple of weeks, a couple of months, until they sorted themselves out. When we sat in the evening watching the news about Bosnia, it was like sitting in the cinema. We would watch the terrible things shown on the telly, then open up about our own experiences. I heard so many different stories that only a few of them stuck in my head, as my brain could not cope with some of the atrocities committed by those with whom we used to live in peace and harmony.

I told them my own story about when Arkan's paramilitaries came to our village and tortured me, and the sadness we felt on our last day leaving home, when we kept turning round to see our house for the last time. On that day when we were ethnically cleansed, heading towards the concentration camp, two young lads ran into the cornfields and were killed with a machine gun. I heard the screaming when they were shot and that sound still echoes in my ears.

While in Zagreb, my dad gave many interviews to the various journalists about the hell that we went through and the humanitarian crisis at the concentration camps, the torture and killings, but it felt like nobody listened and no one seemed to care. He told them that the number of casualties was rising on a daily basis, but no one did anything about it. None of us was brave enough to expose the war to the world as we were worried we might endanger our remaining family members, neighbours and friends who were still being held in camps, but my dad knew the story had to be told and so he put a brave face on and did it for us all.

When the war in Croatia first started, it felt far away from us, but now that we were in Croatia in peace, the war in Bosnia felt far away, as we had travelled for months to get to safety. And, although we were safe now, we were still concerned about the people in the concentration camps. It was a time of reflection and sadness for us too, a constant reminder that we were far from home.

* * *

Croatia soon became flooded with the Bosnian refugees, so different countries agreed to take a certain number of refugees. It was hoped that this would take the burden off Croatia, so the refugees could be released from the centres. My dad regularly visited the centre to get our donation parcels, and he heard from his friend Sami, a volunteer there, that Britain was taking refugees. Sami offered to put our name forward to Human Appeal International, the organisation making the arrangements. Sami was a Syrian medical student who had lived in Kozarac and was married to a Bosnian woman with a child.

My dad thanked Sami for the offer but told him he had to talk to us about it first and would get back to him.

When Dad came back and told us that we had an opportunity to go to England, none of us wanted to go – we all felt we had travelled too far from home already. Auntie Dina worked really hard to persuade us to go, saying, 'Just go for six months and if you don't like it, come back – you are always welcome here.'

We had a big decision to make, and we were running out of time, as the places were being filled very quickly. My dad did not want to leave behind all of our family, including my granddad and grandmother, as we had just been reunited. Auntie Asima and her daughter Mersiha had travelled with us all the way from Bosnia to Croatia, and they couldn't go with us because they had to wait for my uncle, who was still in the concentration camp. It was a very difficult time for us.

My aunt kept stressing to us that we should go and not miss the opportunity of a lifetime. 'As long as the war goes on, your kids will not have any future here,' she told my parents. 'The education system in Croatia is overcrowded with refugees from Bosnia and they will face discrimination.'

My dad thought about this, and alarm bells started ringing in his head. 'Mirsad struggles with mental issues, with PTSD and flashbacks; he will at least get treatment there. In Croatia, he will get no treatment,' he said. 'We should treat this trip to the UK like a holiday after everything we've been through, and if we don't like it, we can always come back to Croatia.'

'And we don't even know how long the war will last,' my auntie said. 'If it lasts for two more years, Mirsad will be sixteen years old and the Croatian army will conscript him.'

That was the deciding factor for my dad; he had to make the biggest decision of his life to leave Croatia to save me from being sent to fight against the Serbs.

So it looked like we were making another move.

We started crying and this time very loudly. Strangely, all the way through the war, we had been crying silently. But I don't know why; maybe it was fear, maybe we were trying to be strong for each other. I felt bad leaving my family, my grandparents, Uncle Aladin, with whom I got on really well, my cousin Mirza and my auntie.

In the end we knew we had no choice; my dad had no job and no money, so we were constantly relying on donation parcels and who knew how long they would last? Dad did odd jobs, but nothing where he could make a living, as he was ill, struggling with his heart problems again. We were all emotionally as well as physically drained, and something had to change. In the morning the final decision was made: we were heading to the UK.

Dad went to see Sami to confirm our places, and he was very happy when Sami told him he had decided to go to the UK as well; at least he knew he would have one friend.

When Dad came back, he said, 'We are all set to go, we are leaving next week.'

Now the tears really started to fall – we were leaving a lot behind us, our entire family. We were going very far away and a lot of family members were very upset, especially our grandparents, even though we kept reassuring them that we would be back in six months. We spent the week getting ready to go, but we had no luggage really, as we hardly brought anything with us from Bosnia.

On the day we were due to leave, our auntie dropped us off at the camp centre where the two coaches were leaving for England. Our grandparents came along to give us our last hug. It was a sad moment for me leaving my grandfather again, but we didn't have much choice. We had been through so much together with our family: Hasnija, Kada, Asima and Mersiha, and now we were leaving them behind once again. I never heard my grandmother Hasnija cry so loudly and bitterly, as though it came from the bottom of her soul. My grandfather, like most men, was trying to be strong, but he was crying silently, the tears rolling down his face and hiding in his wrinkles. I could not stop looking at them all, thinking it was probably the last time that I would ever see them.

All too soon, it was time to go. We got on the coach and I sat down near the window, so I could wave to my auntie and grandparents. I became their framed picture: a little boy full of tears, moving further and further away from his home. They always told me that they remembered my face the most.

8

No Going Back

The coach drove off, taking us further away from home. The journey was comfortable, but very long. The coaches were massive and modern, and we had plenty of food, especially bananas, which I couldn't get enough of. The guys from Human Appeal International assured us that there would be lots of food for us to eat in the UK. After being so hungry for so long, I found it hard to believe them, but Waheed, one of the aid workers, promised me, 'Mirsad, you will be able to eat as many bananas as you want!'

I had a huge smile on my face. For the first time since the war started, I was travelling without stress and trauma, and without all the terrible fears. Will a grenade fall on us? Will we get caught behind the enemy's line? Will I be taken out of the bus? Will I be killed? It felt like a dream. People started to relax and enjoy the trip, and we had a fantastic journey. Hell, it was a long journey, nearly forty hours, but it was nothing compared to the one that had taken us from Kozarac to

Croatia. I will never forget an old Croatian couple called Ante and Manda, who were on the coach with us. Ante was a huge man and he ate a lot. Manda had brought boiled eggs with her and she offered me one; that egg was like eating honey, as it wasn't cooked properly, but I loved it, and she said, 'Eggs are just as good for you as eating bananas.' Every time I eat boiled eggs, it reminds me of Manda and what she said to me. Ante had worked in Australia when he was young and he spoke basic English; it was rusty, but he was the only one who was able to communicate with the drivers.

Freedom was a wonderful experience and nothing is better than that feeling of peace, but we were still displaced and traumatised, unsure what awaited us at the end of our journey. The people from Human Appeal International kept reassuring us that we would have everything in the UK and wouldn't miss anything, but we had already started missing our home, as we got further and further away. I soon realised nothing in life can replace your home, the place you were born, no matter how much wealth you might gain.

Everything normal for us felt abnormal and boring with no flow, no excitement, no imagination and no feelings. Fighting to survive had become our life; living with fear and tension, learning how to play the survival game had become the norm. Now it was no longer part of our life, we seemed to be missing it. We missed our country already and we all started talking about it; it seemed like everything we said was funny to us, and I could never work out why. Then I realised it was because now we were safe, out of danger, and we were allowed to cry and laugh and show our emotions. Imagine going through that horror and fear in complete silence, unable to react to the situation like a human being; instead, you become a dead person.

My dad had the biggest laugh and no one could beat him at that. He always loved talking and now he was allowed to talk again. That was a true blessing for him. Even now nobody can stop him talking; he loves people, he loves the world, but now he appreciates the peace more than ever, as he knows what it's like to live without it. Throughout the trip, people were talking about their war experiences again and again, and my dad would say, 'Come on, guys, give us a break – let's all sing!'

So we did sing, but we cried too, as it reminded us of all the good days with our families and friends who never made it. There were plenty of tearful moments on the coach. Everybody had a story to tell and they were all equally hard to hear. For those people who lost their close family members, the biggest challenge was to stay positive. It was almost impossible – even today, after twenty-five years, it is still hard. I guess you never recover from the war, you just bury the scars deep inside you, and some people are better at that than others. As a child, it is even harder, as you have an even longer journey to walk through in life, trying to hide those scars.

As the coach journey went on, we were experiencing mixed emotions about our new life. Who would care about us in the UK? Would people welcome us there? Would they like us? Then people would laugh and say, 'Why would they like us, when they don't even know us?' We realised we would have no one there apart from ourselves.

At this point, I still thought we would soon go back home to Bosnia, but the reality was very different. The war in Bosnia was still raging, and people used to cry and say, 'What will happen to our families who are still left in that hell?'

Old people would say, 'We will never make it back home alive again, only on our backs in a coffin.'

At the time, I couldn't work out what they meant; I thought it was some kind of a joke or an old saying, but, sadly, for most of them, it turned out to be the reality.

I said to my mum and dad, 'I thought we would only be in the UK for six months, like a holiday, then we would go back home.'

'How could you go home when they are still fighting?' my dad said.

'I mean Croatia,' I said.

'Well, Croatia is not your home, is it?'

'I guess you're right, but I thought we would stay with Auntie Dina again.'

I was getting puzzled, as the future looked bleak and perhaps I was just realising that we were becoming homeless. After all, I was just a kid, and I had to follow my mum and dad's instructions. But it looked like they didn't even know themselves what awaited us: our future was in the hands of others.

Waheed, one of the organisers, came up to me and asked me in a mix of broken Bosnian and English why I was upset. I told him I missed my home in Bosnia and it would be a long six months in the UK. He looked at me with a smile on his face and said, 'Young man, this is your new home.'

I still couldn't accept that, so I said no, I would be going home.

'Who else has had the opportunity to be picked up from Croatia and taken to the UK?' he said.

And, of course, he was right; in the history of the European refugees, we were the only ones picked up from the Croatian camp and taken to the UK. We had made history.

* * *

The coach reached France, where we were due to catch the ferry to Dover. We were warned that it would be a difficult crossing as the waves were very high and they were expecting a thunderstorm. We were hesitant to cross in those conditions, but we waited a little while and they showed no signs of improving, so we boarded the ship. Almost as soon as we left the port, we were thrown from one side of the ferry to another on the turbulent sea. Many of us were feeling sick and started vomiting. It reminded me of the rough trip through the forest in the people-smuggler lorry. The crossing was so rough that people started panicking, and it reminded us of the war. It seemed as though any little situation brought back those terrible memories – I guess because of our bad experiences in the war we became very sensitive to any little problem. The organisers were aware of that and they were very gentle, kind and reassuring whenever we had any problems.

We finally reached Dover and saw people on the shore waving at us. It was dark, we were tired and all the children were quiet. The coach drove off the ferry and took us to Immigration, where the staff were trying to register us as refugees. We didn't have interpreters, so we relied on anyone who knew a little bit of English, including Ante. The immigration officers just needed basic information, such as names, addresses, where we lived in Bosnia, etc., and they were very kind to us, but we didn't trust them and we didn't want to communicate with them. Anyone in authority reminded us of the concentration camp guards. Then the officers asked the men if they were war criminals. They didn't understand, so they nodded their heads. Fortunately, Ante intervened and the answers were very simple: 'If I was not at the front line fighting, how can I become a war criminal?'

The questioning seemed to go on forever, and as soon as we got back on the coach, we slept like babies.

I woke at about eleven in the morning, and as I looked out of the coach window at my first proper sight of England I noticed how green the grass was. The little garden lawns looked like carpets. I was a bit disappointed to see how wet and windy it looked, and thought about the good weather we had left at home. Everything I saw I compared it to back home. I was lost in my own thoughts as the coach sped along, when all of a sudden the drivers and the organisers started cheering and singing: 'Hooray! We're home at last, thank God.'

They were happy to be home, but we were crying. We were further from home than we had ever been and there was no going back.

9

A New Country,
A New Life

The two coaches pulled into the car park of Birmingham Central Mosque. We all got off the coach and walked into a big open space on the ground floor of the mosque, where we were greeted by other Bosnians, who had prepared food for us. They had made the same journey a month earlier. As we were eating, we were told that we were being divided into two groups: one group was going to Manchester and the other was staying in Birmingham, and we had to make our minds up where we wanted to go. My dad decided we should go to Manchester, as all our friends were going. Unfortunately, by the time we reached the coach, Waheed told us that the coach was full and there was no room for our family, which meant that we had to stay in Birmingham. We were left entirely alone with nobody that we knew. It was cold and windy and even our clothes were shaking. Distraught and in tears, we watched the coach pull away. Now, we felt more alone than ever, with no home, stuck in the middle of a strange island, broken away from our family and friends, and everything we knew. We walked slowly back to the mosque, to the centre that would be our home until more permanent accommodation could be found for us. This setback on our first day did not seem to be a good omen for our new life in England.

Everybody at the mosque seemed to feel sorry for us and they were constantly giving us pitying looks. I'm sure they were trying to be kind and wanted to help us, but it was a very strange experience. It became claustrophobic, almost like our family were animals in a zoo, there to be stared at. We found it very uncomfortable; we were not used to people feeling sorry for us. People had hated us and didn't want us anywhere near them and their families. Now, these people were giving us funny looks, and we didn't know how to react, didn't know what they wanted from us. We were simply frightened of everybody and everything, even our own shadows. Still very traumatised by our war experiences, we were trying to come to terms with what had happened to us. We didn't speak English, and people were trying to communicate with us using mimes and gestures. My dad was a natural leader, and he was always the best ambassador to put across people's problems. He had learned German in school, which is a bit closer to English than Bosnian, and somehow managed to communicate with people. It was soon noticed that I was always deep in thought and never spoke a word to anyone. Of course, the language was a part of the problem, but my war experiences were the real reason I withdrew from everyone apart from my family. The doctors who arrived to check every single refugee immediately diagnosed my PTSD, and how the trauma and flashbacks I was suffering were affecting my mental health.

My mum and dad tried to keep it secret from everyone else – they didn't want any other kids to know in case they looked at me differently and perhaps started bullying me. But of course kids immediately spot the smallest differences in how you look or behave, and that is precisely what happened; the other kids thought that I was too quiet and started pushing me away, not giving me an opportunity to play with them. My communication with kids was very poor – I didn't know anybody and I didn't trust anybody. I guess my PTSD had already begun to affect my everyday life.

Somebody bought us a table-tennis table and all the kids played except me. I was a lonely child who lived in despair and sorrow. I just wanted to be left alone in a little corner, deep in thought, but it seemed that was too much to ask from the other children. When different people brought us things – clothes, toys, balls, even money – most of the time I never got anything, and if I did, it was usually taken off me by the other kids. Most of the kids would run to greet everyone who turned up at the mosque, but I wasn't interested; I was always the last to meet people and most of the time I didn't even bother. My sister would take care of me and fight some of my battles with the other kids, but, eventually, I had to start fighting for myself, by now against every single child at the mosque. I enjoyed the physical pain, as the pain became part of my everyday life. I was used to living with it, which is probably why the other kids could never work out what was wrong with me. Some of them thought I was weird, but mostly they just thought that I was mad. Our parents were too busy worrying about how the family could start a new life here, so I was fighting my own demons with no one to help.

I knew I had a raw inner strength, energy and enthusiasm, but the war scars were overwhelming and they affected all my behaviour and communication with other children.

At first when the other kids pushed me around, I hadn't retaliated, but one day I had had enough. A boy called out to me, 'Sissy boy, you are a girl, aren't you?'

His two mates grabbed hold of me, while he tried to take my clothes off. I was worried and embarrassed that my mum or my sister would turn up and see, and while struggling to get away from them, something changed: inner Mirsad woke: 'For the first time in my life I must fight back.' I never really knew how to fight, had never needed to; I had used the stones in Posušje to punch people in order to get food, but that was completely different, it wasn't personal. The boys had forced me on to the floor and were on top of me. I grabbed hold of one of the boys' balls and I squeezed them as hard as I could. He started crying from the pain and his tears were falling on my face, but I wouldn't let go. Every single person in that room was hitting me with something, but I refused to let go, not until *I* decided to. As soon as I'd let him go, the boy took his pants off to see if he still had any balls. All the other children were laughing their heads off. He was in so much pain he thought I had taken his balls off. I didn't say anything; my face was neutral and cold. That really scared the boys, and for the first time I felt enormous power and unlimited strength. In my head I saw the images of the soldiers beating me up. I guess I had started to discover myself.

Now the real game began; the war had started at the mosque with all the children. The more they beat me up, the more I enjoyed it. I took regular beatings on the head with a belt, with stones – you name it, those kids used it to beat up the 'crazy child', that's how they described me. I still didn't retaliate; instead, I wanted to show off to them, to make them see that they couldn't do anything to me, that they couldn't scare me.

One day the strongest kid in the mosque, nicknamed Miki, came up to me: 'I heard you said to the other kids that you're not scared of me.'

I nodded. He was two years older than me, and a lot bigger and stronger. No one ever messed with that boy. His other nickname was Tyson, and he could punch. He started punching me, some really heavy punches, and he was shaking me off like a tree branch, but I didn't show him any fear. I remembered the words from my granddad: 'When you are in a fight with someone, never show fear to your opponent, keep a cold blank face to confuse him.' So I did. Now it was my turn. This was my first real fist fight in my life. I imagined I had the stones in my hands and I clenched my fists, then I started punching as hard as I could.

Everybody was impressed – none of them would dare throw a punch at Tyson. I landed a few good punches, but soon my sister and other family members stopped us. We were like two bulldogs trying to take each other's head off, all our clothes were ripped and we were out of breath, but even that was not enough: Miki wanted to destroy my confidence, he wasn't happy that I didn't fear him. He didn't know and he didn't understand what I went through in the war. Anyway, we were too young to understand, just kids; Miki was sixteen and I was fourteen. I had experienced a lot more pain than those punches he landed on me.

After the fight, he said, 'Are you scared to fight me again?'

'No, I really enjoyed that.'

'What! Are you crazy?'

I just walked off.

Later, everyone at the mosque heard about the fight. My dad spoke to Miki and said, 'You are a lot older than him, please leave him alone.'

It still didn't stop the other kids attacking me, but from then on I always fought back, always me alone against a group of them. Nothing stopped me and no one scared me.

Eventually, we were moved out of the mosque into our own houses, and we began to learn a little more about Birmingham. Everything seemed different to us, especially the buildings, which looked dull and miserable, with rows of identical terraced houses glued together. All the houses in Bosnia were detached and different from each other, with white rendering and beautiful shapes. The roads here were really busy and there were cars everywhere. Our parents told us that the whole population of Bosnia is equal to the population of Birmingham. Now we realised what a very big city we were living in and it was difficult to get our head around it. Birmingham seemed very dirty compared to our little village; it was polluted, full of smoke and fog, and there was rubbish and rats everywhere.

We compared everything in Birmingham to Bosnia, especially the food and the weather, and as we struggled with the language, it really began to hit us how different our new life would be. Here, everything looked the same and we were quickly bored with it.

We had lived a relatively insular life in our little village, and many of us had never seen black or Asian people before. They all spoke English but with slightly different dialects, and they all seemed to get on with each other. I found that fascinating and it made me think about Bosnia and the war, how we had kicked off with each other, our own people – the same people, the same race, all from the same country.

We were allocated a house in Esme Road in Sparkhill. Two families had to share one house, and we moved in with a lady called Enisa, who had two children approximately the same age as us. Her daughter, Leila, was the same age as my sister, and her son, Adnan, was a year younger than me. It was OK – my sister and Leila became friends, and Adnan didn't bother me that much; he loved computer games and would spend most of his time in front of the telly playing Super Mario. We didn't have much in common but I didn't play with the other kids anyway; I was always described as a loner.

Naturally, with two families living together in one house, it was hard to have any privacy. We had lots of visitors, people who were trying to make friends with us. To communicate with those people was a real nightmare; Leila was the only person who spoke a little bit of English.

My mum had been hiding my war traumas really well, but we were living in a small community and inevitably people talked about the other children. It soon became a real challenge for my parents to hide my PTSD. Often I heard conversations between the Bosnian parents, with them boasting about how intelligent their kids were and how well they would do in life. I knew my mum always felt embarrassed then, and she kept quiet. Mum's silence was very telling, as everyone wants their children to be the best they can, but what could she say? She knew the terrible pain I was suffering. She'd seen me have to fight with the other kids, who were constantly picking on me, but I was also fighting with my traumas from the war. My mother always stood by me and supported me in the best and worst situations. She didn't argue or fight with anybody and kept quiet instead. People used to say I was like my mother, but that was her trick to draw attention away from me and on to her, and it always worked. When people noticed how different I was to the other kids, how I never played with toys, never played the Nintendo game with Adnan, they found that extremely unusual and strange. They started asking my mum intrusive, personal questions.

Mum thought it was none of their business, but she would always shrug it off and say, 'They're only kids,' but by now, I was fourteen, and, of course, it was nothing to do with my age.

For me the hardest thing to deal with was the nightmares and flashbacks. They were my worst enemy, especially as they became more and more frequent. We knew the other family could hear the distressed noises I made, and my mum tried to disguise them with snoring and sometimes she would put the radio on, pretending they were trying to tune into a Bosnian radio station to hear the news about the war. That worked for a while, but people could sense that I was different from the other teenagers and my behaviour certainly stood out. There were times when I would switch the lights off in my room at night, roll myself into the rug and lie down in that position for hours and hours. Mum would ask what I was doing, and I would say, 'I want to stay in peace; I am hiding from the soldiers.'

'But we are not in Bosnia, we are not in a war, we are in peace now and we live in the UK,' she would say, trying to reassure me, but nothing seemed to help me.

That behaviour went on and on for months and looking back, I can see it was a coping mechanism, but I didn't really understand it myself. My parents thought the best way to help me would be to get me jobs to keep me occupied. The garden of the house in Sparkhill was like a jungle, and my mum gave me the task of clearing it and bagging up all the rubbish. I have always been a hard worker and as soon as I started, I was in there like a bulldozer! I enjoyed the hard physical work, and it helped to take the attention away from my PTSD and to stop people talking behind my back. When the neighbours saw what a great job I'd done, they asked my parents if I could do their garden too. I was keen to get on with the work and cleared their garden in no time. They were very happy, and paid my parents for the work, even though it was more like pocket money. A family in the neighbourhood wanted me to do their garden, but it needed a lot more work. My dad helped me to cut the trees and I got rid of the overgrown bushes. They were very impressed as nothing seemed too hard for me – I just got on with the job in complete silence.

I met their son Omar, who was two years older than me. He was one of the biggest kids that I have ever met, a lot bigger than Miki, with whom I'd had problems at the mosque. Omar was a very lonely child and he never went out apart from to his garden. Like me, he never spoke, but we managed to communicate through mimes and gestures. He was a strange boy, but seemed very kind. I had found a very secret friend. There was lots of wood in his garden and we made a treehouse

– like my dad, I was good at making things like that. Omar was very impressed with everything I did, and he was always giving me sweets, chocolates and all the goodies kids love. I always loved chocolate and I missed it so much during the war; my parents still didn't have the money for such luxuries. He had toys that I had never seen in my life, and the more I got to know him, the more strange I found him. But, of course, that was what some people thought about me. He hardly spoke to me but he would give me instructions, and whenever he needed the garden cleared or his room tidied, he would call me to come round. The friendship was becoming a little too intense for me, and I began to think that I wouldn't like to fall out with this guy, as he would beat me up like a chicken. He had really big glasses and when he got angry he looked really scary; all the other kids would shout, scream and run away from him.

One day, I went to the treehouse before him and I was eating the chocolate that he had given me the other day. He started shouting and saying something I didn't understand. I was in a little corner scrunched up; I sensed something bad was about to happen, just like in the concentration camp, waiting for the beating. Omar came over and slapped me really hard; the chocolate started coming out of my mouth and was spread all over my face. Then he started strangling me. I was choking and nobody could see or hear me; I was at the bottom of the garden and totally defenceless. I was trying to prise his hands off my throat, while he was laughing. Boy, it was scary! I couldn't breathe anymore and there was nothing to hit him with. My whole body started shaking, exactly like that chicken I'd envisaged. He was still laughing, while pinning me down, crushing my little body. My parents didn't have a clue what was going on. They thought I had been through the worst in Bosnia, and that now I was safe from the other kids with Omar, but in fact this kid was attacking me. There was no way that I could get out of this situation. I felt my eyes were on stalks and I was dying. Then all of a sudden he let me go. I started coughing, gasping for breath, my eyes red and full of tears. Omar just looked at me; he started stroking my head like a dog and said, 'You little rat.' I was just glad to be alive; I looked at him sadly, cowed like a beaten dog in a corner. He took some chocolate out of his pocket and threw it at me. I didn't want it; I was too sick to eat it anyway. I stood up to leave but he wouldn't let me go; he wanted me to eat the chocolate. Then I heard my mum calling me: 'Mirsad, come home – dinner is ready.'

I ran past him to get to her.

I didn't tell anyone what had happened and nobody realised anything was wrong as I was always quiet and sometimes I would cry for no reason.

After this I avoided seeing Omar, but the following week he came over to our house with his parents. He acted like nothing had happened, so I did the same but I was wary of him. He wanted to go to my room and he was trying to be nice; he'd brought sweets for himself and chocolate for me, but I was too scared to take it. I felt he would get angry with me again. I gave him my toys, including my favourite pistol, and he gave me the chocolate. Nervously, I started eating it, and straight away, he started hitting me on the head with the gun as hard as he could. Again, he was laughing and I coughed all the chocolate up. Suddenly, my sister came in with some drinks for us, but she didn't see Omar hit me, and as usual, I didn't say anything.

I was beginning to be really scared of this big monster; it felt like I was trapped with this guy. I kept trying to think of what my granddad would do, but Omar was overpowering me in every way. There was no solution to this problem: he would ring the doorbell and just slip into my house to disturb my peace and torment me. There was no escape. My family and his family became very close so he kept bringing food to us through the garden. One day, I was cleaning something in the garden and there was a full bucket of water in front of me. Omar tripped when he jumped over the fence and fell down. I laughed and he got angry with me. He lifted me off the floor and pushed my head into the bucket of cold water. I couldn't breathe and tried to push the bucket away with my hands, but he had his feet on it so I couldn't move it. He was holding me by my legs like a chicken and laughing. I could hear my mum saying, 'You guys must be having fun!'

As he lifted my head out of the bucket, I was shivering and gasping for breath, and panicking about what he was going to do next. Luckily, just then, his mother called him, so he dropped me on the floor and ran through the garden back to his house. I ran into my room and as usual, didn't tell anyone what had happened – I was too scared to tell anybody about these recurring incidents because he kept gesturing to me that he would cut my throat.

It took me a good couple of weeks to recover from that incident, so when Omar's parents invited us to a party at their house next door, I didn't want to go. I stayed at home, until my dad came back and said, 'There's a lot of food cooked for all of us – come along with me and join us. Omar is expecting you too.'

Dad always had a good appetite for food and he thought that everybody else was like him.

I agreed to go to the party, thinking that, if Omar was waiting for me, he might fix up and be OK towards me. In front of our families, he was very kind and never showed any aggression. He kept loading my plate with food and was very generous. Then his mother suggested that we should go and play in his bedroom. At first I was a little bit sceptical, but then I relaxed and thought, Omar seems different now, perhaps he has changed. But as soon as I walked into his bedroom, he locked the door and became aggressive. I looked around to see if I could escape. He smiled and said, 'There is no escape this time!'

I formed the opinion that this kid was a complete psycho.

He had a bench and a bar and some dumbbells, and he said, 'Let's lift some weights.' Then he handed me some tablets – amino acids – and he said, 'Take these – they're good for you.'

I felt I had no choice but to swallow them, as he was taking them too and I didn't want to upset him again.

I was still nervous around him, but I loved weight training as it reminded me of my hero Fikret Hodžić and the days when I was lifting weights with him. So when Omar started lifting the weights, I did too. He seemed rather impressed with my technique and how strong I was. After giving me some more tablets, he told me to take my top off. I followed his orders very carefully as he reminded me of the soldiers. He had an evil smile on his face, as I was taking my top off. I was skinny with very fair skin, and he started laughing loudly, then suddenly his face was like a monster's: he had seen the cross-shaped scar on my chest from when the soldiers in Bosnia had tortured me. He was a Muslim guy and he reacted when he saw the scar. He said, 'You little rat!' then pinned me to the bench and pushed the bar on to my throat. Oh my God, there was no escape! I was kicking my legs on the floor, hoping they would hear downstairs and help me, but they were listening to some music and had no idea what was going on. My legs were gone and my body was losing control; my vision was blurry and I was getting pins and needles all over. I summoned all the strength I had left and pulled his hair as hard as I could. He let go of the bar and slapped me really hard, but then he lost his balance and slipped. I grabbed the bar and tipped the weights to one side, so they fell on the floor, which made a massive bang downstairs.

My mum ran upstairs and tried to open the door. Omar quickly unlocked it, and told her, 'We are just training really hard so the weights came off the bar.'

In our culture, parents always believe what an older child says. I was still recovering from the attack and trying to get my breath back, and my mum asked me why I was red. As usual, I just shrugged my shoulders, but, now I could get out, I quickly grabbed my T-shirt and ran downstairs and went home. I had a shower and went to bed, but I was too upset to sleep and spent all night thinking about what had happened.

From that day my PTSD really kicked in. I avoided Omar at every possible situation, until my sister decided to throw me a little surprise party for my birthday. She invited all the Bosnian children, as well as Omar. When I saw him I was in shock, and I ran outside and hid in the treehouse. My family were really concerned when they couldn't find me, and the entire neighbourhood was looking for me for hours. It was starting to get dark and I was still hiding in the treehouse, crouched in the corner with my head buried between my legs, scared of my own shadow. All of a sudden, I heard someone coming up: Omar. Panicked, I charged at him and headbutted him in the stomach, knocking him off the tree and on to his back. I ran into my house and my worried parents asked me where I'd been. I told them I was hiding in the treehouse and that I'd pushed Omar off the tree. They rushed over to the treehouse and found him still lying on the grass. He told my mum and dad that I'd pushed him off the tree; he said he'd hurt his back and couldn't move. His parents came and helped him inside the house; they were really angry. From then on, Omar always had a problem with his back. He didn't come out of the house much after that, but any time I saw him, I used to run away. My mum and dad realised what I did was very serious and they were concerned about my behaviour, so they encouraged me to do more jobs to keep me out of trouble.

Fortunately, I already had a reputation as a good worker and a neighbour soon recommended me for some painting work. The guy called my dad and offered to give me a mountain bike in exchange for the job. He agreed as I hadn't had a bike since before the war, and I happily started the three-week job. Then, one day, while I was painting, Omar turned up at the door: it turned out this guy was Omar's uncle. I was that scared my hand started shaking and I couldn't even hold the brush. I ran out of the house and straight home. The following day, the guy came over to talk to my dad; he advised that it was best for me not to mix with Omar. That was good for my mum and dad to know, and solved the problem.

I went back and finished the job. It was hard work and the guy was very demanding, but he was very pleased with it. I was a perfectionist at any job I did, so people were always very happy with my work. He gave me the bike, as agreed, and I couldn't wait to start riding it. I kept that bike clean, and all the kids knew me by my yellow mountain bike, but I still didn't socialise with them, and kept to myself as usual.

One day I was standing outside my house with my bike and one of the neighbours' kids came over to ask if I could fix the broken chain on his bike. I called my dad, who said he would fix it. Dad repaired the chain and charged the boy £2.50. Word spread quickly, and soon our garden was full of bikes. Tyre punctures, welding, changing brakes, and painting and servicing bikes – we did it all. It certainly kept me out of trouble and it kept us both busy. We also made some money out of it.

But I'd lost the little confidence I had since meeting Omar. I was very thin and had been easily overpowered by him. I wanted to put on some weight, get stronger, and build a wall of muscles around me to protect myself from the bullies. I'd grown up around bodybuilders and knew that weight training would be the best way to bulk up so I got myself an old chimney and some bricks to use as makeshift weights. I used the chimney as a bar, holding it at each end and lifting it above my head. I cut out pictures of Arnold Schwarzenegger and I put them on the wall in my bedroom, and that gave me the inspiration and focus I needed.

I spent every evening in my room, silently pushing the

weights. My dad could see my potential, so he bought me a bench and some plastic dumbbells. Weights became my best friend and Arnold's posters my motivation. I became so drawn into it that on a number of occasions I spoke to my pictures of Schwarzenegger. I'd heard stories from our relative Fikret Hodžić about Arnold and I always dreamed of meeting him but I didn't really believe that would ever happen.

Weight training became a big part of my growing up, as it gave me some power over those kids who tried to bully me. Soon, I began to notice differences in my muscularity, and definition started to show on my skinny body. Kids started noticing the little 'eggs' on my arms and began calling me Little Bruce Lee. The training became like therapy for me. Whenever I would get panic attacks and anxiety, I would start lifting weights. The exercise would help sweat out those problems and calm me down, but really I was just learning to suppress them somewhere deep inside me. Those moments would appear on a daily basis, but somehow I dealt with them.

At this young age, I had already realised that I was facing many barriers in everything I did because of my PTSD. The one thing that I was able to control was my physical strength, but I knew that I would never use a weapon in a physical confrontation with anyone. I knew in my head that if I had access to weapons I would probably end up being the worst terrorist on earth. My terrible experiences in the war and the violence and trauma I had suffered had damaged me deeply, and it would take many years to learn to live with the effects. There was also the danger that I could become self-destructive. Somehow I needed to find a way to harness this inner energy, strength and endurance and turn them into passion and love.

A new challenge was about to present itself, and I would need all my inner strength to cope.

10

Beating the Bullies

It was time for my parents to enrol me in school and I agreed to go. It was a family decision. I was fourteen by now, and perhaps they thought the school would give me a direction, a better future, and I would learn English. My parents knew I would face difficulties with my PTSD, and that making friends would be a big challenge for me, especially as I couldn't speak English. They thought the best solution was to put me in a school with other Bosnian children, where my sister Meliha had started a little while before.

On my first day at Waverley School, my dad came with me and introduced me to the teachers. I said nothing as usual. For some reason the teachers were never told about my past and that created real problems. I don't know if it was so that I wouldn't be singled out, or whether my parents were still wary of authority, of giving too much away, but it meant the teachers couldn't understand my unusual behaviour.

As I didn't speak English, I was based in the Language

Development Base – LDB. There were kids there from many different ethnicities, as well as some Bosnian kids I already knew, including my sister Meliha, Leila, Adnan, Elvis, Sead, Mirza, Amir, Almir, Alma and Miki, the big guy from the mosque. However, many of them, including my sister, settled in well enough to move out of the LDB classes to mainstream lessons quickly, and soon the only kids left there were the badly behaved ones and the ones who couldn't speak English – I had both problems.

Even on my first day, I felt the teachers didn't like the look of me and I thought they would give me a hard time: I was right. I took all the blame for everything that went on. Miki showed he hadn't changed by turning all the tables upside down and beating up all the kids. He didn't touch me that day, but I'm sure he just wanted to let me know he was there and show me he was in charge. When the teachers came into the classroom, the room was in such a mess it looked like there had been an earthquake in there. They started shouting at me, like I was responsible for all of the mess made by the other kids. They all thought there was something wrong with me because I didn't speak to anyone and Miki had told everyone I was crazy, so I was an easy target. They then made me clear it all up and put me in isolation. I sat alone in a little room for the whole week, filling in paper sheets with one sentence, which I didn't even understand. I absolutely hated it. I remember teachers were swearing at me in Bosnian without even knowing what they were saying. The other Bosnian kids had taught them those phrases pretending they meant 'Please be quiet' and 'Get on with your work'.

My sister would appear now and again, making sure that I

was OK. She thought I was in isolation to learn English, not because I wasn't fitting in.

For some reason, all the teachers thought I was a problem. Almost as soon as I got out of isolation, I found myself back in there – it was like a prison and I hated it. Most of the time I didn't do anything; they would give me something to read, but it was always in English, which of course I couldn't read, so I was bored to death. But I never complained, I just got on with the punishment.

When I was back in the LDB, the other kids took everything off me: pens, pencils, papers, etc. Whenever Miki came in, he seemed to be looking for a fight, but I stood up to him again. I lifted up a chair and swung it at anybody who came near me. When I was fighting, I imagined I was in a war and I fought for my life. Everybody thought I was a complete psycho, including my teachers, and that's why they seemed to give up on me completely. They didn't even know how to punish me anymore.

One of the teachers decided that my punishment should be picking up the litter on the sports field. While the other kids had their PE lessons, I was out on a cold morning, picking up their rubbish. It felt like I was being punished for the whole school's bad behaviour. I was developing grudges against all the teachers. Oh my God, it was cold and quite often it was raining too. I was out alone with a litter picker and massive black bag, which was bigger than me. It was so cold, my hands turned blue. At times I couldn't even hold the litter picker as my hands were shivering so much.

One day, I had been picking up the litter on the field for a couple of hours, when all the kids rushed me and got the bag off me. They ran into the changing room and threw the rubbish all over the floor. This great big lump of a teacher came over to me and shouted, 'You, come with me!'

He made me pick up every single bit of rubbish and then wrote a report about me. For a whole week, I had to come into school twenty minutes early and clean the changing room and do jobs for him. One day, while I was on the floor cleaning, another group of kids ran into the changing room and every single one of them kicked me as hard as they could. When the teacher came in, he thought I was putting on an act to get out of the punishment, even though I was badly hurt and bruised. I made up my mind as soon as I saw those kids again I'd get them with my litter picker. The next morning, I waited in the changing room, and as soon as they came in for their first PE lesson, I started hitting them on the head with the metal picker, as they ran around me, bumping into each other, trying to get away. Now it was my turn to dish out the punishment and I was showing no mercy. When the teacher came in, I froze. I looked around me – every kid was hurt and shocked. He made some hand gestures towards me, which I think meant that I would go to prison. That didn't scare me though, and that seemed to confuse the teacher even more.

Again, they punished me. This time I had to clean all the football boots for weeks and weeks. I sat in a dark little room with a big pile of boots and a brush and water, trying to get all the mud off. There were bags full of mud from those boots.

Another day, a group of kids jumped me again, throwing punches and boots at me. I picked up a boot and started hitting anybody who came near me, trying to get them to back off.

All of a sudden, I saw the teacher's face. He was gesturing to me: 'Come on, hit me!' But he knew I wouldn't dare hit him.

It was an endless cycle of punishment from the teachers and daily attacks by the other kids. I couldn't see a way out. More teachers got involved to try to deal with me but none of them seemed to know what to do. I'm sure if I'd told my parents what I was facing every day they would have taken us out of that school straight away.

Although the PE teacher was struggling to deal with me, he had seen something in me. He didn't say anything to me, but I now know he recognised that I had unbeatable inner strength. We had shared values without even knowing one another. He had a strong Jamaican accent, so few people could understand him, but I didn't need to understand for he knew what it meant to be an outsider. He used to scare all the other kids with his deep voice when he shouted, but I wasn't scared of him and that is probably what he liked about me. I wasn't scared of anybody and I always stood up for myself. He liked that too.

One day, this massive kid, Kemal, came in. He was another kid nicknamed Tyson. The teacher said to him, 'Listen, Kemal, if you can tear apart this little tiger, you can have a lunch on me.'

I looked at them blankly. By now I had picked up enough English to get the gist of what people were saying, although I never replied, but I understood and I was up for it. Everybody feared Kemal and Miki, but I stood up ready to fight him. Nobody could believe it, and all the kids started saying I was mad. The teacher laughed and asked me, 'Are you scared of the big boy?'

I shook my head. Like a proper Northerner, I stood up

to Kemal, beckoning him over with my hands. He froze and started sweating, and all the kids started booing him and saying, 'You sissy boy! Look who you're scared of.'

The teacher looked at us and said, 'No, I didn't mean for you to fight. I want you to compete to see who can lift more weights.' He pointed to the bench press machine, an old-fashioned multiple-use unit, and said, 'I'll stack all the weights at the bottom and whoever lifts it more times is the toughest kid in the PE department.'

I was like a hungry wolf that wanted to eat – not only Kemal, but the machine too. But now Kemal was excited – he was bigger than me and he started taking the piss out of me and my skinny little body, but I knew how to beat him. I grew up with bodybuilders, and I knew how to sit on the bench and arch my back to make a bridge so that all my strength would come from my legs. And I knew I could demolish him with my endurance.

Kemal got on the bench. He was big, but he didn't have a clue how to lift properly; he just used his body power to shift the weights. Puffing away, he was squeezing everything. The other kids were so excited they started counting for him. He managed to do ten reps and everybody was really impressed, including the teacher.

Now it was my turn. As I started to warm up, circling my arms, with my Little Bruce Lee muscles, they were all laughing their socks off, even the teacher. The laughter didn't last long, though. I got into position, with the correct posture and breathing technique, and started squeezing the weights.

The teacher said I'd do twenty, so I did. There was complete silence in the changing room as I easily beat Kemal, and my expression didn't change a bit.

I earned a new nickname – Tiger – that day, but it gave me an unwanted reputation and just brought more fights my way. Straight after school, Miki came up to me and said, 'Listen, Tiger, don't think because you've lifted some stupid weights that you're tougher than me.'

I didn't respond, just kept a blank face, but he didn't expect me to say anything anyway.

Another day, a kid came up to me and asked if I was scared of Miki. As usual, I shook my head. This got back to Miki, and I heard the other kids were stirring it, trying to arrange another fight.

My friend Sead Alimajstorović was worried about me, and he said, 'Don't be stupid – you can't fight Miki, he'll kill you.'

'I don't care. I don't fear him – after all, I don't fear anybody.'

'But I know a secret way out the back to avoid Miki,' he said.

'No, I'm going home alone the same way.'

I knew I couldn't back down, and my plan was to attack Miki first and land a few punches on him. That was my only chance, as he was much stronger than me.

As I met my sister outside the school gate as usual, I spotted Miki. As soon as he saw me, he started walking towards me, stamping his feet to scare me, shouting, 'You're not scared of me?'

I just kept a blank face, remembering my grandfather's words: 'Get a punch in first to shock him and the rest is easy.' That's exactly what I did. I managed to give him a few digs, and before he could even get one back, my sister and her friend Leila jumped in between us, trying to stop the fight.

Then suddenly the teachers turned up and stopped the fight. Someone had obviously told them that I was going to get beaten up again. Miki was furious but there was nothing he could do.

From that day on, Miki never came near me again and over the years he gave me respect for standing up to him. But other people soon came to take his place and I found myself fighting on a daily basis. It was a destructive cycle; it affected my wellbeing and I never received any education. I was punished every day for something and the teachers didn't seem to have the time nor the inclination to look deeper into the real problem and find a way to resolve it.

* * *

Outside school, things were just as bad. Sorrow and anger were deeply ingrained in me and I often struggled to cope with the effects of my PTSD.

Many times in my life, when I am in meditating mode, quietly embracing the peace, I feel my brain and my body are like a steady sea, the waves gently lapping the shore. Then I think I can control my PTSD, I can control my anger. All of a sudden, I hear the angry voice harshly spoken: '*We will meet again*'. Instantly, it wakes those bad memories and I start panicking and shaking like a little boy. I feel like I am on a big ship with no captain, in a thunderstorm. The anger fills my body, controlling every single muscle. I feel it destroying the ship; the ship is falling apart, and losing its course. I cannot control the ship and it is sinking. That is when the PTSD kicks in. I cry uncontrollably from overwhelming feelings of anxiety, anger and frustration. There is no one to help and the pain becomes even harder to bear now than when I was tortured. These feelings invade my body for a couple of minutes before they disappear.

The aftermath is always scary, devastating and disappointing. Then I see a gentle hand and it's my mother stroking my back and saying, 'Mirsad, are you OK?'

I look at her but I do not answer; I enter the world of silence, shame, fear and frustration. I'm too embarrassed to say anything, but my look is enough for my mother to register my sorrow, my pain. Only my dearest mother can put the fire out and calm me down.

That was still her biggest challenge – to be discreet about my PTSD, so the neighbours and friends did not find out. Concerned about the stigma attached to mental illness, especially a few years ago, she feared it would affect my future. She hoped that I would grow up to live a normal life, and have a family of my own, and she worried that people would hold my problems against me. She always cared the most, and just wanted me to be well and happy.

People know that I am an all-or-nothing kind of person – anything I do, I give 100 per cent. My very good friend Sead Alimajstorović, who came to the UK from Sarajevo at the same time as me, always said, 'Mirsad, if you became a soldier, you would be the best soldier and you would become a hero. The only problem is you would get killed very quickly!'

I thought long and hard about his statements and what he was trying to say. I looked up to Sead, as he was a very intelligent kid and I hung around with him quite a lot. Always a committed friend, I would give everything for the people I cared about, whether in a fight, money or doing someone a favour. I cared about others more than myself because I knew what it meant to be hurt – I never wanted anybody else to get hurt. My sister saw that in me and she always wanted to get close to me, but I didn't allow anybody to get attached – my feelings and emotions were too dangerous, raw and unsaturated. It was my problem to deal with, and I didn't want anybody else involved. Most of the time I tried not to involve my family, and would go into my quiet zone, pull away from everyone for a couple of weeks. I always felt alone, although at the back of my mind I knew my parents were there for me and tried all they could to help me. In any situation I always relied on myself – I guess that's what made me the very strong, independent person that I am today. Over the years I have learned never to be disappointed with anything or anybody and that's what made me this person.

One day, I went to the local park in Highgate with my friend, who was nicknamed Elvis Musić. We rode our bikes there, and laid them down on the ground near us while we played on the swings. As we were chatting, a guy walked up to Elvis's bike and sat on it, obviously thinking he could get away from us. I jumped off the swing and landed on top of him; I wrestled him on the floor and took the bike off him, while Elvis sat watching, not knowing what to do. I sat on the bike, making my way over to Elvis, when all of a sudden someone hit the back of my head with a bat. I fell off the bike and lost consciousness, while Elvis took his bike and ran off. When I came to, I had cold blood splattered all over my face. My bike was next to me – they didn't want it because it was only a cheap one. I couldn't ride it so I started to walk home, wheeling my bike beside me. A passing bus driver noticed the state I was in, and told me to get on the bus with my bike. He dropped me near my home, and told me to call an ambulance, as I was still bleeding. When I knocked on the door my face and my top were covered with blood, and my mum collapsed in shock on the doorstep. My dad called an ambulance straight away, and I was taken to the nearest hospital. I had eight stitches in my head but I was perfectly all right. People were concerned at the hospital and at home, but it didn't bother me at all: I've been through worse, I thought. I didn't blame Elvis for leaving me – I knew how scared he must have been to run off like that.

I met another friend, Enes Arifagić, who also came from Kozarac. Enes didn't have parents, and he came from Bosnia with his aunt. He was two years older than me, but we got on very well. Neither of us had any friends or any money; we stood up for each other in every situation. More importantly, we understood each other because we had been through the same ordeal.

Enes told me his story, how he was separated from his parents and put in a concentration camp at the age of fifteen, in the same place I stayed with my family. I felt sorry for him, and I thought at least I'd had my parents. Enes told me what had happened to him at the start of the war. Soldiers would turn up at his house on a daily basis and make him take things out of the neighbours' houses and load them on to a tractor for the Serbian paramilitary troops.

The soldiers were scared to enter the house in case someone was inside protecting it and might shoot at them or in case there was a booby trap, so they would send Enes in first to take the risk. While he was getting stuff from the house, the soldiers were getting drunk. On one occasion they bumped into another Serbian paramilitary group, who were also taking things out of the house. All of a sudden Enes felt someone jab him with a rifle: 'Stop and turn around!'

He turned around to see a soldier pointing a gun at him: 'What are you doing here?'

'I'm loading things for the soldiers outside.'

'Get out of my sight before I shoot you in the head.'

Enes walked out with his head down, hardly able to believe what had just happened. 'This soldier would have actually shot me in the head without any hesitation,' he told me, his eyes full of anger and tears pouring down his face. 'How can someone do that to a child?'

As I was listening to his story, I was reliving my own experiences. I realised we had a lot in common – we had lived through the worst, there was nothing else to scare us.

Enes often borrowed my bike, but he really wanted his own, and when he'd saved some money, he asked me to go and look for one with him. We went to a second-hand shop, where there was a bike on display, and we stood in front of it for at least half an hour, staring at the bike as if we wanted to eat it. The shop owner came outside and shouted at us like we were going to steal it. Even though we told him we had the money to buy the bike, he just told us to move on. As a child that experience stuck in my head – it was a horrible day. We would never go back to that shop again. In the end, my dad helped Enes to buy a bike somewhere else, and then we went everywhere together on our old bikes; riding by the canals, parks and on the streets.

Both of us felt really sad, disappointed and disorientated

by the experience at the shop. It seemed to be just another indication that nobody wanted us; we were poor, struggled to communicate and full of negative experiences from the war. We felt alienated from English society and had great difficulties being accepted, so we stuck closely together. It was hard, but we accepted the fact that nobody seemed to want to hang out with us. We also wondered if maybe this was part of everyone's growing-up process, and perhaps things would have been the same for us in Kozarac. Our experiences in the war had made it difficult to know what was normal anymore. We observed the community and often felt sorry for ourselves and each other as we felt so excluded. Often we would stand by the ice-cream van, watching other children buying and enjoying ice cream, without thinking about how lucky they were, just as we had done in Bosnia when life was normal. Somehow we knew better days would come. I wouldn't say that I was angry at the world, but I was disappointed and frustrated that we couldn't have basic things like other kids had. At a young age I had realised that you have to accept things the way they are, otherwise you will turn against the world in a negative way and become a cynical, negative young man, but it wasn't easy.

I was very emotional, going through a lot of issues in my head about acceptance, integration and different values in life. Often I felt overwhelmed and just wanted to block out the world. Why can't I be a normal human being like other kids? Why is everybody picking on me? I thought.

Now I decided that the only way to deal with that anger was to fight anybody who attacked me. I found it very difficult to find inner peace. First, I had to let my friendship with Enes go. We had endured the same terrible experiences and were facing the same struggles, and I began to realise we weren't helping each other. In fact, our friendship was starting to affect my PTSD. In negative situations, it actually hits me even more, so I try to avoid them whenever I can. One of my biggest challenges was to stay positive – I need positive energy, warm feelings and emotions. I never asked for help, and I often wonder why I didn't ask for my family's support – I guess I wanted to show them that I was brave and strong, that you can throw anything at me and I can cope with it. I did not realise that this kind of behaviour was destroying me inside.

But my family knew more than I realised; they noticed the differences in my behaviour and were very concerned about my mood swings. They knew me so well I couldn't hide anything from them, especially my mother, who knew how I was feeling just by the way I looked at her. My sister, Meliha, also knew all the little signs; she would touch my hand and if it was too warm, she knew I was deeply buried in my PTSD, my heart racing and my blood pressure high. My head would feel like it was going to explode and everything was racing at a hundred miles an hour. Inside, I was always fighting to defuse the situation, to control my inner conflict.

I used to take the bus to school with Meliha, and she always sat next to me and made sure that I was protected. Even though she was older than me, I always thought it was my job to make sure that she was protected too – I used to look at her and think, if anybody touches her, I'm prepared to kill them. One day, on the bus, I had been lost in my thoughts when I suddenly heard Meliha screaming. I looked up and there was a guy pointing a knife at my sister, trying to grab her bag. I glared murderously at him, and drew his attention to me, gesturing for him to strike at me. He looked at me confused, while Meliha started crying loudly to get people's attention on the bus. No one even looked, no one reacted, and no one stood up. I felt blind fury: I could see the soldier torturing me again, but this time the soldier only had a knife. I was thinking, that knife cannot shoot, there is no bullet. If needs be, I can eat that knife. There was now complete silence on the bus. The man began to pull away; he had seen my furious eyes, knew I would not back down. He hadn't bargained for this. I jumped at him, and grabbed the hand holding the knife. Then I squeezed it so tightly that the knife fell out of his hand. The other passengers started applauding, but for me that was not the end, it was just the beginning.

I began to kick and punch this guy mercilessly. Meliha picked up the knife and started trying to get me off the bus, but she knew I wouldn't – couldn't – calm down. She ran to the driver and showed him the knife. 'Call the police! My brother will kill this guy!' she said.

The driver stopped the bus and people started getting off, but I kept hitting the man, punching him, and the blood splattered everywhere. He was calling for help, but the people on the bus ignored him. I grabbed hold of his neck and started strangling him, when suddenly I heard my mother: 'Mirsad, calm down.'

In fact, it was the bus driver trying to get me off him, but the thought of my mother had been enough to make me stop. I picked the guy up and threw him down the stairs and ran down after him, looking for Meliha. She was downstairs waiting for me, and dragged me off the bus, saying, 'Come on! The police are on their way – they will take you away.'

A police car shot past us to get to the scene, but Meliha had already rushed me away from the bus.

I was shocked at what I had done. Where did I get the energy to fight like that? I guess the turmoil and terrible anger inside me had to be released somehow. That guy must have been terrified and he was lucky that I didn't pick up the knife and use it on him. Even when I experience these PTSD panic attacks, I am still myself and keep the same values. Somehow, my brain always sends the signals to my body not to fight with any tools and never to use a gun. In the past I have been hurt with both a knife and a gun, and I would never hurt anyone else in the same way.

The next day we got the bus to school again, and, as soon as I got on, the passengers started applauding and saying, 'Well done! That guy will never get on the bus again.'

For the first time since the war, I felt positive healing energy, which was overwhelming and difficult to explain. I felt like a hero, proud to help others, especially my family.

* * *

At school, I decided I had to take matters into my own hands, and my only education came from writing my own dictionary: I would write down any new words I heard people say, then find out what they meant and write the meaning in my own language. It was the best way for me to develop my vocabulary and remember new words. I got the idea from my uncle Hasan – he was my favourite uncle as he always brought me chocolate. On one occasion when he was going out with my aunt Sebina, he came to our house when I was trying to remember a poem, but it wouldn't stick in my head. My uncle said, 'You're tired and exhausted now, but just take a pen and paper and write out that poem. When you get up in the morning you will know the poem by heart.'

I didn't believe him, but the next morning when I got up I was reciting that poem like a parrot. I'll never forget my uncle's words of advice as they helped me to overcome my language barriers.

I remember one day my dad came to school and he was shocked to see what was going on and that I was not receiving any education. My options were limited because of the surroundings and bullying that was going on. I had already wasted the whole year in this place without learning anything, apart from writing my own dictionary. Dad realised that I was spending all my time fighting the bullies instead of getting an education, and he knew it couldn't go on.

My dad was learning to drive with his friend Tariq, who had grown up in the area. He trusted his advice, and asked him if I was allowed to change schools. Tariq said of course I could, and Dad knew that was what I had to do and as soon as possible.

One day, during my dad's driving lesson, they drove past a school and my dad asked Tariq about it.

'That's Moseley School,' he said. 'I went there as a child – it's not a bad school, I came out all right!'

My dad decided to enrol me there, and Tariq came along with us as our interpreter. I guess I was lucky the school had spaces and they told us that I could start the next week. I hoped this would be my final school.

11

New School,
Same Challenges

As I put on my new school uniform and blazer, I was very nervous about what awaited me, and starting all over again. My dad also had concerns about me. Like any parents, they tried to advise me not to get in any trouble. Dad told me to run away from any bad situations and fights. With hardly any English and my communication problems, that seemed an impossible task, but I would try my best.

The school was huge, with an east and a west wing, and it took five minutes to walk from one end to another. On the first day, I was a little overwhelmed, trying to get my bearings, and more importantly, looking for any escape routes I could use if I got attacked. Already I'd noticed there were many little corners and blind spots. As I wandered round, I noticed the other kids looking at me like I had just dropped from Mars. I wanted to fit in quietly, and was trying not to make the same mistake as in the previous school; I knew I would have to try and play a different game here. The school was predominantly full of Asian and Afro-Caribbean children. Who would I turn to for help? Who would back me up if I got attacked? There were hardly any teachers walking around, considering the size of the school. I knew there had to be a way to make a new start in this school, but the kids were already giving me strange looks. In my head I started thinking they were provoking me already.

I met my first tutor, Mrs Hatton, who was nice – she pretended to be a very strict teacher, but I soon worked her out. She just knew how to deal with young boys really well. I was taken to the Language Development Base, where I met Mrs Heatherington; she was very calm and healing, and she had this enormous energy around her. I always thought she brought us all together.

But the kids had already noticed I was different – it was only the first day and they had decided I was very strange and peculiar, and the bullying soon began again. The kids were asking me questions, but I didn't really know what they were talking about, so I would just mumble something back in Bosnian.

I remember my first PE lesson with Mr Manda. All the kids were laughing at me, pointing to my skin, saying that I was too pale, and he was trying to divert their attention to my muscles – I was still weight training at home in my bedroom, and I was developing a good physique.

At the end of the lesson, this big black kid, Nathan, was giving me dirty looks and, as usual, I just stared back at him, showing no fear. This time around, though, I guess my granddad's tactic didn't work. It was almost the end of school classes, and we were walking to the tutorial with Mrs Hatton.

There was massive congestion in the corridor and Nathan was pushing everyone out of the way to get to me. I didn't even have a chance to turn around fully towards him before he launched a punch at my face, but I pulled my head back and he didn't catch me. I struck straight back at him with a dig in his teeth. Nathan fell back with his mouth bleeding and landed in Mrs Hatton's arms. She'd seen me punch him and I thought I was finished.

'You got some anger in you, young man,' she said loudly in her Jamaican accent. 'What did you do that for?'

I just shrugged my shoulders.

'You come with me,' she said to Nathan and me.

As we followed her, a couple of girls shouted, 'Mrs Hatton, we saw what happened.'

She told the girls to come too, and we all sat down in her office.

She gave Nathan a tissue, and he kept dabbing the blood out of his mouth and saying it hurt.

Mrs Hatton sucked her teeth. 'Look what you've done,' she told me. 'I'll have to call your parents. You will have lots of explaining to do and this is your first week in a new school.'

Shit, if she calls my parents, I'll be in a lot of trouble with my dad, I thought. I'd promised him that I would make a new start in this school and avoid any trouble. Dad had told me this was my last chance with the schools and this school would be my very last school. He warned me that, if I got into any more fights, I'd be taken into a mental institution.

I had a good feeling about Mrs Hatton, as she reminded me of my mother, and I loved it when she shouted at me with her Jamaican twang as it sounded like a Bosnian mother. Nathan found it strange that I was not scared of Mrs Hatton, but he had a reason to be scared because he bullied all the kids. The girls were very happy when I gave Nathan a beating, and told Mrs Hatton that he hit me first. She dismissed us and we walked away with a handshake and without speaking another word.

All the school was buzzing that this new kid has knocked out Nathan. That was exactly what I didn't want to happen as this could lead to more and more fights.

The next day, in PE, Mr Manda smiled at me, saying, 'We have a new boxer in the class, I hear. Perhaps you can join me on the boxing bag.'

Mrs Hatton also greeted me with a smile, but she said that I should apologise to Nathan. So later that day, I walked up to Nathan and said sorry in my broken English. All the other kids laughed, but I never knew if they were laughing at me because I apologised to Nathan or because of my accent.

Mrs Hatton had noticed that my communication skills were very poor, so she spoke to me a lot to try and help me. She was my favourite out of all the female teachers. One day she asked where I was from. When I said Bosnia, I think she finally understood my background and my frustration with the other kids, and perhaps she realised why I acted the way I did. Looking back, it's strange no one had told her, and that no one seemed to know what we'd been through as refugees. She always spoke to me as if she was telling me off, and I loved her loud Jamaican patois the most: 'Mirsad, you are crazy,' she would say. I didn't even know what it meant, but she made me repeat it, just to tease one or two words out of me, as I never spoke. I really liked that and I started to trust her – she was the one who really got me speaking English.

Mrs Hatton had Jamaican values and she commanded respect in her classroom. She always made sure that all the kids were well behaved and obeyed her rules. She noticed that I was writing my new words in my own dictionary, and she could see I wanted to learn, so she invested a lot of her spare time to help me extend my vocabulary and learn more words. She was expert at that, as she taught English and she was always reading books. Every week she would give me ten new words to learn: how to spell them, how to pronounce them and the meaning of those words. Eventually, the whole class was doing it and it became like a quiz.

Although my language was gradually developing, I was still struggling to make any friends as I couldn't speak to anyone and I didn't have any siblings in this school. Also, I was still getting into fights. I felt like somebody was setting those kids against me and I always thought it was Nathan. Already I had wasted a year at Waverley School, and I could not follow my normal lessons, so Mrs Hatton and Mrs Heatherington suggested that I should go back and do Year Ten again, so I would have a chance of getting better results. It was a good idea, but it meant that I would have to start all over again, meeting new classmates, which meant more bullying and more fights.

One day, I was in a geography lesson with a guy called Raymond, the biggest kid in the school. He always used to borrow my massive eraser, but one day he decided not to give it back. I walked up to him and gestured that I wanted it back. He threw it at my face and, as I was trying to catch it, he punched me. I saw stars and I couldn't fight back. The geography teacher shouted at Raymond and asked me if I was OK. I just nodded like nothing had happened. Then I remembered more of my granddad's advice: 'You have to be a man to be able to receive a punch.' Granddad was right because Raymond was surprised that I didn't cry, and I didn't look scared of him. I knew if I punched him, I could have been expelled from the school, and this was my last chance so I didn't want to blow it. Somehow I knew that I would deal with him later.

The bullying didn't stop until I dealt with a guy called Shafik, a Pakistani in the sixth form, who loved beating up younger kids. He always used to ask kids for money after school. I would run off but one day he caught me on a bus and put his hand out. I opened my bag, pretending to look for money, but instead, I grabbed hold of a brick and whacked him on the head. I always had a brick in my bag for protection, but I told the teachers that I trained with it at lunchtime in school. After I hit him, I opened the emergency window and jumped out of the bus. I ran home and didn't go to school for a week, telling my parents I was ill. Then I started going to school on my bike, knowing what happened on the bus. I tried to avoid Shafik, but then I saw him on a sports activity day and he looked embarrassed when he spotted me. The other kids had found out that the Year Ten kid had beaten him up, and his reputation had taken a hit. Shafik had had a month off school, so that brick must have really hurt his face – no other kids messed with me for a while after that.

But the peace didn't last. One day, I was sitting on the grass next to the basketball court, eating my sandwiches, and this big fat Asian guy walked up to me, and said, 'Have you got a problem?'

I kept quiet, but he kept going on and on. I didn't understand half of the stuff that he was saying, but I didn't care.

Then he said, 'Tom told me that you called me fat.'

I didn't know how to swear in English so I said just one word I'd heard other people say: 'Paki.'

Furious, he jumped on top of me, pushing me into a big pile of sand next to the court. I tried to get myself out, but I was squashed underneath him and had no chance. All the kids had gathered around us, and they were cheering and shouting, 'Come on, Sajid, finish him off!'

Then I heard another voice: 'Sajid, it wasn't him! It was an Afghan boy that called you fat.'

As Sajid stopped for a second to listen to this kid – Tom – I grabbed a handful of sand and threw it in his face. He cried out, and while his eyes were full of sand, I got as close as I could to his face and gave him my best shot. Afterwards, he told some other kids that he saw stars when I punched him. That was my last fight for a very long time in that school.

All of a sudden, some of the teachers appeared and separated us. Sajid's eyes were full of sand and one of them was bloodshot, where I'd punched him. One of the teachers said, 'What have you done now?'

Tom told them that Sajid attacked me because he thought that I called him a fat boy.

The teachers seemed puzzled and one of them said, 'He never talks to anyone.'

Sajid said, 'He called me a Paki.'

I nodded and confessed straight away, and I was taken into isolation.

Sajid's mother made a formal complaint to the school. I

apologised to Sajid and I wrote him a letter explaining that I didn't understand what that word meant.

Isolation gave me an opportunity to reflect on my actions and to try not to make the same mistakes again, but at the same time I was happy that another of my granddad's tactics had worked again.

On my first week out of isolation, I walked over to the same spot behind the basketball court where we'd had the fight, knowing no one would bother me here again as I had marked my territory. I started eating my sandwiches when Tom turned up, bouncing his basketball. I didn't say anything, but I knew he had saved me from being expelled permanently from school that day.

Tom started playing on the court. He shot and missed, and the ball landed in my lap. Basketball had been my favourite game since my Serbian teacher in Bosnia had taught me how to play. I threw my sandwich on the floor, picked up the ball and started showing him my basketball skills. He looked amazed and had a big smile on his face. Then he started clapping his hands and saying, 'Well done, Mirs!'

The more he supported me, the more skill I showed him. Before you knew it, the playground was full of kids and teachers watching my performance. I showed all my best skills: two strides jumping and scoring, slamming the basket, slam dunk, double flicks in the air, and a lot more. Then I stood on the other side of the court with the ball above my head with one hand, and I scored sideways. Nobody could believe my skills. I even heard some girls saying, 'Look at his muscles!' as I rolled up my sleeves. So then I took my shirt off completely, and stood there in just my little white vest, showing my muscles to the girls. They were smiling, giggling and whispering, and that boosted my confidence. The next day, all the kids were talking about my basketball skills.

I made a few friends through playing basketball – we didn't really talk but some of the boys were happy to play a game with me at breaks. One day, I was on the court playing against Luke Brown, a popular boy at the school, who knew me vaguely. He had a very good physique, and his muscles were popping out from his little red T-shirt. Nobody ever bullied Luke – his dad had taught him to box and he knew how to protect himself.

It was a warm afternoon and I was wearing shorts. A few girls were sitting on the grass, admiring our skills, jumps and moves. As we were playing, I noticed a group of boys coming behind the basket where the girls were sitting. Straight away I lost my confidence because this group of lads had picked on me in the past. I never asked anybody to help me to deal with them so I knew they would pick on me again. The girls were cheering and applauding, giving me support – even if nobody could ever pronounce my name, they knew exactly how to lift my morale. But as the bullies approached, my court skills deteriorated, and it was obvious that I was scared of them.

We were playing three against three on one basket and Luke's team started winning. I was trying to keep an eye on the bullies as well as on the basket and Luke. Whenever we played on opposite sides, I always covered him; he was the strongest and most skilled player in the other team. We were about the same height and same build so evenly matched. For a minute all my attention was on Luke to stop him scoring and to get the game back in our hands. I ran towards the basket to score,

I jumped and, while in the air, one of the lads grabbed my shorts and pulled them down. It was the most embarrassing moment in school – I was mortified. I think it was even more embarrassing to me than when the soldiers had stripped me semi-naked and beaten me up. The boys were pointing at my private parts, saying, 'Look how small it is!', while the girls were laughing – they seemed to be more entertained watching me in my underwear than watching the basketball.

It seemed to go on for ever. I was desperately trying to cover my underwear with my hands, and begging them to give me my shorts back. They were passing my shorts around, kicking them to the ground, making them dirty. It was a good twenty minutes before a teacher came to stop them, and it was the most embarrassing twenty minutes of my life. For months afterwards, wherever I went, the girls were laughing and whispering about my private parts, my private pride. It was another very damaging incident and self-destructive for me, but as usual I somehow managed to get through it, although I never trusted the girls in school again and lost all interest in them.

I had never really spoken much as my English was poor, but now I chose not to speak, to avoid the other kids laughing at me in the playground.

I had to get back on the court and get my confidence and my pride back. I had also started to make some friends, slowly bonding through basketball. My communication skills were still poor, but sport was our common ground, and they were happy to play basketball with me. I didn't want to lose these friendships before they even started properly.

I had a plan, but I would need another pair of shorts so I

asked my mum to buy me a pair, but she said, 'You have a pair and I haven't got money to buy you another pair. We have to send the money to Bosnia. Our family hasn't got food to eat and you are asking me to buy you another pair of shorts!'

I understood, of course, and I didn't want to worry her about my problems in school, so I asked my sister if I could borrow her shorts. I put her shorts on first and then put mine on over them – if they tried to pull my shorts off again, at least I wouldn't be stripped down to my underwear.

That day, I started playing basketball with Luke again. The girls always sat on the grass near the court to eat their sandwiches and they were admiring our basketball skills, but after they'd laughed at me I wasn't really interested in them anymore. I had been nervous about the boys ambushing me again, but I couldn't give in to it, and I slowly started to enjoy myself.

I always loved playing basketball – I was very skilful, but now it was also a release for me. It helped me control my anxiety, anger, frustration and embarrassment. Luke was always calm, hopping around me, doing his best and enjoying the game, but that day I was winning easily. I was having such a good game I started to forget about the bullies, and started using my best moves, jumping, and spreading my arms like wings, like I owned the court. All of a sudden someone from behind tackled me. I knew how to deal with tackles, ducking underneath them or jumping above them, but there were too many hands touching me – this wasn't part of the game.

I stopped, just froze, holding my ball. I was in a trap; they were all holding me, not letting me go. Overpowered again, there was nothing I could do. The basketball court emptied in minutes and I was left alone with the boys pinning me down, ripping my shorts off again. All I could see was girls giggling and looking over to see if I was naked yet.

My shorts were off already and this time they had ripped them to shreds. My sister's shorts were showing – worse still, they were pink. They all started laughing and saying, 'Oh my God, we knew he was a girl! Even the last time he didn't have anything to show!'

The girls were pointing at me, helpless with laughter, as I was trying to pull on my ripped shorts, but it was hopeless. I'm not sure if I've ever felt more alone. I was trying to save my pride and not cry. I sat down in the middle of the court in despair and embarrassment, not knowing what to do. As I put my head between my legs, holding the torn pieces of my shorts, I was thinking, how am I going to explain this to my mother?

I don't know how long I was sitting there on my own, but then I heard footsteps. I turned around and got up, ready to defend myself if they'd come back, but this time it was a friendly hand, patting my back.

It was Luke. 'Are you OK?' he asked.

I said yes, but one tear silently dropped from my right eye. He gave me a firm bump with his fist, and I knew that meant respect. That little gesture was enough for me to know that now I had backup.

I went home thinking I should be happy that Luke was my friend, but my confidence and trust in people had been worn down so far that I even wondered if it might be a trick, that he might be part of the gang of bullies. I was finding it hard to care anymore.

I made up my mind that if they came near me again, I would attack them on the court in front of everyone.

I couldn't play basketball anymore because I didn't have any shorts, but I could still watch. However, the bullies wouldn't even let me do that in peace. The next day, I was sitting on the grass watching Luke and his friends play, and the gang arrived, shouting and showing off to entertain the girls. They started on me straight away, pointing at me and saying, 'Look, all the girls are sitting on the grass!' The girls started laughing, and one of the boys shouted, 'Ah, the girl in the pink shorts can't play anymore!'

That was it. I thought of my granddad and I knew what I had to do. I got up and grabbed two handfuls of sand from the pile next to the court and started running towards them, screaming my head off in Bosnian: 'I am not alone, I am not a loner! I am not a girl and I am not afraid of you! I will beat you now!'

I knew my granddad was watching over me and guiding me not to show fear. His words ran through my head: 'Strike with your left, punch with your right, kick with your leg from your hips.' They were expecting me to fight like that, but instead I threw the sand at them as hard as I could, and they started ducking down and rubbing their eyes, like a swarm of bees had attacked them. The other kids around me stood frozen, wondering what would happen next. Now it was my turn to show them who was a girl and who was a real man. I started swinging punches and kicking them like a programmed robot. Then I realised Luke had joined in on my side and the boys were hitting the floor like tree trunks cut down by a chainsaw. In minutes we had dealt with the bullies for life.

All the girls were now cheering for me and clapping their hands, saying, 'Beat the bullies, our Little Hercules!' That became my nickname for the rest of the time in school.

My mum still couldn't afford to buy me new shorts, so I had to play in my sister's pink ones, but now that I had beaten the bullies I couldn't care less. In fact, those shorts seemed to make me even more popular with the girls. Those were the two worst and best experiences I had with the girls in school.

Mr Manda was the first person to engage me in extracurricular activities linked to basketball after school. It was great as I didn't need to speak to anyone – I just needed to play and actively engage in the game. I became very close to Mr Manda and he used my skills to demonstrate proper basketball techniques to the other kids. Happy at being useful, I was starting to make friends through the sport too. I've always believed sport brings people together, especially children: you develop special communication and teamwork skills that you cannot learn anywhere else. Mr Manda introduced me to Mr Hebdon, who was in charge of the weight-training club. He became another favourite teacher as I loved weights and weight training. My muscles were already starting to show, and Mr Hebdon saw my potential straight away; he got me to help him out with the lunchtime weight-training club. The word went around to the other teachers that I was good at sport and very kind in helping the other children with the sports activities. Now all the bullies wanted to be my friends and I didn't have a problem with that. Luke also went to the weight-training club; he became my best friend and we used to train together. With the teachers' help, from being a place of torment for me, the school was fast becoming my favourite and safest place to be.

As the other teachers saw how I had begun to thrive in sports, they worked hard with me to try to transfer that success to other subjects. Mrs Heatherington and Mrs Hatton worked the hardest to help me shine, and they showed the other teachers that everything was possible with this little Bosnian boy. I showed courage and commitment, especially with my dictionary and learning my new words. I had become friends with Tom playing basketball, and he helped me to pronounce new words, although he always took the piss out of my pronunciation – I didn't connect any sentences, I just spoke them out one word at a time to get the meaning across. In return, I became Tom's protector and learning mentor for basketball. Finally, the word had gone around the school that no one should mess with this Bosnian boy, who was very well built now and played basketball really well. I wanted to stop having to fight for survival and I wanted to be noticed for my academic achievements instead, which ultimately was what my parents always wanted for me. Now that the kids were leaving me alone, I was able to access good secondary education, and I was determined to make the most of it.

I worked really hard in the LDB with Mrs Heatherington. She had worked in a professional theatre company and she encouraged me to take on drama to develop my speaking skills. So I joined her after-school drama club, which she ran with Sangita, who was in charge of bringing drama to the local community, and I loved it. I had always dreamed of being an actor, but my dreams had got lost during the war. She definitely knew what she was talking about though, and my English slowly began to improve. The teachers' encouragement started to pay off, and as my language skills developed, my confidence grew and that gave me the drive to continue with my academic studies.

Mr Manda and Mr Thacker also pushed me to succeed. They wanted me to participate in a school assembly and say a few words about the Bosnian War from a child's point of view. It seemed an impossible task for me, as, although my language was improving slowly, it was still poor. I expected the children to laugh at me, and not in a jokey way like Tom did. My worst fear was that they would start to pick on me again and I would be facing the battlefields again. I thought long and hard about it and I felt under terrible pressure to do it: those teachers had already done a lot for me and I owed them one. On the other hand, if I didn't cooperate, I thought they might lose interest in me and not put as much effort into my education. I knew it meant a lot to the teachers, but I don't think they understood how difficult it was for me. But how could they? How could anyone who had not experienced my trauma understand it? Sometimes in life you have to do things without asking too many questions, and so I made up my mind I would do it.

The night before the assembly, I couldn't sleep – I was preparing myself for making my first ever public speech, and it was to be in a foreign language I was still struggling with. However, when I started practising my speech in front of the mirror, I felt emotionally embarrassed. I didn't even know what that meant at the time, but I was getting angry with the negative feelings and emotions crowding my head. I guess that was my biggest problem, and one of the reasons why I couldn't communicate with the other kids. I would want to say something so I'd build myself up to do it, then all that negative energy flooded my head and when I tried to connect the words, I'd get a complete block, and start stuttering then go silent. Most of the time I just went blank, and that's exactly what happened that day in the assembly. I felt like I was a little baby attempting to speak for the first time; my jaws were glued together and my tongue froze. Raging with anger and frustration, I couldn't speak. The kids could see I was struggling, but no one was laughing at me, and I felt their encouragement. That gave me a little bit of hope and confidence. I looked around the hall and all eyes were on me; the children and teachers were silent, expectant. I had never seen this kind of behaviour in the school. They all wanted me to speak; they wanted to hear about the Bosnian War and what I went through as a thirteen-year-old child.

'My school in Bosnia, I had terrible time...' I began hesitantly, wanting to find the right words, needing them to know the whole traumatic story. 'My sports coach tortured me and my family... I lost many family members... I saw people killed in front of me... I lost my close family, uncles, aunties and neighbours in the war... I have no one here to protect me... I am all alone in this school... This school became my family... I love this school... I hate the school in Bosnia, I was tortured there... I hate Bosnia... I hate soldiers with guns... I hate guns... I hate bad people. I fight for good people.'

As I finished my final sentence, I looked nervously around me, and at least half of the children and all the teachers were crying. For me, it felt cathartic, like a confession, everything had come out at once. For the kids, it was a revelation – they finally understood me! The teachers congratulated me and told me how proud they were of me and how brave I'd been.

The next day, all the lads told me how touched they were by my speech and they kept asking me questions about the Bosnian War. All the girls were hugging me and asking if I was OK. I was a bit embarrassed by all the attention, as I was so used to keeping my head down, and I didn't always understand what they were asking me, but I understood the smiles and handshakes. I didn't talk, but at least I listened to them and nodded my head, pretending that I understood. Later on, the kids learned how to speak to me slowly and use very basic English words.

It had been very difficult for me emotionally at the time, as the war was still raging in Bosnia and I had lost a lot of family members, but I guess the teachers were right to encourage me to do it. It turned out to be a very clever way to deal with those kids that were constantly on my case, and helped draw a line under all the bad feelings and anxiety at the school. Finally, the school truly became a safe haven and a healing place for me.

The teachers had been so impressed by my speech that they encouraged me to speak in front of the whole year groups in assemblies about children caught up in conflict. After my own experiences, I became an anti-bullying ambassador in the school. I talked about the war and the terrible things my family had seen and endured, things they could never have imagined, and my own experiences of being bullied while I was still traumatised. The kids were very interested and engaged with me, and I like to think it encouraged them not to bully other kids.

At the same time, I had improved so much academically that I was ready to take my GCSEs. I achieved eight GCSEs, all A–C. I had walked into that school like a complete loser and I came out with great qualifications. The bullies became my friends and the teachers became like my family. At the end, they were all proud of me.

The final part of my education in Moseley School had sped by, because I had fun and I enjoyed myself. Those were my best times in school and couldn't have been more different to the early days. I made many unforgettable friends, and found some peace. When I left after my GCSEs, I made a promise to all my teachers that I would return to the school as a teacher. At some point in my life I knew I would come back and give something back to the children – I always kept my promises. I didn't close all doors to Moseley School, as I was still attending Mrs Heatherington's after-school drama club, but I was going to study for my A-levels at Joseph Chamberlain Sixth Form College in September and I couldn't wait. I could finally look forward to the future.

Unfortunately, our life at home had not been going quite so well.

12

The War Had Come
to Us Again

We were still struggling to settle in Birmingham. Here, everything was different for us – even the food didn't have any taste, unlike Bosnia. People had a dry sense of humour, which we didn't really get for a long time, and as none of us spoke English, communication was impossible. My dad still used the German he'd learned in school to talk to people, but it wasn't easy. He always hoped for the best and he is a very optimistic person, but I knew sometimes he was just trying to be strong for us and he was facing his own demons. Our parents couldn't give us the upbringing that we'd had in Bosnia. They never really took us out and they didn't give us the attention we needed. We had to cope with new surroundings ourselves. We were dreaming of better days, but they seemed to be far away.

The war in Bosnia lasted until 1995, and our family numbers were getting smaller and smaller by the day. Shelling was an everyday thing, which killed many people; the rest were victims of snipers. There was no way out; Bosnian people were under siege in most cities. The embargo put in place by the UN meant Bosnia couldn't buy arms to defend its people. We were slaughtered like animals, while the world stood by and turned a blind eye.

We had very little news from home, apart from what my dad heard from his sister in Croatia about the situation in Bosnia. We felt how tense our parents were, although they did their best not to show it. Often it felt like they were hiding something from us – looking back, it was probably to protect us – and when they spoke it was in whispers and through tears, especially when my mum's two brothers, Atif and Junuz, were killed. A new wrinkle seemed to appear on Mum's face for every family member who passed away. Sometimes she would dream her brother was alive, only to wake up and realise the sad truth. Distraught, for days she wouldn't speak with anyone. All we could hope was one day it would all stop.

We tried our best to help and decided not to ask for anything. Mum and Dad would send every bit of money they had to our aunt in Croatia to send on to Bosnia. We didn't have any toys and never really had any desire for them. As strange as everything was in the UK, at least we were safe from the battles still raging at home, and we felt for the guys who were still stuck in this cruel war. With all of this in our heads, we had struggled to integrate and start a new life in the UK.

I heard one old man, Kasim Brkić, say, 'I wouldn't mind dying in Bosnia, at least there I had a reason to die, but here there is no reason.'

He was very intelligent and always told us stories about

Bosnia and what a great life he had there. When the old people got together, all they did was talk about their past – they always had massive grins on their faces, sitting in each other's gardens in these traditional British terraced houses, reminiscing about the good old days in the Balkans for hours. They had the hardest time integrating. What you have to understand is that most of these people came from the countryside, where they had lived and worked all their lives as farmers. All of a sudden they were taken away from all of that and dumped in big cities like Birmingham, stuck in an overpopulated, polluted island full of strangers.

I could imagine those guys at home in Bosnia enjoying all four seasons: very warm summers, beautiful springs, rainy autumns and freezing-cold snowy winters. Here, the weather was always the same: rain and wind, with an occasional glimpse of the sun.

I loved listening to the old people's stories as it reminded me of my granddad. One day, Kasim told me that my granddad had beaten him up back home when they worked in a paper factory. He said, 'Your granddad was not the biggest bloke, but for sure he was the strongest. He was fearless and nobody messed with him. Instead most of the people feared him.'

Granddad still had respect after so many years.

Kasim liked me a lot, because he could see my granddad in me. What I was happiest about was the fact that I was able to remember all the stories that Granddad had told me. At times I'd thought he was exaggerating when he was telling me his stories, but now I knew he wasn't. That made me happy and gave me the willpower to carry on.

* * *

It was time for us to move to a new house again. It was a sad day, as we had got used to our peaceful neighbours and quiet community in Sparkhill, and apart from the trouble I had with Omar, no one had bothered us. But we were living in private accommodation and the landlord wanted us out, so we had no option but to go. I had both good and bad memories from our first house in England, but we needed a fresh start and something positive to happen in our lives.

Dad got the keys for the new house, and my mum packed all our possessions – just clothes, crockery and bed sheets. It felt strange moving house without anything, just hand luggage. Our new home was in Braithwaite Road in Sparkbrook, which we soon discovered was one of the worst areas in Birmingham, deprived and full of crime. It was a traditional area for new settlers: Irish, Asian, Jamaican, and now Bosnians. People used to call it rough, but we didn't know anything about it at that time, and we just wanted to settle in our new home.

We made the move from Sparkhill to Sparkbrook by foot, carrying our few belongings. It reminded me of the war, when we were walking to get to safety. People were staring at us, giving us funny looks. We ignored them and carried on with a smile, but it seemed we would not get a warm welcome here. There was something in the air, negative energy. I had to figure out how I would get to school from the new house without any help from my parents, and I was worried about walking home when it was dark. Meliha was even more concerned as she had just started college.

The house was divided into four flats. Our flat had a long corridor, with the bedrooms on the right-hand side and the toilet, dining room and kitchen on the left. There was also quite a good-sized garden. We were the first people to move into that building, so it felt a bit lonely, but my dad fixed up the place as much as he could. We did a fair amount of work in our flat: stripping all the wallpaper, decorating, painting doors and windows to make it feel like a home. We were told that previously it was a care home for teenage kids, and the building was a bit tired. It still felt like the kids were around and people kept turning up, looking for their friends and family, which made us a little wary.

When we woke up after our first night there, we found most of our windows looking on to the garden were smashed. We slept to the side of the house where the street was and those windows were fine, but it was strange that we didn't hear them. We concluded it must be kids, as the stones were everywhere, and we thought they would realise that we were living here now and back off.

We cleared all the mess and never bothered calling the police, but we did call the housing people to install new windows. That took them longer than we thought but we were happy that they did it in the end. One of the things that stayed in my head was that when all of these attacks first started, we never called the police and tried to deal with them on our own. I guess my mum and dad were still living in the war zone in their heads and were dealing with the attacks themselves. Maybe they still didn't trust authority after how we had been treated.

We didn't know where the attacks were coming from or why we were being targeted. I guess we did stand out back then, wearing shabby old clothes, walking down the street with our heads down and having great difficulty integrating – we felt we didn't belong anywhere and nobody wanted us. Looking back, it seems strange we never had any social or community workers to help us to settle down in a new country, facing new challenges and language difficulties.

This community was much bigger than we were used to back in Kozarac. It was a big culture shock for us and it led to a cultural clash. I remember my dad walking down the street and greeting everyone with a friendly hand gesture like he used to do back home. But people found that very strange – they seemed angry and it drew even more attention to us. I knew they were calling us freaks, strangers and foreigners, and saying we didn't belong there. Of course, we couldn't understand the words properly then – but we knew what their faces and gestures were saying.

My uncle Ismet and auntie Asima Solaković came to visit us from Switzerland. Just as we did, they found everything in the UK strange. One day, my uncle and my dad, together with my little brother Jasmin, who was only five years old, were walking from our house towards the park. Two young men came up and spoke to them. Dad smiled and said thank you. The young guys thought that was hilarious and they were doubled up with laughter. Jasmin was young and had found it easier to pick up some English, and so my dad asked him why they were laughing.

My brother said, 'They just called you two big old horses, and you said, yes, thank you.'

Dad got angry and started chasing them, but they ran off.

After fleeing Bosnia, for a very long time we were used to that behaviour; even now we struggled to find peace anywhere. But this was now our home and we were determined to protect it. We would stand our ground and defend ourselves against attackers. There was an old rule in Yugoslavia: if anybody attacks you in front of your house and disturbs your peace with witnesses around, you can kill them, as long as you are defending your home and your family. We were brought up with that rule and it was very hard to get out of that way of thinking, especially my dad.

We had hoped that the window breaking on the first night was just kids, thinking they were messing about with an abandoned building, but it soon became clear we were being targeted. We found ourselves in a civil war with our new neighbours. Our lives changed overnight and we became tense, looking over our shoulders whenever we left the house. Whenever my sister went out, I followed her to make sure that no one would hurt her. She went to Joseph Chamberlain Sixth Form College and I would walk with her on the way to my school. If anybody looked at her, I would growl at them, giving them a menacing look. After school, I would go directly to my sister's college to wait for her, sometimes until five in the evening.

One day, as we were walking home through the park, two guys started following us, saying things we didn't understand. One guy was on a bike and the other was walking. We ignored them and kept walking, but it was getting dark and we were really worried about what might happen to us. The guys were getting closer to us, not giving up. My sister was shouting at me to hurry up, and I was trying to use my granddad's tactics of not showing them fear, giving them a sharp look. Suddenly, they made their move and started pulling my sister's bag. No one hurt her. I had Arnold Schwarzenegger's bodybuilding book in my bag and I hit one guy on the head with it and he fell off the bike. His mate punched me and I saw stars, but then my little protector jumped in. My sister hit him with her bag and started pulling his hair. She was strong, a little woman packed with muscle and no fear – she has punched guys in the past with her rings on, her hand knocking their teeth out! So I guess these guys were lucky just to get a few whacks. We knew how to defend ourselves and we would do anything to protect each other. Those attackers had picked on the wrong people and they got what they deserved.

We arrived home full of anxiety and stress. Mum was waiting at the front door. She knew what time we should be back from school and college, and when we were late she knew that something was wrong. Our faces told her without any words that we were attacked again.

In many different ways, life was sometimes even harder in the UK than in the war. In a war, all you have to worry about is staying alive to face another day. Here, we were facing so many new challenges all at once that it was often hard to handle them.

The following week, there was another incident at our flat. In the middle of the night, some thieves managed to get in the house through the garden. Somehow they took the whole window out – it looked like they cut it out and got inside while we were asleep. We didn't have much, but it was a lot for us, considering we were refugees. They took our TV and stereo, and some jewellery of my mum's – basically, everything we had. My dad was going to the toilet that night and he bumped into the thief. He managed to get his wooden bat out and hit him a few times with it, enough to scare him and make him jump out of the window.

Fortunately, after that it was quiet for a couple of weeks, and we hoped we might be left alone permanently.

* * *

In the meantime, we got some new neighbours. More Bosnians joined us and all of a sudden, Bosnians occupied the whole building. The Mujkanović family, who came from Kozarac, moved in upstairs. They had arrived in Scotland from Bosnia before moving to Birmingham. My dad and grandmother both knew them from home – my grandmother had the same surname and came from the same village. We felt more at ease and more at home when they moved in. The Šarčević family from Sana, a neighbouring town in Bosnia, lived in the flat above us. They were also really nice and I made friends with the sons, Edis and Elvis, and over time I became very close to Edis. Irma and Una, students from Sarajevo, moved into the last flat, and we helped them decorate and get settled in.

Now we were no longer alone. We became stronger, more resilient and unified. We knew the attacks were inevitable, but at least we had more people on our side to defend us. Now all four flats were occupied, nothing could get past us. We were more relaxed and we spent a lot of time making sure that our building was immaculate. We painted all the doors and windows ourselves, and finally started to feel like we belonged there. That must have upset our attackers even more, as they began to smash the windows again in the middle of the night. We made sure that we showed them resistance and that we were not giving up. At least we were no longer alone, and now there was always someone at the building. There was never an empty flat now to give the attackers the chance to smash all the windows.

Around this time, we found some work on a farm. Each day during the summer holidays, the farm van would collect me, Meliha, Edis and Elvis at 5am, and drop us off late at night, sometimes 8pm. We would work during the holidays and every weekend in the fields in Evesham and Brown Hills, doing various jobs, from onion and strawberry picking to packing apples and pears. It was very hard work, but it reminded us of back home, and it gave us a break from our house, which was constantly under attack. It also gave us some pocket money, so we could buy kebabs. We bought ourselves new bikes, too, but we gave most of the money to our parents, who sent it back home to their families, who didn't have food to eat.

We were determined to protect our homes and families, and Edis and I worked out that most of the attacks happened at the weekend, so we took the law into our own hands. We would stay up in Edis's room all night and wait for the thieves. When they turned up, we would throw bricks at them. That came to the attention of the police, who started making regular patrols of our street. One evening, the thieves tricked us – while they were distracting us from the front of the building, their mates took everything from the back, including mine and Edis's new mountain bikes, and the money that we'd earned working on the farm. They even took the satellite dishes from the walls, which meant our parents couldn't watch the Bosnian news and naturally, they were very upset.

We strongly believed that we deserved some peace after what we had all been through in Bosnia during the war. Every family who lived in that building thought the same way: why are they bothering us, why are they attacking us? We didn't cause any harm to anybody; it wasn't our choice to leave our home to come to this country – the war forced us here.

Our childhood was difficult in so many different ways. I got on with Edis because he was a very shy and vulnerable child. He never spoke a word of English with anyone and I completely understood him, because I went through the same thing. I tried to protect him, as quite often the other children took advantage of his generosity. He trusted me fully but perhaps relied on me a little too much. It took him a very long time to be independent, and even then he was always vulnerable when he was alone.

One day, he was on his way to school on his bike and someone stopped him in the street. He said something that Edis couldn't understand, then took the bike off him and rode off. When I saw Edis come back from school on foot later that day, I knew straight away that someone had taken his bike. He told us that he thought the guy wanted to buy his bike but he wanted to try it first. Now, that would be a completely normal thing to do in Bosnia, as we all lived in a small community and it was easy to find people. Everybody knew everybody else, and no one would scam anyone. But Birmingham was a big city and everything was different. I felt sorry for Edis, but he quickly learned not to give his bicycle to anyone. That meant we had to work even harder on the farm so we could save some money to get him a new bike.

People really liked us on the farm because we didn't speak much and we just got on with the work. The main boss, Ian, was Australian – he liked us a lot and he started picking us up in his Land Rover every weekend. On occasion we brought our parents along to help us out and we all had a lot of fun away from the problems and stress at home. My dad loved the farm – it reminded him of the good old days in Bosnia. In particular, he loved working with the tractors and he could do any job with them. Eventually, more Bosnian people joined us on the farm and for all of us it was a healing process, an escape from reality. We shared stories of good times in Yugoslavia and it brought a smile to all of our faces

It was the summer of 1994 and it was the best summer for all of us.

Unfortunately, that happiness didn't last long, as Ian's farm didn't do well and he went back to Australia. We all missed him as we were hoping to get regular employment on the farm and we had lots of skilful people who could do those jobs. We were back to square one – stuck in our house with miserable faces, facing those thieves and thugs on the streets of Sparkbrook.

Things had started deteriorating again at the flats, and the attacks were happening more or less every night – our windows were broken, the doors were damaged by the heavy stones, we even had people's waste put through our letterbox. The two Bosnian students had decided to move out, as they couldn't handle the constant attacks. They were terrorising us, and we didn't know how to stop them. Edis and I were facing huge challenges in school and we needed to focus our energy on that.

One evening, as I was coming back from the shop, I saw some guys throwing massive stones at our door. The noise was unbearable. By now, we had called the police so many times that I think they were getting fed up with us. Once again it was time to take matters into my own hands. I went around the back and attacked the guys with the stones, and that taught them a lesson.

Another day, Edis and I found someone in our garden spraying the walls with graffiti. We went straight up to him, and Edis grabbed his spray can, so he couldn't spray it in our eyes. There was a full bucket of water nearby that we used to clean our bikes, and I grabbed his head and I shoved it in the water. I held his head underwater for a couple of seconds and then got him out. He ran out of the garden like a headless chicken.

All of those attackers were different ages. I began to wonder if someone was sending them for a reason to get us out of the building. But after that last incident, they gave us a little break, and we all started to feel more relaxed.

It was now the summer of 1995 and we would spend a lot of time sitting in our garden at the back, drinking coffee. We had been living there for a couple of years now and we were the longest occupants out of all the Bosnians. We were all talking, laughing and joking as if we were back home in Bosnia. My mum went inside to get some sugar for the coffee, and all of a sudden we heard her screaming, so we ran to see what was wrong. My dad was the first one inside the house, where Mum was sitting on top of this man, screaming her head off, holding on to the bag full of our personal belongings he was trying to steal. In my life I had never seen my dad fighting, but what I saw him do that day was really disturbing. He started punching the thief, and didn't stop until Fehim Šarčević, Edis's dad, and our other Bosnian neighbour, Esad Mujkanović, managed to drag him off.

Dad was a big heavy man, weighing seventeen stone, and when he pounded the guy, he had no chance of escape. It was like my dad was taking all his rage out on him; all the anger and frustration that had been building inside him for those two years while we struggled to find peace finally erupted when he saw his wife in danger. When they pulled my dad off him, the thief was covered in blood and was begging us, 'Please call the police!'

When the police arrived, Dad was arrested immediately and taken into custody. We didn't have any interpreters at that time. I could speak a little English by now, but not fluently, and I had to try to translate as well as I could. In the police station my dad told them about the law in Bosnia – if someone attacks you in your house, you can kill them, as long as you have two witnesses. The police officer listened politely, but then said, 'Well, now you live in England and you have to follow our law. Otherwise you will end up in custody again and in serious trouble.'

The thief was also in the police station, covered in blood, and a doctor was trying to clean his wounds. He was shaking and my dad didn't take his eyes off him.

Dad told me to say to the police and to the thief, 'If I see him again near my house, near my kids and family, I will kill him with my bare hands and that is not a threat, it's a promise.'

The police officer said, 'Tell your dad, if any thief ever comes again to rob your house, you need to sit in a corner and call the police.'

We went round in circles for a little while, with my dad insisting that the law in Yugoslavia was much better than the law in the UK, and the police officer saying, 'You don't live in Yugoslavia anymore, you are in the UK now and you must obey our law.'

Eventually, they let my dad off, but the thief was released

soon after him, which made the situation even worse. After a couple of weeks, he was brazenly walking around outside our house, showing the scars on his face and making gestures that he was going to burn us all alive. But that didn't frighten us now – something had changed for my dad, and he wouldn't be pushed around anymore.

* * *

The Bosnian War ended in 1995, and Edis's family decided to go back home. It was a sad moment for me as he was one of my only friends. Perhaps one of the reasons they went back was because of what they experienced in Sparkbrook. They told us, 'We lived through and survived the war, but we will never forget these attacks on us in a peaceful country like England.'

I started a collection to help Edis's family make a new start in Bosnia. I made a speech in a school assembly and we did really well. All the teachers gave £10 each and the kids brought in as much money as they could. We managed to raise over £2,000, and I was very pleased I was able to do this for Edis, one of the best friends that I ever had in my life.

The family were booked on a coach back to Bosnia, and on the day they left, I cried like I had when I left my grandparents in Croatia. Edis was gone and I was left alone again.

After they left, there were only two families in our property, us and the Mujkanović family upstairs. The other half of the building was completely empty, and within a week the windows were broken and graffiti started to appear. We complained to the housing association, and they boarded up the windows and doors, so at least no one could get in through the empty side of the property, but the house started to look really rough. After that, the vandals set fire to the Mujkanovićs' car with a petrol bomb, and we were lucky that we heard the vehicle being set ablaze, so we could put it out. The car was parked near our bedroom window; if it had exploded, we would probably have been killed. How ironic would that have been? Refugees from Bosnia survive a war but are killed in an arson attack in Sparkbrook. It would definitely have made a good headline on the news.

This was the final straw for the Mujkanović family, who decided to move back to Scotland, and once again, we were left alone, under siege in a rundown and battered building. The state of the building just attracted more attacks and more confrontation, which resulted in the police getting involved again.

The *Sunday Mercury* newspaper also wrote about us: 'Refugees dumped in a Sparkhill area left alone by themselves, no aid has been given to them'.

There had been so many attacks on us, all of them logged by the police, that the council finally moved us to a new house. It was only two roads away, but it felt like moving to a completely different area, and we lived quite happily within that community; in fact, my mum and dad still live there today. Now my sister was safe going to college and I felt reborn. I felt almost overwhelmed that I could sleep at night without being attacked again.

After a couple of days in the new house, my dad said what we all felt: 'I feel like we're coming out of a war again.'

13

College Days

It was time for me to leave school and move on to college. My difficult start at Moseley School had a happy ending – I'd made friends, and achieved all my GCSEs. I was now going to study for my A-levels in drama and performing arts at Joseph Chamberlain Sixth Form College. I had to say goodbye to so many good people, as well as the bullies and those who had made it hard for me in secondary school. I guess that's life – you have to go through the journey with good and bad people.

It was the beginning of September 1996 and all good things happen to me in September, because that's the month I was born. My good friend Luke from Moseley School later joined me and as he was taking the same A-level subjects as me at college, we had the same teachers: David Henson, Debbie Bird, Marcia Carr and Bev Sokolovski.

We were like brothers: both strong, good-looking and ambitious, and we were always together, training, eating and studying. The girls always wanted to hang around with us; that just gave us more confidence to train harder and show off our little muscles in the tight tops that we wore to college. We used to sit in the college canteen during the morning break, drinking our favourite coffee, cappuccino, and flirting with the girls. They were always asking us: Who has bigger biceps? Who has the bigger chest? Who has more developed abs, and so on. We just used to smile at them; we weren't really interested in answering the girls' questions, but we did enjoy the attention – we felt our arms growing bigger with every compliment.

We used to work out in the gym at Birmingham Sports Centre next to the college after our classes. Nobody hassled us when we were together, not even the older guys, but they had all seen how hard we worked on the punchbags. We became very popular at the gym, and the staff often took our photo for their leaflets. Luke was already modelling with the Louise Dyson Agency and he got me on board as well. He appeared in Argos catalogues advertising weights and sports clothes, and I followed in his footsteps.

Luke gave me a lot of encouragement, and he introduced me to his agent, Louise Dyson. She said that I had very nice hands and she could use them for adverts in catalogues.

I started gaining my confidence from modelling. During our break time in the canteen, we would give our phone numbers to the girls, and they would giggle and whisper to each other. Every day after college, when we were heading to the gym, all the girls would run up to us and say they'd seen our pictures in the catalogues, or that they liked our muscles. It was innocent fun and we really enjoyed those moments.

More boys eventually joined us at the gym. There were many girls that we fancied, but my favourites were Katie and Saima.

College life was good; my communication was much better and I made lots of friends at the college and the sports centre. I still didn't speak much, but here it wasn't used against me, and I became a very popular young man. Modelling had opened different doors for me and my self-confidence was growing.

One day, my teacher asked me if I would take part in a charity event by walking around the school topless. The girls from the art department drew graffiti on my body, and every time somebody drew something on me, they had to pay to the charity. On that day we raised £100 for BBC Children in Need. It was probably one of my best days at college. I became well known and all the girls called me the Bosnian hunk. I didn't really know what it meant, but by the looks on their faces I knew it was something nice! Overnight, everyone in the college knew who I was and they started to relate to me in a very strange way, like we were friends. At first, I was hesitant, because of my negative experiences during the war and in school. I had learned to stay away from people and create a distance, but this was completely different.

One morning, I walked past a college security guard who said, 'Hello, big man!'

I said, 'What?'

He said again, 'Hello, big man!'

'Big man? Where did you get that from? You're bigger than me.'

'I saw your body the other day; you're massive.'

'OK, thanks.' I was really happy to hear that from a big security guard who was much bigger than me.

One Saturday evening, Luke and I were modelling clothes for a catwalk show. My sister Meliha came with us and we all had a great time. They had overall winners that evening and Luke came second and I was third. It was my best day with Luke while we were growing up. We met many good people who gave us lots of compliments and encouraged us to continue with our training and modelling.

When we got home that night, I was really excited to show my mum and dad the photographs from the show. They were sitting in the living room, looking too serious for my liking, and they simply said, 'We need to talk.'

My face fell, and I said, 'What's wrong now? Who died in the war now?' But I didn't even give them the chance to answer. 'Mum! Dad! I've had enough listening to you every day about every single family member that dies in the war. That is enough! I'm too young to handle that. After all, it is a war and they will all die and we cannot do anything about it.'

I had never seen my parents more distressed and angry with me. They were furious, even angrier than they'd been during the war. There was a moment of silence. I froze and then I realised what I'd said. My mum and dad were crying inconsolably. I hugged them and said, 'I'm sorry, I didn't mean that.'

I didn't mean to hurt them but I just wanted to have a normal life, and after the carefree fun and laughter of the show, it felt like everything was always being spoiled.

When they had calmed down a bit, my dad wanted to speak. 'This is very serious. We need to talk,' he said. 'You need to sit down and listen.'

'What is it?' I asked nervously. I didn't like the sound of this.

'Do you have a girlfriend?'

'No!' I said it so fast that it sounded like it was wrong to have a girlfriend.

My mum started crying again and she said to my dad, 'I knew it! I told you, but you would never listen to me.'

By this point I'd lost my patience. 'What is this about? Why is this your business? What is your problem with me now?'

Mum seemed to be choosing her words carefully. 'Well, hmm,' she said slowly, 'why do you have all your walls plastered with pictures of naked men?'

'Naked men? Mum, these are models. You know I've joined the modelling agency. These guys just inspire me.'

Then they both started firing questions at me: 'What do you and Luke do in your bedroom?'

'We lift weights, we train with the chimney and the bricks.'

'What else do you do?'

'We eat together, we dress together and pose in front of the mirror.'

They looked at each other, then my dad asked, 'Do you sleep together?'

'Yes, we do sleep together.'

My mum started crying again, and she shouted at my dad, 'I told you he is gay!'

'Gay! Who? Me? Gay? What are you talking about, Mum?'

'Well, we heard from some people in the community that you and Luke were walking semi-naked at the college, holding hands, and you had some writing on your body. Everybody is talking about it, all your friends and the Bosnian community.'

'Mum! Ask Esmir!' Esmir was another Bosnian guy who hung around with us most of the time, and I thought they would listen to him. I felt like I'd been caught out in something, although I knew it wasn't true. 'Mum, Dad, Luke is my best friend at college. We are always together training or doing our homework, doing modelling and everything. When we get tired from the training in my room, then we watch TV and we fall asleep at times, that's all.'

The next day, when I told Luke what my mum and dad had said, he couldn't stop laughing.

I thought long and hard about the people in my community. I could never understand them. They all knew about my struggles and no one had helped me in the past. Instead, they had told my mother that I was crazy and that I would never be a normal child; I would never get an education or be able to have my own family. Now, when someone like Luke helped me to cope with my traumatic childhood, the PTSD and all the fighting, even that was no good. It was as though they wanted to find the faults in me. I didn't care anymore; I knew what I wanted to achieve in life and I didn't need them to do it.

College had given me new hope, better stability and an opportunity to pursue my dream of an acting career. I was getting positive ideas and started writing my own quotes in my dictionary diary. I framed those positive thoughts in my head so that the negative thoughts would disappear.

Luke was always around me and that helped me, because he understood me better than anybody else. I had the same approach to people as in school. If anybody attacked me, I would hit them back with all my force. I didn't see any threats personally at first, but the college was rough. There were a few Bosnian kids there, and, strangely, they were the first ones who tried to bully me. In a million years, I would never have expected this grief from my fellow refugees. Every time I walked past them they had something to say, and in the end I had to deal with them. I was walking upstairs to my lesson minding my own business and I heard Bosnian voices being sarcastic towards me. There were five of them and they always hung out together. I always just said 'hi' and 'bye' and walked away from them but on this occasion they had surrounded me and were saying inappropriate things. 'That's enough. Now leave me alone – I just want to get past,' I said.

I tried to get to the door, but before I managed to grab the handle to open it, one of them said, 'Or what will happen?'

In my head I heard the soldier's voice: 'We will meet again.' That was all I needed to switch into fighting mode. I grabbed the guy and threw him over my shoulder down the stairs. He was a skinny guy and he flew over me like a balloon. I grabbed hold of the rest of them, one by one, and they all ended up down the stairs. The last person put up a bit of a fight, but I smashed his head on the radiator.

Two security guards ran towards me, shouting, 'Hey! What did you do that for?'

'They deserved it. Every day they say things to me, doing my head in. Now, they got what they deserved.'

What was interesting was that only one of them fought back, the rest were in shock. They couldn't believe where my strength and energy came from. They said themselves: 'Dragon fire came out of Mirso Solak.' That was the nickname they gave me that day, and from then on, we got on OK.

The security guards, Mark, Dave and Phil, had to record the fight in their incident book, but they said they wouldn't take any further action as long as it never happened again.

They knew I was a nice guy, and, as there were five of them against me alone, they decided to turn a blind eye so as not to damage my reputation and destroy my education. I knew I was lucky to get away with it as the guy whose head I hit against the radiator could have been seriously hurt. Now, I knew I needed to stay away from situations like that. That was not healthy for me. I owed a massive favour to the security guys who saved my arse that day. If it got back to the principal, I would probably have been expelled permanently. I didn't want to ruin my last chance at an education so after that I behaved myself; I would walk past the reception unnoticed.

A couple of weeks after that incident, when I got to college, there were lots of people gathered in front of the building. They were checking everyone's passes and they said, 'If your pass has expired, you need to go and queue outside.'

I handed my pass to Mark, the security guy, to check, when, all of a sudden, some students started shouting and someone screamed, 'Knife! Watch out!'

One of the students had been stabbed and the attacker had run into the college, shouting, 'Where is he? I'm going to kill him!'

Everyone was panicking and Mark shouted to me, 'Mirsad, get out of the way!'

Mark was calling Dave and Phil for assistance, but it was too late for me to go anywhere: I was alone behind the guy with the knife. The doors were locked with magnets and neither of us could move from the reception. Before the guy turned around, I thought the best thing would be to jump on his back and try to get hold of the knife. I grabbed hold of his forearm with both my hands. He was much stronger than me but I knew Mark and the other two lads were coming, so I just had to hold on. As soon as Mark put the walkie-talkie down, he ran towards us and went straight for the guy's arm. He took the knife off him with no effort whatsoever, then pinned him to the floor and we held him until the police came and arrested him. When Phil and Dave arrived, they couldn't believe that Mark and I had got the man down already. The security guys were all really impressed by my bravery and they thanked me for helping them out.

That was on Friday. By the Monday, I couldn't get near the college, as all the students had gathered at the front of the building waiting for me. As soon as I arrived, they started calling out my name: 'Mirsad, Mirsad, Mirsad is our hero!'

I walked into the reception area, and the principal called me over. 'I want to thank you for risking your life to stop the intruder,' she said.

'That's OK,' I said. 'I just did what I felt was right at the time.'

She then asked me to come and have a word with her after college.

When I went to her office, she said, 'The whole college can't believe what you did last week. As a result of that, I would like to offer you a job as a security guard. Will you accept it?'

'Of course!' I said.

'There is one condition, though,' she said. 'You can only work when you have a half-day off in the morning or the afternoon. There will be plenty of work during the weekend. You will get paid £6 an hour.'

I couldn't believe it! My sister was working in a retail shop at the time for something like £2.50 an hour. I came out of that office the happiest guy on the planet. The security guards greeted me at the reception and said, 'You're one of us now!'

For the first time in this country I felt accepted for what I was, and I couldn't stop smiling. My confidence went through the roof.

I ran home and told my mum and dad, 'I'm a security guard!'

'Have you gone mad?' they said. 'Calm down! You can't be a security guard, you've only just turned eighteen.'

'Yes, I can! The principal has given me the job for special events and weekends. I can help out the lads when I am free from my lessons in the mornings or the afternoons.'

I didn't tell my parents about the guy with the knife because I knew they would be scared for me and wouldn't let me do the job. I knew I wouldn't have to worry about anybody with Mark by my side – he was a great big lump and he could fight anybody. This was the guy who taught me how to fight properly. He looked clumsy when he walked, but when he started throwing punches, he was like a machine gun firing out bullets. He was also a professional dog handler and he had some dangerous dogs that could take you down in seconds. I would experience that a few times with Mark.

Every morning, I would come to college very early, about 6.30am, before my lessons and sign in for a couple of hours working with the lads. They pointed out the troublemakers among the students, so I could keep an eye on them and let the security guys know when any fights were likely to happen. Luke and I would find out everything from the lads in the gym and we would report back to Mark and the other lads. Most of the fights we heard about happened on a Friday afternoon

Above left: Granddad Ramo does a little jig at a family wedding

Above right: Uncle Sefer Solak in 1974 with his *klapa* (gang) members; left is Husein Solaković (Osman's father) and right is Redžo Duračak

Middle right: (left to right) Mehmed Tači, Mirsad Hodžić, Iliaz Tači, Osman Solaković; the person in front, unknown to the author, is from Trnopolje.

Below right: The Solakovićs: granddad Ramo Solak, grandmother Hasnija, father Mehemed, mother Zumra; I'm in front with the ball with my sister Meliha. Taken in front of the house in Balići.

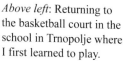

Above left: Returning to the basketball court in the school in Trnopolje where I first learned to play.

Above right: This railway boxcar, used to transport civilian prisoners during the Bosnian War, still sits rotting at the station in Trnopolje to this day.

Middle right: Trnopolje school 'Osnovna škola Hrnići' 1985/6 – I was seven years old. Second from the teacher Fikreta Muranović in a white top, Mirsad Balić; last person middle row with a yellow top is myself.

Below right: Fikret Alić, a starving Bosnian prisoner in the concentration camp at Trnopolje – a press photograph that shocked the world into recognising the true horrors of the war.

(© ITN/REX/Shutterstock)

Left: Fired houses are still in evidence today, twenty-three years after the war ended.

Right: The Memorial Complex in Kozarac, Prijedor Municipality, which bears the names of 1,226 citizens who were killed during the conflict.

TO THE INNOCENT KILLED CITIZENS OF KOZARAC 1992 - 1995

Left: Me and my sister Meliha (both standing at either end of the front row) during an anti-war demonstration in London, 1995.

Left: Osman Solaković's bones were discovered in a mass grave. In all, around 2,100 victims have been identified and given a reburial.

Top left: Arnold Schwarzenegger and me with the letter of condolence that the former had sent to Fikret Hodžić's son after his father's brutal murder.

Top right: Suada Hodžić lamenting for her husband, brutally murdered in the atrocities.

Middle left: Fikret Hodžić, our unbeatable champion, believed that it was best to train outdoors.

Below right: In tribute to Fikret, I transformed my body to enter an amateur bodybuilding competition.

Top left: Above: Mrs Heatherington, my Language Development teacher, visiting the family home in Esme Road, Birmingham, in 1994.

Top right: My sister Meliha with the weights, me and brother Jasmin plus cousins Adnan Menković and Ramo Elkazjpg.

Middle left: Circuit training classes with Peter Lee and Kelly in 2008.

Below left: The Bosnian community kids I grew up with in Birmingham: Adnan, Amir, Miske, myself, Faruk and Elvis.

Below right: The Sarčević family leave Sparkbrook. They told us, 'We lived through and survived the war, but we will never forget these attacks on us in a peaceful country like England.'

Top: My teacher-training class at Moseley School.

Middle left: My Graduation Day at Coventry University in 2001 is witnessed by my proud parents.

Middle right: Staff from Birmingham Sports Centre in 2008. Back row, left to right: Siforth, Shabina, Barry, Donna, Gill, Denice, Peter, Darren; front row: Dave, Trâcï, Paul, myself and Lee.

Below left: With actor and friend Greg Hobbs, talking roles.

Below centre: With my good friend Luke Smitherd celebrating our Graduation together.

Below right: Sharing training with my friend Luke Brown.

Top left: From left to right: Joe Egan, Mehemed Solaković, Meliha Solaković, Cass Pennant, Zumra Solaković and Mirsad Solaković, Kozarac, 2018.

Top right: I present the Bosnian flag to Iron Mike Tyson. He said to me: 'People that have never been through pain will never be able to understand your pain.'

Middle left: Solak Gym members pointing at Arnold Schwarzenegger's signed belt, living the legacy.

Middle right: With my good friend Mirsad Balić at the Sarajevo Film Festival premiere of *Ja sam iz Krajine, zemlje kestena* ('I am from Krajina, the land of chestnuts').

Left: Here with Grandad Ramo and my brother Jasmin in Balići, 2014.

At home in Birmingham with my wife Lejla and our daughter Jasmina.

Inset: Today I find myself speaking to different organisations, sharing my life experiences.

(© Tony Banks Photography)

for some reason, so we would close the college early to let the kids go home and avoid the problem.

Soon after I started, all the lads, including Mark, were contracted to run the security staff privately, and it was even better for me because Mark gave me more flexibility and more hours. We were like an unstoppable army; we kept an eye on everyone and made sure there were no fights at the college, so the kids could feel safe and receive a good education. I was fully protected and I felt like I was part of the team, one of the big lads. Those were some of the best days of my life.

I felt like I'd come home; I was accepted for the first time in my life, I was receiving a good education and I was respected for the job that I did. I was also very proud to be able to provide my parents with money – they were sending lots of money to Bosnia to our different family members to rebuild their homes. And things were about to get even better for me.

14

A Life-changing Job

One day, I turned up at the gym to train with Luke, and I noticed a lot of older guys staring at me. I felt uncomfortable, and didn't really know what to do. I knew everyone had heard about the knife attack, and I was on alert, ready to fight if anyone wanted to challenge me as a tough guy, but at the same time I was thinking, I cannot retaliate because I am here every day. I am still a boy and these men are a lot older than me. I knew one thing, though: no matter what, I would not let them get near me to bully me. I would have to win the hearts of the people at the gym to be able to manage the hard knocks, the tough guys, the hooligans, the drug dealers and gangsters.

All of a sudden, a big shadow appeared in front of me. I tried not to look, avoiding eye contact, while aware that the whole gym was watching me. He was already in my face. 'Can you talk?' he said.

I looked at him, this big scary face in front of me; this guy was not to be messed with. I said, 'I will talk, but not here.'

'Come to my office.'

I followed him like a naughty boy who had been told off by his daddy, but not knowing what I'd done wrong. I was worried they might want me to stop using the gym. After the knife attack at college, the word had gone around that I was a tough guy. I was already preparing what to say to him in my head.

We walked into his office. A man with a moustache and glasses was sitting behind the desk. He looked directly at me, then said to the big guy, 'Is this Mirsad?'

The big guy said yes.

'We want to talk to you about something.'

I put my head down. 'Yes, no problem,' I said nervously.

The big guy introduced himself as Peter and the guy with glasses said, 'I'm Barry. We'd like to talk to you.'

I thought, here we are now, I'm going to get kicked out of here as well. I felt like crying inside but I was holding myself together, trying to put a brave face on. The gym and training were a big part of my life and I didn't know of any other gyms in Birmingham. I didn't want to lose this place. I was prepared to do anything, as long as I could stay at the gym to train.

Barry said, 'We would like to offer you a job at the gym.'

'What?' I was so prepared for bad news, I wasn't sure if I'd heard him properly.

'Would you like to work here?'

'Sure! Yes!' I walked out of that office with the biggest grin in the world. That same smile lasted all of those years that I worked at the Birmingham Sports Centre.

Quite often, people asked, 'What's wrong with this guy? He is always smiling, day and night, early in the morning and late at night. You can say anything to him, he would still reply with the warmest smile covering his young face.' The customers with angry faces, the gangsters and thugs and the polite people, they all got the same treatment – I just got on with the job and the people around me. But one thing I knew for sure was that for the first time Barry, Peter and Mark, who worked here as well as at the college, protected me. The job didn't feel like a job, it felt like my second home and my second family. I was looked after properly and that's what I cared about most. I worked hard at the sports centre and the college and it reminded me of the work that I did on the farm with my granddad. The land occupied by the sports centre and the college was huge, so there was a lot of gardening and litter picking to do, which I loved. I became very close to Mark, Peter and Barry and they used to say I got away with murder already. When Barry had his bosses coming round, he always spoke highly of me and told them that I never came to work without a smile. They loved that and the customers loved it even more because they could actually say anything to me and get away with it; I wouldn't get angry.

I got on really well with Barry: he understood me, and he had a lot of time for me. He was very regimented in everything he did. He had served in the army for ten years and he liked my discipline and commitment to the job. Over time, we became very close, and I opened up to him quite a lot, talking about the Bosnian War and what we went through.

I spent twelve to thirteen hours a day at the college and sports centre, seven days a week, working late shifts, early shifts, weekends, and also covering for people when they were ill. Mum and Dad used to complain that they didn't see me anymore, but they knew that I was happy there and I loved it, so they just let me get on with it. I managed to complete all my homework there and still kept the place clean and tidy. The management even paid for me to go on a course to become a fitness instructor.

One of my great friends at the sports centre was Elvis, known as 'Kelly', who is committed to training and keeping fit and loves martial arts. Kelly is one of those people you cannot walk past without noticing his muscles. He was always smiling and joking, and I looked up to him.

Peter, Kelly and I ran our own keep-fit classes every Monday and Saturday morning and they were always the most popular sessions. We also put on circuit classes, where we set different exercise stations.

I loved any physical exercise – it always made me feel on top of the world – and I wanted to share that feeling with everyone. Young and old, disabled, ill or well, we encouraged everyone to exercise and keep fit. We always made sure our classes were entertaining, and integrated dance movements into aerobic moves with steppers, like an early version of Zumba. We used all sorts of music: reggae, Bosnian, Spanish, English and any other music that would give us a good beat for the exercise and get people moving and having fun. Everyone loved our classes and as the numbers grew, we added an extra session each week. Our motto was always: 'If you want to be happy, healthy and lively, come and join our happy class!'

Kelly and I were the perfect partners – we welcomed everyone and they loved our enthusiasm and our passion for training and for the community. Peter had lots of experience in training, as he had trained professional athletes in powerlifting for most of his life. He was always there to correct us and develop our ideas further, making suggestions on how to make the class harder for regular members or more interesting and accessible for beginners. The three of us were the perfect little team and our classes were always popular. Those were some of the happiest times of my life in the UK.

Working at the sports centre, I felt like I was back home in Bosnia and I enjoyed every moment of it. I made lots of friends there and I was the happiest member of staff. I wanted everyone to feel as good as I did at the centre, and I always felt very protective of the staff and customers.

One day, I turned up to work at the sports centre to find a group of people gathered around the reception, talking loudly to Gill the receptionist. There were five lads and she was alone at the reception so I walked past them to see where Peter was. I saw him at the office and told him the lads were demanding money. By the time Peter and I reached the reception, one of them had a knife in his hand, threatening Gill. She was terrified and handed over the cash in a bag. Peter pressed the panic alarm, which alerted the police that we were in trouble. I jumped over the counter, locked the door and got hold of a broomstick. The lads were looking at me, thinking, he's crazy – we've got a knife and he has a broomstick. I was confident that Peter could overpower most of the guys and with my help we stood a chance. The guy with the knife started heading towards me, but he didn't even reach me – I was scared of what he would do so I hit him as hard as I could over the head. Peter had already got hold of the knife, and the other lads started to panic, shouting at us to let them out. Peter and I were throwing punches like there was no tomorrow. When the police arrived, we unlocked the door and they arrested all of them. They told us that they had been after these guys for a very long time because they were using the same strategy to rob the other leisure centres and they were using bikes to get away. I can tell you one thing: those guys never came to rob us again.

It was a multicultural community and we all got on well with each other: Asians, Afro-Caribbeans and English people. My motto was to make everybody happy, to treat everyone the same, and to love everyone equally. People have seen that in my personality and I was accepted and protected by the customers too.

The Bosnian Association started booking parties at the sports centre and I played a major part in dealing with them. For the 1 May Bank Holiday weekend, they would organise football tournaments during the day and have a Bosnian party in the evening. Barry, Peter and I were the main organisers of the event and we did double shifts until the early hours. I was helpful to them because I spoke the language and dealt with the Bosnians directly. There was always a lot of work and not enough staff, but we always managed to get everything done without any complaints; we helped each other and we never complained. I developed a particularly close working relationship with Peter and Barry. Over the years we learned to trust and rely on each other and we made everything possible. If ever there was any trouble at the Bosnian parties, Peter and I would get stuck in when they would kick off against each other late at night. Often, we would have to ask certain people to leave and make their way home and that was the most challenging job, as it caused embarrassment to the families and they always objected. I enjoyed assisting my own people and giving them an opportunity to have a good time. Over time I became a familiar and popular face among all the Bosnian communities in England as people attended those gatherings from everywhere.

Strangely, it was here that I finally seemed to earn the respect of my own Bosnian community. The Bosnian parties at the sports centre became very popular, and I became known for hosting such incredible events that brought Bosnian communities together from all over the UK.

We built the best reputation in Birmingham for organising and running community events. We also put on Jamaican parties, birthday parties, christening parties and even funeral receptions – we did it all.

My bosses liked and supported me and I soon became known for my permanent smile as much as for my hard work. I never complained about being tired or not being able to do something. I was still working security at the college with Mark as well, and I enjoyed every moment of it and made the most of the experience.

I made lots of Jamaican friends. We learned about our cultural differences and similarities – what we had in common, and about our native countries. However, I was always very competitive and I wanted to be the best in everything, especially bodybuilding. The Jamaican guys used to call me 'The Little Man with Big Muscles and a Big Heart'. I wanted to surprise everyone and show them a different side of me to the tough guy – the bright, gentle, caring side of me – and I was able to do that there. I loved telling them stories about Bosnia and how peaceful it was before the war and the unbelievable freedom we had there as kids. Those kids had grown up on the rough streets of Birmingham and they admired my love for my home country. The older Jamaican guys shared the same history, having come to the UK in the sixties. They left behind them their close families, a beautiful warm country and one of the cleanest seas in the world for the rainy little overcrowded island of Britain. Of course, my reasons for being there were slightly different, as we were ethnically cleansed from Bosnia, while the Jamaicans had come for work. We shared our cultural values and we always stood up for each other at the best and worst times.

Of course, the job wasn't without its problems. I had a confrontation with a guy called Roy, who had a speech impediment. He started bullying me and everyone warned me to watch out for him. I was never going to allow myself to be bullied again but I had to be careful about any trouble at the sports centre, as I would risk losing my job. Roy was a massive Afro-Caribbean bloke, all muscles and bad attitude. Every day, he started picking on me, grabbing me, but he tried to make it look like a joke. One time, my old coach Uvin, who became my very close friend, got involved and he gave Roy a high kick, knocking him into the gym lockers. I have never seen a big man like that flying backwards. Uvin was the most skilled martial arts expert at the gym and nobody messed with him. But he had embarrassed Roy and I knew he would want to get his own back; he was just waiting for the opportunity to strike at me again. Uvin had retired from the gym and only popped in occasionally, and Luke didn't train as much as me, so I would have to face the biggest guy alone.

He had most of the gym guys on his side, and for Roy it was all about who ruled the gym. I had just taken over Uvin's job and I was not interested in any of that – I just wanted to keep my job. Roy started taunting me in front of the whole gym, calling me sissy boy and running up to me like a bull. I had no alternative but to put on a show. I ran towards him – to shake the big tree, using my granddad's old trick. Somehow a miracle happened and I got the big man off balance. Fuming, I was giving it to him large: 'Come outside then, big fella! I've dealt with bigger guys than you!'

If I laid a punch on him, I would be out of a job instantly, I knew. Getting him outside would cause me less embarrassment if I was going to get punched by this big guy.

Dave, a coach at the gym, tried to calm things down and said, 'Mirsad, you don't want to do this, he'll kill you!'

I didn't care – I wasn't going to be pushed around anymore.

There was a huge courtyard outside the gym they called the prison yard, and I led the way, showing Roy I meant business. I always found myself more capable fighting outside than indoors; it's a cultural thing. In Bosnia, most of the fights would be arranged outside, so you don't break anything inside a public place and you don't hurt innocent bystanders. I stepped outside first and I was calm, but ready to go. Roy followed me, but most of his army were still training inside, thinking the fight would never happen, that I would be too scared to lay a hand on him.

Now I had no choice; I had invited him outside, I had to get in the first shot. What worked to my advantage was that as soon as Roy walked outside, he lost his confidence. He lost his earlier swagger and I knew I had to dig into him first. I had a lot of space around me and I knew Dave would save me if he got on top of me.

I took my top off, exposing my muscles, showing him what I'd got. Then I ran up to him with my biggest, most exaggerated swing, hoping for the best. I knew my punch wouldn't touch a guy his size, so I tricked him into thinking I was going to hit him, so he would pull away. That gave me the greater distance to elbow him in the chin, making him collapse on the floor. He fell down like an apple from a tree. The whole circle around us froze, unable to believe that the big man was on the floor. I acted like it was no big deal and walked back inside. Everybody agreed that it was a fair fight and congratulated me on dealing with a bully. I knew there could be repercussions, but I really didn't care what happened next; I had stood my ground and achieved my objective.

Roy went home through the courtyard and people encouraged him not to go back to the weights room that day.

I went back to work in the gym, and about five minutes later, Peter and Barry appeared in front of me, looking furious.

'What have you done?' Barry said.

I smiled.

'I can't believe you're smiling. We saw everything on the camera. You were fighting customers while you were working – it's automatic dismissal.'

'Barry, I wasn't fighting inside the gym and I didn't wear the uniform.'

He sighed. 'Come into the office.'

We sat down in his office and I had to write down a statement of exactly what had happened. I put in my statement that he attacked me outside of the gym while walking to start my job, so I defended myself – I was lucky it happened just before my shift started at seven o'clock and I wasn't wearing my uniform.

Barry said, 'If Roy presses charges, you'll be out of a job for good, no questions.'

That was fair enough, I thought, and I was happy with that.

Fortunately, Roy was too embarrassed to come to the gym for a couple of weeks, and people started spreading rumours that he was not allowed back. When he finally showed up, he wanted to speak to Peter and Barry. Roy said all he was interested in was getting back in the gym and training. Barry and Peter agreed that he could come back as long as he shook hands with me and left it at that.

In years to come, Roy became one of my good friends. That earned me a good reputation so all the big guys would back off from me. Roy told them all I was the crazy, fearless guy from the war!

Uvin later became my coach and he taught me martial arts, self-discipline and self-belief. He was in his sixties, but he looked after himself so well that he looked more like someone in his thirties. Uvin was the man I respected the most in the gym and the one from whom I learned the most too. He taught me how to be calm and to control my temper, as well as about positive energy and my posture. I still suffered with PTSD and his techniques helped me when I struggled to cope.

As I gradually gained respect and understanding from other people, I slowly learned how to trust people once again. This was my biggest challenge. My dad had never lost trust in people, despite everything he went through with us in the war, and I admired him for that. I wanted to be able to connect with people positively and share my humanity.

In many ways, I believe being at the sports centre and college saved my life. I had been going through some terrible dark times. I didn't speak to anyone about it, but I had become suicidal at school; the war experiences, the PTSD and the relentless bullying had overwhelmed me and I couldn't see any way out. I had been locked in my own deep silence and despair for too long, and I began to believe I would only find peace by killing myself. As desperate as I was, there was still something strong inside me though, and the people at the sports centre and college believed in me, saw the good in me, and it gave me the confidence and self-esteem to believe in myself.

In total, I would work at the sports centre for seventeen years, and I was devastated when it closed in 2014. It was a stable part of my life, the one constant in my ups and downs over all those years. It will always be the most memorable place where I spent most of my youth, with people who loved me for who I am without being prejudiced. I think of it as the place that made me who I am today.

15

University Life

Good things were happening for me academically. I had always wanted to be an actor – in fact, when I was eleven, my grandmother had said that I would be an actor, although I never asked her how she had managed to predict that. With Mrs Heatherington's encouragement at Moseley School, I had taken the first steps to pursue my dream at her drama club. At Joseph Chamberlain Sixth Form College, I had worked hard at my drama and performing arts A-levels. As I grew in confidence at college, my drama teacher – Marcia Carr – saw my potential and encouraged me to apply to university. I achieved good grades and was offered a place on the Theatre Studies & Professional Practice degree course at Coventry University in 1998.

I was lucky enough to be able to continue working at the sports centre all through my time at university. I enjoyed the work and loved the camaraderie with the other staff, but earning my own money was also very important for me, as it gave me independence and meant I could pay my own way through the three-year course.

It was a big move going from the college where everyone knew me to start all over again at university, and I was very shy about facing new people, the new environment and new challenges. Luckily, once again, my smile won me many friends at university, many of whom will be friends for the rest of my life. The ladies especially loved my shy approach and mysterious looks. I was still a bit reserved and quiet, partly because my English was still a little shaky and not completely polished. It all added to the fun for the girls, who wanted to get to know me.

The first friend I made was Luke Smitherd. He was a great guy – very funny, inquisitive and good-looking – and we hit it off straight away; we became very close and he also helped me with my academic studies. Through him I met Chris (nicknamed 'Chubby'), Steve, Richard, Tom and Nick, who were all great guys to work and study with. At the weekend, we would all go out and have a brilliant time. I still remember how amazed they were the first night they saw my secret tough-guy side. We were in a club and some guys started picking on the lads. I was furious and steamed straight in, sweeping the attackers aside like rag dolls. We already had a strong friendship, but the lads gained a new respect for me after that night.

On one occasion, Luke and I were at a freshers party and as I came back from the toilet, I saw this guy grab him at the bar. From a distance, it looked like he was beating him up, so I rushed over and punched the guy, who fell on the floor. Luke pushed me away, shouting, 'Mirs, that was only a playfight! He's my friend.'

When the guy got up, he said, 'What did you do that for?'

'Luke is my friend and you were beating him up.'

He looked at Luke and said, 'You have a good friend.'

'It's OK,' said Luke. 'This is Mirsad from Bosnia – he takes things seriously since the war.'

Later on, Luke and Chubby were the first people that I took back to visit Bosnia with me, as they were very interested in my past because of the stories that I had told them. I met up with my childhood friend, Big Mirsad Balić, and they were amazed at what this monster can eat. One of the most memorable evenings was when I took the boys to a prestigious hotel in Sarajevo. A fight broke out and Big Mirsad carried on eating while all the tables and chairs were flying around, until he stood up and the fight stopped.

'Let's go,' Luke said. 'Leave the food.'

'How can I leave all this meat?' the big man said, smiling.

So we stayed and finished our meal, and we still laugh when we remember the big man and his meat at the hotel.

It was funny how some girls at university used to love seeing me get into a scrap with the lads. The girls felt safe and protected with me whenever we went out. Girls were not my priority at the time – I treated them like my sisters, rather than girlfriends; that was as far as I wanted to take things with them. They could never really understand me – my wild personality, but with a shy approach to everything. It puzzled them most of the time, but they all knew that I had a big heart. At times I ended up putting myself in dangerous situations, just to make sure the girls were protected. I took pride in it and after all I had been through in life, that behaviour was natural to me. At night, I still struggled to sleep, going over my experiences and thinking, I couldn't protect my vulnerable family members who were caught in the war. But I knew I could protect these girls and treat them with the maximum respect. I had earned their trust so much that I could sleep next to them and they would feel safe with me, knowing I wouldn't try to take advantage of them sexually. I had no interest in that; all I wanted was to get a degree and to make many friends at the university. At that time I felt that I needed a lot of people to love me and respect me, and that was more than enough for me.

Siham was another of my very close friends who worked with me at the college, and she also helped me with my assignments. It was only after I started university that I found out I was dyslexic, so it was no wonder I had struggled so much at school.

Those three years sped by, and I had the most amazing time. My university days were uplifting for me and I learned so much about hard work, discipline, strong friendships, teamwork and dealing with young women.

My parents felt very proud standing next to me in my graduation gown. At this point they realised that I had changed and was heading in the right direction with everything. I felt on top of the world. Having come to England deeply traumatised and unable to speak the language, I had overcome relentless bullying and worked hard to achieve what had not seemed possible.

After university, I felt all my community started looking up to me and respecting what I had achieved. They knew where I had started, with all the struggles with my PTSD, and now they saw how much I had accomplished in such a short time.

They started to use me as an example for their own children. I even heard parents telling their children off in front of me. They would say, 'You should be ashamed of yourself! Look what Mirsad has achieved after what he has been through in his life. You should be more like him!'

It made me so proud and drove me to push myself even further. Wherever my parents went, my family and friends praised them, commending them for how well they had brought up their children, especially me with my PTSD. Even after the war, when people went back home, they all knew my story in the village, that I was 'the little boy who said nothing'. It was so satisfying for me to hear after the gossip my parents had had to endure about me and my behaviour.

* * *

After graduating from university, I wanted to hone my acting skills, and I applied to Birmingham School of Acting, now part of the Royal Birmingham Conservatoire. I auditioned and was offered a place at my first attempt. It normally takes people a couple of auditions to get in, so I was very proud. I had put the hard work into my academic studies and it had paid off in the end. My biggest obstacle was my accent. I had developed a Brummie accent when I learned to speak English at school, and now it was hard to get rid of it. I worked really hard with my vocal coach, but then I ended up with a foreign accent.

The course was very intensive, covering all aspects of performance, and the teachers were always supportive but pushed us hard to do our best. My favourite teacher was Daniele Sanderson, who worked very hard with me on my improvisation skills. I did very well in the nineteenth-century workshops delivered by Louise Papillion. David Vann was our history teacher, and he spent a lot of time delivering different modules on history and period theatre. He had a great approach to learning and an engaging way of teaching history. My television tutor, Andrew Higgs, always told me that I had an excellent screen presence and that I was very photogenic – in acting terminology: 'the camera likes me'. Stephen Simms was in overall charge of the course and he kept our enthusiasm going; he was also our tutor, making sure we all made individual progress. We had ballet, as well as keep-fit and aerobic classes, where I stood out because of my weight-training skills and keeping fit at the gym for years.

Life at drama school was very special; we were disciplined and motivated to compete against each other in every module. There were no limits to how much we could achieve or how much work we did. We would start early in the morning and finish late at night. In the morning we would normally have aerobic, ballet, period dance and keep-fit classes,before starting our other modules. I loved the discipline and it reminded me of working hard at all the chores I had to do when I was a little boy on the farm with my granddad in Bosnia.

I made a lot of friends at drama school, including Nigel Boyle, Dhafer L'Abidine, Karen Tween, Catherine Garner, Rachel Dealtry, and too many more to mention.

The students were from all over the country and they all had different accents. Having encountered so many different people since leaving Bosnia aged thirteen, I managed to adapt to this environment pretty quickly. But I had a real problem with my smile, which in acting terminology they would call 'corpsing'. The smile had been my coping mechanism as I grew up, and I had used it to hide my problems with PTSD. It had served me well when I needed it, but now it was causing issues for my acting. In no time my teachers and vocal coaches had spotted the problem and they were trying to deal with it. Every time I practised for a different role, the smile would kill my character onstage. When I had finalised and developed it fully, my smile would just break out from nowhere. I couldn't control it and it would destroy a character that I had been developing for weeks and weeks. As it became more noticeable, I had to do something about it. The pressure was building and it would cause me huge embarrassment in front of the whole class. Then, one day, it became too much and I was getting very emotional. I ended up in Stephen Simms' office to discuss what I could do about my smile.

Claire Fiddler, one of my voice coaches, decided to deal with the situation herself. She tried many techniques with me for weeks and weeks in different workshops and none of them worked. Then one day, she handed me a drawing and said, 'This is your head, this is your character,' and told me to write all the information about my character in the picture. It was the breakthrough I needed. When I did that, it made me think about character and I realised nothing else should enter my thoughts and emotions when I was onstage. Finally, I had managed to lose my smile and stop corpsing permanently.

It just made me realise how hard these teachers worked to get us through drama school with the best results that they could get out of us individually. We all had different talents and different problems. My Tunisian friend Dhafer used to help me with facial expressions in front of the camera and I helped him with pronunciation. Dhafer spoke English with a French accent and it was very difficult to understand him. Bearing in mind that he had lived in England for only a couple of years, he was doing really well. Although I had similar problems, I had been developing my English language skills ever since I was in secondary school. I was able to pass on to Dhafer the techniques that I had used to develop my English speaking and writing skills.

We became best friends and we worked really hard in drama school. Both of us faced more obstacles than our classmates in finding acting jobs because of our accents. We still had hope and confidence in our talent, and one could say that we had different qualities to offer onstage and in front of the camera. One thing was clear: we stood out in the crowd with our accents and versatile approach to acting, because of our backgrounds.

Money was always tight and our tutors warned that it would be even more difficult when we finished drama school. They told us, 'Actors have to become the best beggars in order to survive in this game.' I never really understood that phrase, but after drama school it soon became clear: the only actors who make it are those who go for the jobs and don't take no for an answer. I also believe you need sufficient talent to go with it, but you must be persistent in chasing every little part on stage or in a film to be noticed in this field. Certainly, some of us are more determined than others, and I guess with experience you become better at it.

In acting, your character, no matter how big or small the part you get, has a big influence on the role you might be offered next. I am a strong believer that you have to start with playing the small parts in order to develop yourself and your confidence in front of the camera to play the bigger roles.

I will never forget our last day in drama school. Our teachers gathered us all in one little dance studio. We were like kids crammed in on top of one other, over a hundred of us looking at our teachers as though they were about to give us gold. Instead, they told us, 'Only a couple of you will become professional actors and the rest of you, within a couple of years, will change your careers.'

None of us really believed it, but it was the scariest lesson they had taught us since we started there. The reality of an actor's life is very cruel and I know they were letting us know just how hard it can be. I think some of the students were disheartened by this and immediately began to think they wouldn't realise their dream, and even I wondered, what was the point of giving us all that intensive training and then telling us that we wouldn't be able to use it? All my life I have had to struggle, and at the very start of my dream career I was being told it would be a struggle – how ironic is that? But the war had been the most terrible time in my life, and nothing could be worse than that. So, I embraced it – I thought, what could be better in life than not knowing what's around the corner and what you might achieve the next day, the next week or the next year? That thought carried me through to each new day. I always hoped for the best and believed if I was persistent, my time would come in front of the camera or onstage. The only thing that worried me about this career was that I wouldn't make a good beggar. In fact, there were only a few people in that small room who I thought would be good at that part of the game. But there is always that little hope sparkling in your head.

The biggest challenge is getting a good agent who will send

you for the right auditions for roles that you are capable of delivering. The same agent has to recognise your ability to push you further in order for you to reach your limits. Then you can overcome your obstacles and meet your challenges. Your agent should be like a second parent and adapt to the way you are working, learning about you so they can sell your qualities and get the most out of your potential. I am from the first generation in this country and the expectations from my mum and dad are quite high, but they had no contacts or people around them who could point me in the right direction in my acting career. At the same time, I wanted to surprise my parents and achieve something that they never expected from me.

We had a showcase in London at the end of the final year, which would be our opportunity to sell ourselves to agents, film directors and different production companies. It was standard procedure for all drama school students to show off their skills and potential in the West End in front of the people who could make or break their future careers.

My teacher Daniele Sanderson had always thought highly of me; she pushed me to the maximum and gave me the best advice on what would work for me. I trusted her with all my heart and became very close to her; I took on board all her recommendations and advice. One day, in London, while I was rehearsing my monologue for the showcase, she came up to me and said, 'Mirsad, I want you to run quickly to a shop to get a tight top, and I want you to wear it. That way, we can expose your muscles and that is your selling point.'

At that point, I realised just how much she cared about my success.

I found a tight top that showed off my arms and the rest of

my muscular frame and wore it for the auditions. My exposed muscles were shining out of the pitch-black theatre space, and I stood out from the other actors onstage, so I guess I was offering them something different.

The next day, Daniele called me to say that a director from America, who was making a film with Sean Connery called *The League of Extraordinary Gentlemen*, was interested in me. We had a couple of good conversations and we were all convinced that I would be the best candidate to play one of the Russian villains. It would have been a good beginning for me, with massive exposure, as the film would be seen in cinemas all over the world. The whole drama school was buzzing – both teachers and students – about what a great opportunity it was; they all seemed as excited as I was. Unfortunately, nothing came of it, and we never really got to the bottom of it. All I know is that we lost contact with the director, who flew back to LA the following week. It was an early lesson in how hard the acting world can be, and how quickly opportunities come and go. But it just made me more determined and gave me the drive to carry on. I strongly believed that other chances would come my way, as long as I persevered.

The only three people that I know of from my course that made it in acting are Nigel Boyle, Dhafer L'Abidine and me. Nigel is a regular actor, known for TV dramas *Peaky Blinders*, *Line of Duty* and *Humans*. Dhafer and I were perhaps the least likely people to survive in this industry because of our accents, but Dhafer's career took off quickly when he got a part in *Dream Team*, the Sky drama series about football players. Dhafer had been a professional footballer in Tunisia before deciding to pursue an acting career, so the role was perfect for him. More importantly, it opened doors for him, and led to many different parts, including a role in the Hollywood film *Sex and the City 2*, which in turn led to him being cast in Egyptian dramas and soaps. Now, this is the reality of the situation. You struggle every day to secure auditions and jobs, and every little helps you to climb the ladder and get any role you can in films and get yourself an IMDB listing.

It was a scary and often dispiriting time, but I was determined to follow my dream. I have done many different jobs since I was a child, but for me acting is a way of life and I enjoy it the most. It doesn't feel like a job to me and I get completely involved until I make or break the character that I am developing. That is how I work and everything revolves around that.

I also wanted to achieve something recognisable for my country, which would make me feel proud of the place where I was born. After all the bad experiences that I had in Bosnia, I was considering moving to America to pursue my dream. I knew that American directors liked English-trained actors with an Eastern European twang.

One day I sat down with my mum and dad and told them about my plans, but that reality hit them very hard. I never heard them disagree with anything that I wanted to pursue in the past, but this time it was definitely no. Mum started crying and said, 'We lost all our family in the war and we cannot afford to lose you now.'

My dad said, 'If you go to America, you will never come back. I know a lot of people who went there and never came back.'

They said everything they could to put me off: 'You will be

alone, you have to make a new start without your family and loved ones to support you. You will have to work very hard and there are lots of guns in America, with a lot of crime.' My mum said, 'Don't forget, you are still dealing with PTSD, and with that many guns around you, you will not stand a chance, as it will remind you of Bosnia and the war. After all, there is no one to help you to deal with your PTSD.'

I knew a move was the best thing for me at the time, but I wanted to make my parents happy. I felt sorry for them, and realised I couldn't leave them alone, especially after we had all rebuilt our lives in the UK and had stayed a small, close-knit family all through the tough times so a move to America was out of the question, but I always had other plans in mind. I knew that I had to re-engage with an agent and start auditioning for acting jobs. It felt like starting all over again, now it was clear that I hadn't got the part in *The League of Extraordinary Gentlemen*. In the meantime, we had planned a different trip. For the first time since the war, we were going home.

16

Return to
My Homeland

In 2001, it was time to go back home to Kozarac and reconnect with my past. At first my parents thought it might be too soon and were worried that it might trigger my PTSD, but they accepted that it was my decision. My dad always encouraged me in everything that I set out to do and he realised it could be good for me. My parents took great pride in encouraging their successful kids to see their roots and reconnect with where we came from.

It was interesting arriving home and finding the whole village occupied by the Serbs, who had fled other parts of Bosnia. All my relatives and loved ones were gone and new faces had taken over our village. Most Bosnian people paid the Serbs living in their houses to move out and go elsewhere – it was the easiest way of getting your home back peacefully. Otherwise there was the fear that they could set it on fire, just before they left. I could understand them as well: the Serbian people had also been forced to leave their homes and find somewhere else to go. There were many Serbs in the village who always showed us respect and care, because their experience must have been similar to ours. None of them burned any of our houses down and they always welcomed us to visit our home. However, we felt a little uncomfortable with them around us. Many people died in that village, killed by their Serbian neighbours, paramilitary soldiers and civilians, and it is very difficult to trust them at all, after what they have done to us. The village felt empty without our close family and neighbours, and not like our home.

Soon it became apparent to the Serbs that they were no longer welcome to stay there, especially the ones who told us their personal stories of being soldiers in the Serbian army and how they lost their arms, legs, etc. They said that the Serbian government had given them our houses as a reward for their bravery during the war, that some of them were injured soldiers with gold medals, and that they had nowhere else to go. I found all that very hard to listen to; I thought some of these guys probably killed our family members during the war, that they had earned their medals at our expense. Now they were walking freely around our village, pretending like nothing had happened. I was distraught and found it very hard to sleep during the night.

We stayed with our families in surrounding villages until our house was finally cleared and the Serbs left.

Having seen what had happened in our absence, my dad said to us, 'Listen, children, if you don't come home to your motherland regularly, you will never be able to claim your land and it will fall into their hands.'

I had been so upset to see our village overtaken that his statement always echoed in my head and I made it my business to make sure that we got our home and land back. Our granddad had worked hard all his life for this land, why should we let it fall into their hands for free?

* * *

Reunion with our family in Bosnia gave us an opportunity to catch up and share our experiences about the war and living abroad. We also began to hear the stories of what had happened to our family and friends during the war, as we had lost many family members, and some were killed by their best friends. There were many told and untold stories about the genocide in Kozarac and the rest of Bosnia. The people who survived told some of their stories but many of them have never been written down or recorded, and that was the plan from the top: to completely wipe out the intelligent and capable people, while pretending to care for and spare the old and vulnerable.

One of the most heartbreaking times for me on my first visit after the war was meeting Suada Hodžić, who was working in a little paint shop in Kozarac, and finding out what had happened to my hero Fikro, his wife Suada, and their children, Džemal and Elvisa.

When the ethnic cleansing had started in our area and they were rounding us up in concentration camps, Fikro had still felt safe and wanted to support his community. He joined the local Red Cross, which was based at our school in Trnopolje, and tried to help everybody. One of the things that he will be remembered for was going to our village's local farmers to get milk and taking it to the concentration camp for the babies.

Fikro went backwards and forwards from the camp,

helping out everyone that he could. He loved and cared about others, especially his own people from Kozarac, who he trained in his gym. Those were the people that he least expected to get trouble from. Indeed, he carried on like there was no war, loving, caring and sharing. We were brought up to love everybody and not to discriminate against anyone, but the war brought a completely different way of thinking to many people, and those who were once our best friends became our worst enemies. That was certainly the case in Kozarac; it was a little town and everybody knew everybody, so the war was a perfect opportunity to get rid of anybody who was perhaps in your way. Fikret fell into that category, being the unbeatable champion.

At the concentration camp people were filtered out: most educated people immediately disappeared; rich people were killed; and influential people were used to persuade everyone else to follow the militants' orders. In the end, they all fell into the same category: their last station was a death camp.

There were many stories told about our hero Fikret, but the truth was that everybody saw him at the camp helping vulnerable and wounded people. He went backwards and forwards from the camp to his home to check on his family, and his beloved wife Suada told me what happened on his last visit home. On that day, they were ordered to leave their home with all the others from the village of Trnjani. The army told them to head towards the concentration camp where Fikret had been helping out others. As Suada was telling me this, tears were streaming down her face.

'As we were walking away from home with our two kids, Džemal and Elvisa, Fikret was behind us, when one of the soldiers said to Fikret: "You, stop." When we turned around and looked, it was a guy that he trained at our gym before the war.'

The kids looked at their father in despair without saying a word. The Kalashnikov was pointed at Fikret, motioning to him to move away in the opposite direction. That was the guy that he trained, the person Suada cooked for, the same guy who was treated like their family. The future of the champ was in his hands.

At first, Suada thought and hoped he would save Fikret and spare him from Arkan's paramilitaries. In fact, they put the first bullet in his back only five metres from his wife and children. The champ didn't even scream; he still stood facing back to his beloved family. It took five bullets to get the big man on the floor; even with his last breath, without looking at his children, he showed no fear. Gasping for breath, he fell in a pool of his own blood in front of his house and died on his doorstep. The true Northerner gave his life away for his people and his village. He had been warned that he needed to get out of Bosnia just before the war broke out. He had many celebrity friends telling him to leave, that there would be a bloody war in Bosnia. But he never listened and never believed that his neighbours and most beloved friends would kill him like that in front of his whole family on that fateful day, 9 July 1992.

The whole of Bosnia was shaken, and the shock spread to Europe. Arnold Schwarzenegger tried to get hold of Fikret in 1993, but by then it was already too late. In 1993, Schwarzenegger visited American troops based in Žepa in Bosnia, and it was only then that he found out about the death of his friend. He made an effort to find Fikret's wife, and through the Austrian Embassy in America he tracked down the refugee centre in Austria where Suada was staying. He sent a condolence letter addressed to Fikret's son, Džemal, and some pictures, with clothes for the children.

Suada showed me Schwarzenegger's condolence letter, which I will quote here.

April 1, 1993
Džemal Hodžić
C/O Mr Eugene Tuttle
First Secretary, Embassy of the United States of America
Vienna, Austria

Dear Džemal,
I learned of the death of your father, Fikret Hodžić, through the American Embassy in Vienna, and I cannot tell you how deeply sorry I am. This is a tragedy beyond words, and I wish there was something I could do to change what happened. I am thankful that you, your mother and sister were able to escape and find sanctuary in Vienna.
I am very much aware of your father and what a great bodybuilding champion he was. You can be proud of him. We in the bodybuilding community all had great respect for him and I remember well when your father won 3rd place at the 1981 Mr Universe Contest in Cairo, Egypt. He was in his greatest shape ever then!

As much as this will be difficult, you will need to put

this tragedy behind you, Džemal, and go on with
your life. Try to keep in mind that your father, Fikret,
would have wanted you to lead a happy, constructive
life and always do those things that would have made
him proud of you. You and your sister will be a
source of comfort for your mother, who has lost her
beloved husband and she will need your strength as
she tries to make a new home for all of you. None of
this will be easy for you, but for reasons beyond our
comprehension, some of us are dealt more difficult
cards than others.

With the hope that this might help to add a glimmer
of cheer to your life, I have enclosed some little gifts
for you and your family, namely 3 World Gym sweat
shirts, which I hope, will fit each of you. I have
also signed a couple of pictures for you to keep as
inspiration.

My very best to all of you.
With regards,
Arnold Schwarzenegger

After I heard about the letter from Arnold Schwarzenegger,
I was very emotional. I remember it like it was yesterday.
My heart was heavy and I felt really bad for Suada; she was
alone, full of tears, fighting for existence. At one time, they
were the most respected and most popular people in Kozarac
– how things had changed and how the war had destroyed
lives. The most rich and powerful people became the poorest,

and the poorest people before the war became the most rich and powerful.

It was an honour and a privilege having a family member like Fikret Hodžić, who brought peace, love and recognition to our little village of Kozarac. My memories of him will never be erased until my last breath, and I am sure Arnold Schwarzenegger would say the same thing about him. After all, he went looking for him while the war was still raging in Bosnia. I am sure that if Fikret was still alive in 1993 when Arnold visited Bosnia, he would have got him out. It just shows how recognised and respected Fikret Hodžić was in the bodybuilding community all around the world.

When the family received that letter at the refugee centre, everybody looked at them differently and started to respect them more. I am talking about people who didn't know this family, especially Austrian people.

Sadly, there was even more heartache for this brave family to deal with after the war. They had everything in Austria: stability, money, good healthcare and education, but young Džemal wanted to do something that would have made his dad proud of him, and he wanted to continue the tradition of bodybuilding in his birthplace. Arnold's letter inspired him to return home and, with help from his mother, he set up a gym in his father's name: Fikret Hodžić gym. Schwarzenegger's words touched the young man's heart and reminded him of what his father loved most in his life: number one was bodybuilding and number two was Bosnia.

It was a very big and risky decision for a young man, but his mother Suada supported him and accompanied him to make a new start in Bosnia. Her daughter Elvisa had got married in Austria and she remained there when Suada and Džemal took the big step to return to Bosnia. Džemal had a good way of communicating with people and he was a likeable person, just like his father. He had a lot of support for the gym from local people.

Without his father he faced many challenges, but his mother spent a lot of time with him, helping him with his training, preparation for competition and his diet, just as she had helped her husband. Džemal had to work as a waiter to support his strict regime, including his diet plans and nutrition, which all comes at a price. He was quickly recognised for his hard work and commitment in his local community. His training regime was military, as he inherited his intensive training routines from his dad. Džemal had a huge advantage, not only that his mother trained him, but also that he had good genes like his father, and the older guys were already calling him a mini Fikret. He was born with the same V-shape back and tennis balls on his arms. I can say the same thing about my muscular frame; I guess it runs in the family. In no time Džemal became a new champion on the stage. The more recognition he achieved, the harder he worked, and the more trophies he won, the more he wanted to win.

Sadly, tragedy struck this family again in July 2000 when Džemal was killed back of the café bar near the river Sana; he was walking with his friend when they were both shot. His friend was wounded, but survived, but there was no hope for the new champion. Džemal joined his dad in eternal peace – two champions gone in no time.

It is very difficult to come to terms with Džemal's death, and we heard so many different stories, it is difficult to believe any of them. When the killer faced the court, there was no justice for the family. Apparently, he was mentally ill. It was said he was paid to kill someone, but he killed the wrong guy. Even today, the case remains a mystery, but we know that we lost two great champions: one Yugoslavian champion and one Bosnian junior champion.

From that day on I tried to take care of Suada as much as I could. One thing that I promised her was to take that letter to Arnold Schwarzenegger and thank him personally on behalf of our family. When I said that in front of many other people, they laughed and didn't believe me, but I would fulfil my promise to her not once, but twice, of which

* * *

We made a couple more trips back home, and decided we wanted to give something back to our community, and my friend Edin Paratušić and I came up with the idea of setting up a weights room in Kozarac. It didn't take me long to establish myself in the community and earn respect as someone successful from the UK, who wanted to invest in Bosnia. We wanted to provide the same sort of facilities as Fikret Hodžić used to have there, to continue his legacy and honour his memory.

Training and regular exercise has a variety of benefits and is proven to keep us healthy and minimises various illnesses. It can also improve our mental state, our moods, concentration and overall success in life. I certainly reaped all those benefits from weight training when my PTSD was at its worst, and running the exercise classes at the Birmingham Sports Centre had been some of the most rewarding times of my life. I wanted to bring all these advantages to the people of Kozarac, to give something back to them and to share my passion for exercise.

We also wanted to unite all our young people, Serbs, Croats and Bosnians, to help them build good relationships with each other. Memories of the war were still fresh, and it was important for these youngsters to integrate and try to put the past behind them. They needed to learn to live together in peace and harmony to ensure a better future for the next generation. I wanted to bring them all together again and help them bond through sport.

In 2004, my dad found the premises for the gym on the top floor of the shopping centre in Kozarac, and we opened United Citizens – Solak Gym in 2005.

In the early days, the nephew of the first person who went to The Hague as a war criminal for torturing Bosnian civilians in the concentration camps started training at the gym, and we had no problem with that. We wanted it to be a welcoming environment for all Bosnians, whatever their background.

Over time, we would expand from a little weights room to a full fitness centre, occupying the whole top floor of the shopping centre, but more of that later. For now, we were happy to have taken the first steps towards reconnecting with our family and our homeland.

17

Nights on Broad Street

Back in the UK, I was feeling a bit lost. My acting career had not taken off as I'd hoped and although I still had my job at the sports centre, I needed a new challenge. My good friend Luke Brown noticed how down I seemed and got me to open up to him. Luke had always kept an eye on me since school, and he came up with a plan to help me.

A few days later, Luke came to visit me and invited me to his house to meet his family. I was up for that just to get out of the house. I met his father Joe first. He was one of the nicest people that I had ever met, and I quickly became very close to him. Joe reminded me of my own dad. He looked almost the same too: a big guy, with a big smile and a good appetite! We got on like house on fire, and I trusted him straight away. I felt in my heart that he liked me too. We had similar personalities and in a strange way it felt like we'd always known each other

As soon as I got home, I had a phone call from Luke. 'My

dad asked me if you would be interested in doing some security work for him.'

'Well, I don't know,' I said. 'I've done the security work at the college and sports centre, as you know, but that's all.'

'Don't worry, my dad thinks you'd be good at the job.'

'OK, I'm not doing much at the moment – I'd like to have a go.'

Joe was a great charmer, and an even better boxer. I started boxing with him at New Town Gym, where occasionally Frank Bruno would turn up. I never got to meet him there, but it gave me a great buzz, knowing that he went there and that gave me the drive to work harder in the ring. I learned so much from Joe and I was certainly getting my confidence back in everything – he'd picked me up at a low point in my life and helped me carry on. Joe was a big character, larger than life, and he loved his job as a security man. I couldn't think of a better person to learn from.

My first job with Joe was working the door at Sence, a nightclub in China Town owned by a guy called Albert. Doing doors was similar to working at the sports centre; you had to have a good team around you to be able to manage it. I had picked up lots of skills from Mark at the college and the lads at the sports centre. That and learning from Joe's experience was the perfect combination to make me a good doorman.

Joe was wider than he was tall, and he was a tough guy. He knew all the good guys and bad guys, and he certainly knew how to manage them all. He told me all about the different gangs in Birmingham, such as the Zulus, Burger Boys, The Johnsons, etc. This underground world was all new to me and completely different to what I was used to. I didn't have a clue what was going on around me, but fortunately, everyone else seemed to think that I knew exactly how to do the job.

I put on my serious face and kept my smile hidden as soon as I started that job – I knew in that environment the smile would not help me. Quite often the Jamaican gangs used to call me the Russian guy, as I always wore a warm long coat and had a stony face. It didn't take them long to start testing me to see how much I could take and what they could get away with.

Joe prepared me for all of that and warned me, 'It's better to play the easy game. If you play the hard game, you become the tough guy, and how long can you keep that up? You'll get tired of playing the tough guy and then eventually you have to give in, but that means they will break you completely and you will be out of the game, which means out of the job.' He knew all about my temper from Luke, and he knew that would be the best approach for me to take.

I was always a bit stubborn though – it was my way or no way – so, even though Joe had twenty-five years' experience working on the doors, I didn't follow his advice for a minute. One evening, a guy turned up and walked straight into me, barging into me like I was nothing. I said in a very calm way, 'Where do you think you're going?'

'I'm going upstairs!'

'I don't think you're going anywhere,' I said, and used all my force to sweep him out of the way. He was a big guy but he bounced off like the wind had blown him over.

He was furious. 'Do you know who I am?' he shouted.

'Mate, I don't really care who you are,' I said. I'd quickly learned that all the guys used to say that to scare you into letting them in the club.

He came close to me again, which was a bad sign, as I was alone with no backup and I'd already embarrassed him in front of a few bystanders. I was on my guard and waiting for him to strike. I was scared he might have a knife, so my arms were up and I was already warning him not to get any closer to me. That was the best advice that I got from Joe: never allow an attacker to invade your personal space; always keep a metre and a half away from him. If he gets too close, you've had it. Then an attacker can do whatever he wants to you – stab you, punch you, throw you, push you, bite you, strangle you.

In this situation I knew what to do. I thought I would trick him with my left jab, which was the most powerful weapon I always had. Joe had discovered my jab in the ring and he taught me how to use it. My jab went out and the big man bounced off again, this time straight on the floor.

As I was standing over him, Joe appeared behind me. 'Mirsad! What the fuck are you doing?'

I didn't answer.

'Do you know who he is?'

'Joe, I don't give a fuck who he is! He was threatening me, barging into me; he got what he deserved.'

Suddenly, the whole club was outside, shouting and calling to this guy – Blue Guy. He was bouncing around me like a bull, but I didn't take my eyes off him, just kept staring at him to show him there was no fear in me. All the Burger Boys were shouting, 'Come on! Get the Russian guy!'

Now all the doormen were standing behind me, and they were angry with Joe. 'We don't need this, Joe,' one of them said. 'Why did you leave the new guy alone on the front door?'

Joe kept quiet, watching what was going on. But the

moment was lost and Blue Guy came up to me again, saying, 'I'm coming back.'

It was the same sentence used by the soldiers when I was tortured and I hated it.

'Well, I'm here now,' I said to him. 'You do what you need to do.'

Within twenty minutes, three brothers turned up, and came straight at me: 'We've come to deal with you.'

'Come on then,' I said.

They looked confused by my attitude; that I wasn't backing down.

Joe called one of the guys over and said, 'Look, this is my new guy. I left him alone to man the front door while I got a drink and I told him not to let anybody in. It's not his fault, he was just doing his job and he tried to prove himself to me.'

I could see the guy was happy with what Joe had said and he accepted that, but then one of the brothers said to me, 'Come out alone if you're a man!'

I left the front door and stood in front of all three of them and said, 'Now I'm not a security guy, I'm just an ordinary guy right in front of your face.'

All three of them looked at me and smiled. They probably liked my confidence, and decided to give me a chance and leave me alone.

I learned a lot from this situation. It seemed to me that these guys just liked my behaviour and the fact that I had a mellow soft voice with not the slightest hint of fear. The standard procedure for letting the guys back in the club after an incident like this would be to ask the lads to call it a night so everyone calmed down, but they would not be barred.

These guys didn't seem to understand that I came from a war and doing the door work didn't really mean anything to me. From what I have seen, to work on the door you have to be a tough man. But I was beyond that. I never saw myself as a tough guy, I just got on with the job, but never tolerated anybody taking the piss out of me or messing me about. If you were soft, they would certainly take advantage of your generosity and walk all over you.

The club work was very different to working at the sports centre – long hours and few rewards, apart from working in a good strong team and making friends. Quite often I asked myself: who would choose to work with customers who were often drunk and at times would break the law, and why? There is no real answer, but I guess someone has to protect the weak and vulnerable members of the community at night. The police can only do so much with their hands tied, and so we stepped in where we could. You saw everything working on the doors: drugs, thugs, gangs. You name it, we had it, and we had to deal with it.

It didn't help that the club we worked in was known as a tough old place, but that was all part of the job. I'd had my first test, but I knew it wouldn't be the last. In fact, I soon realised we'd be tested every night by different members of the gang. We tried to keep the bad guys out, but if they could force themselves through the door first, the rest of the gang could follow them at some point in the night. The hardest nights were when the club was quiet and the club owner had to make some money, so on those nights he would tell us to let them back in, and the bad boys had a perfect opportunity to invade the club and act up.

One night, one of the Burger Boys kicked off in the club because one of his gang had been shot. He found a person to blame and took all his anger out on him. This guy started punching and kicking a new member of the gang so badly that I thought he would kill him. I stepped forward, but Joe stopped me and said, 'Don't get involved.'

I must have looked confused, but he just said, 'Do you want it as well?'

I stepped forward anyway, and the guy smiled at me but he continued the abuse. He was drunk, short and stocky, full of muscle. Someone said, 'Leave him. He's very drunk, full of emotions, and he's teaching the other guy not to make the same mistake.'

I didn't know what that meant but I always hated to see anyone being bullied.

The attack continued on to the balcony and tables started flying everywhere. I ran at the guy as fast as I could, lifting my right arm like I was going to slap him. He stumbled into the balcony fence, went over it and fell from the first floor to the ground floor, landing on three massive rugby players, who stopped him getting hurt. I don't even know how I got away with that – I guess no one saw me running into him. I admit it was a nasty move on my part, but I hadn't meant to knock him off the balcony like that. It was an accident, but I was a bit shocked when I thought I could have killed him. The police arrived but there wasn't a scratch on him, and he said he'd fallen off the balcony. Then the police checked his hands and saw his bleeding knuckles. They realised that he'd been fighting, and took him away.

When the officers came back to question us, nobody knew

anything. Even the young guy that he was picking on said they were just playfighting and that he was punching the walls because he'd lost his friend. No one knew what I'd done, and I was too scared to admit to it. People don't realise just what kids from a war are capable of doing. If you have no fear, you have no limits. I had seen atrocities, genocide, people being executed in front of my eyes at the age of thirteen, and these little gang members thought they could scare me. But I learned my lesson that night and I had a very lucky escape. I began to realise that when people are drunk, most of the time they don't even know what they are doing.

I guess like any other job you get used to it and you accept what you've got, rather than looking for a better and more peaceful job. There were times when we stood at the door and said, 'This door is too boring – we need to go elsewhere to find a door with more action.' We all found student nights the most boring, standing around all night, kicking our heels and yawning. But, as they say, be careful what you wish for.

I learned how to do my job safely, bravely and correctly, but this was nothing like the sports centre with its close community and people who wanted to get on with their training and professional athletes who just wanted to be the best in their sport. Doing the security job was dangerous, and your base could change at any time – you had to be ready to start all over again at any time.

Your reputation plays a vital part in this job and you have to have good backup. All of this falls into place naturally when you do the job for a while, but before that you have to take a few digs, beatings, punches and bruises, and learn how to carry yourself. Your job is to be responsible for the other people in your venue: your staff, the people around you and the public late at night. When we talk about gangs, it's a different game altogether. I was never part of any gangs and that was potentially difficult, because I didn't know how the gangs operated, so I didn't know how to deal with them, but I was lucky that I knew most of them from the sports centre. They knew my face very well and they knew how I operated. I was a straight guy and many of them knew that I came from war-torn Bosnia and most of them respected that. They would call me all sorts of names, but most of the time they would call me a soldier, because I was strict with them. I regularly challenged them and didn't let them get away with anything, but there was mutual respect between us.

After a while I was moved to the taxi rank, making sure people queued up for the taxis and behaved themselves. I was by myself, but I got a bit of a pay rise. It was nearly always cold and often wet, but the biggest problem was that I was working alone on the streets and everything that goes with it. One night, a guy barged past everyone and stood at the front of the queue. Everyone started complaining and I had to try to calm the situation down quickly. I had many different strategies and tactics to deal with people but the best way was always to pick someone out without them knowing what you were trying to achieve. You had to trick them to get your job done and move them to where they were supposed to be. The last option was to get physical with them, but you had to be careful because you wouldn't know how many people were together in the queue.

I used my firm, clear voice to the guy who'd jumped the queue. I knew he'd fall into my trap, as he was young, strong and full of testosterone. I said, 'You need to move from there, before I move you.'

'Who do you think you're talking to?' he said.

'I will not repeat myself. I was talking to you, and you know why. If you think you're a big man, step up to me.'

He ran at me, shouting and threatening me, like an angry dog. I had done the hardest job of getting him out of the queue, but now I had to calm him down. He was a bigger challenge than I expected – he was in my face and he was physically stronger than me. I was also cold and tired, and wrapped up in a lot of clothes, so my movement was restricted and slow. The guy was swinging left, right and centre, and I knew that if I got caught with one of those punches, I wasn't getting up.

The entire taxi queue had become our audience, forming a ring around us. I was wearing very good strong boots to keep me stable in wet conditions, but this guy was in his summer trainers, with no grip, and I knew I had to get him off his feet. I had an advantage knowing Thai boxing, which saved me that night. 'Give me your best shot,' I said, and he came at me with a powerful punch. I ducked down, making him miss, before kicking him in the shin as hard as I could. People heard him scream at the end of the street. Then I gave him another dig to the other leg, making sure he couldn't come back at me. His scream echoed so far that the police patrolling the next street heard him and came to see what was going on. I pretended nothing had happened and said I hadn't seen anything, but I told them he was drunk and behaving disorderly. I must admit I was lucky, because back in those days they didn't have that many street cameras.

I strongly believed that I was doing something good for our community and the local people. The job was very difficult at times, testing your mental and physical strength. You have to have limits on how much abuse you will take before you put yourself into a defence mode and start protecting yourself and the people around you. My parents and friends regularly asked me why I did that job, considering all the qualifications that I had, but I was doing other jobs at the same time, so that part of my life was fulfilled too.

The other thing that might seem strange is that I had wanted to be a soldier, but never spoke about it with my family and friends, because I was too young when the war broke out. I did join the British Army Cadets when I was sixteen, but that didn't last long, because of my PTSD. I wanted to prove to the world what a true soldier is. A soldier hurt me, so I wanted to become a soldier. My schoolteacher hurt me, so I wanted to become a teacher, just to prove to people that soldiers and teachers don't do those kinds of things. I also needed to prove that to myself more than anybody else. I believed in people and what we can achieve together to help one another, without hurting each other. That was my mission statement for life, my approach to everything I did. For me, doing the security job was more than just earning the money. I met all sorts of people on the streets of Birmingham and did my best to help all of them, and most people seemed to respect me for it.

One evening, when I was working at the taxi rank in the cold, a man came up to me and started chatting. His clothes were old and shabby and I guessed he was sleeping rough. He told me his name was Steve; he was very polite and softly spoken, and asked me all sorts of questions. For me those questions turned out to be life-changing as they made me think about my life and the things I do.

'I've been watching you for months,' he said, 'and all of my homeless friends think you're a hero.'

'Why?'

'You always have a smile on your face and you're always happy. You treat everybody the same – us homeless people and the clubbers that give you a tip. That is a very good quality to have. Don't let that go, not many people have that.'

I always listen to people – another thing I learned from my granddad. He used to say, 'Knowledge is in people – you just have to find the way to access it. The old people are wise, but they are also selfish, so you must learn how to talk to them.

'Always share what you have and make people aware of that. Then you will win their trust and they will know that you are not greedy. That way, they will accept you for who you are and they will never be jealous of your personal success. That way, you will build bridges between good people. Always remember this in your life. It is a very simple formula: without people around you, you are nothing, and there is no space for you to develop any success!'

I've never forgotten my granddad's wise words, and I always tried to live my life by them. I used to share my tips with the homeless people and bought them warm drinks and the odd burger. I was happy to help them out, but at the same time I knew, if something happened to me, they would be my best witnesses. I did exactly as I was told by my granddad. It was educational, but also rewarding. I was also proud to live by my Bosnian values and to be a good citizen in this world, treating everyone fairly and respectfully, no matter where they found themselves in life.

Getting to know Steve and his friends and hearing their stories taught me so many things about life. In many ways their experiences as homeless people mirrored ours as refugees fleeing a war-torn country. I'd see them on the streets with their tents and bags, their only shelter that little corner of a building where drunken clubbers urinated. That would be the only time when the rough sleepers would have short conversations with the strangers who used to throw them a few pence after they'd finished urinating. It reminded me of when we were refugees and everyone avoided us, saying we were smelly and dirty and that we didn't belong anywhere. I always sympathised. Perhaps more than anyone I knew that life is hard and no one knows what's around the corner; everything can change overnight. Steve told me he'd had a big house, a family, children and a lot of money. He started having problems with his wife, which led to him developing problems with drink, which in turn resulted in him losing everything that he had worked for all of his life. Again, it was very similar to our experience in war-torn Bosnia.

Steve took an old, creased picture out of his pocket and passed it to me: it was a photo of his kids, who he had not seen for over ten years. Again, I thought of our family in Bosnia, who we hadn't seen for years. He had opened up to me, and I ended up telling him my life story, about the war and my experiences as a child.

All of a sudden, someone said, 'Why are you talking to a druggy scumbag?'

I turned around to see the security supervisor, one of the

guys who used to drop by to check on me. 'You're a loser, a hypocrite, pretending to be better than them and you're not,' I said sharply. 'Tomorrow, you could end up like them.'

I really didn't want to talk to people like this guy. As you can tell, he was one of those people who thought his job title made him better than other people. I had no time for people like that – I'd rather chat to the homeless guys.

The next day, Joe Brown phoned me and said, 'Mirsad, the supervisor was there and he is the big boss; he's not happy with the way you're doing your job.'

'What do you mean?' I said.

'He said that you ignored him, pretending you can take all of Birmingham on your shoulders.'

'Joe, I don't mean to be disrespectful to you and the company that you work for. I'm grateful that you have found me the job, but that guy that came around last night is a little prat! He told me not to talk to a homeless guy and I didn't agree with him. Then he started making stupid statements about himself; who he is and what he has achieved in life, and I said to him, "You're telling me all of this and you still work here on the street!" That's all I said to him. He got angry and walked off. I am a true man and I say to people to their face what I think about them – especially when they are rude and disrespectful to someone like a homeless person, who they know nothing about.'

I had a long conversation with Joe and I got really angry.

In the end, he said, 'Mirsad, just be careful. Remember, you are alone there and if you become too confident and cocky, you will have problems.'

'I know that, Joe,' I said, and put the phone down.

I was furious, thinking about the supervisor: little rat, who does he think he is? I can choose who I want to talk to and why. I certainly wouldn't open up to an idiot like him.

I did think about what Joe had said to me though but in a strange way I had always felt protected, like somebody was watching over me.

That night, I was back at the taxi rank, standing out in the cold again, and someone tapped me on the shoulder.

It was Steve. 'Hi, Mirsad, here's a coffee for you. I just bought it from McDonald's.'

His hands were dirty and he was smelly, but I didn't mind – I thought of the war when we were passing through the mountains for days in that lorry and we all looked the same. 'Thank you, Steve,' I said.

'Listen, Mirsad,' he said, 'I really appreciated the way you spoke to that guy when he was rude to me.'

'Don't worry, Steve, that's what friends are for and you are my friend for life.'

He hugged me and left. This world isn't fair, it's so cruel, and all of this country has been built on different classes. I don't belong here, I want to treat everybody the same with respect and dignity, I thought afterwards. In the end, I had almost as many confrontations with people attacking the homeless guys as I did with people jumping the queue.

One of the biggest problems I had was with the taxi drivers. If the clubbers were a bit drunk and only going a short distance, the drivers would find any little excuse not to take them, because they couldn't make any money out of them. I had many rows with the taxi drivers, especially in the early hours if it was raining, and everyone wanted to get home as soon as possible and the drivers were just interested in making as much money as they could. One night, when it was getting to the end of my shift and I was tired, a row broke out in a taxi. A group of lads had got in the cab and the driver started shouting at them to get out, saying they'd done a runner the last time he took them. It was about 4am and people were desperate to get home. Without thinking, I ran straight over. I didn't know what was going on and I didn't know that those guys were all together, all I could see was a taxi driver shouting and swearing in a threatening manner, while a guy stood on the pavement, pissing into his cab.

The driver had got out and was making his way to the other side of the cab. I thought he would help me if I got stuck, which the drivers usually did, so I grabbed the guy who was pissing into the taxi and pulled him away. As he turned towards me, he started pissing on me as well. 'Stop that!' I shouted.

He was a tough-looking guy with scars all over his face. 'I'll kill you both!' he screamed. 'I've killed people before!'

Now I could see that this guy was dangerous. I had to fight now, because he was already swinging his massive fists at me. I kicked him in the balls, and all of a sudden something hit me hard from behind – it felt like a metal bar. When I turned around my vision was already blurry and I was disorientated and dizzy. I was struggling to stand, but I knew that if they got me on the floor, I could die. There were five massive lads in front of me, growling, screaming their heads off, pointing at me and shouting, 'This is the guy!'

The driver had locked himself back in the cab, and I banged on the window, shouting, 'Mate, let me in! I'm struggling here.'

He nodded and I thought he was going to unlock the door, but as I tried to grab the handle, he drove off as fast as he could. Oh my God, now I was in trouble! My vision was blurred and I was bleeding from the back of my head. One trick I learned in this job was to strip off all your clothes, so you become lighter and more mobile, but that wouldn't be enough against five of them. I was looking around for anyone to help, but the street was deserted and I knew I had to get away. I ran unsteadily towards the shelter where Steve and his friends usually slept, hoping they were there. The best strategy in those situations is to call any name you know, so at least the attackers think there are people around you. It didn't stop these guys, though, and they were close behind me. I could always run faster than an average person, especially these guys, who were heavy and drunk, but I was injured. One thing that always went through my mind was: if you don't have witnesses, they can kill you and no one will ever know, especially back then when we didn't have that many cameras in the city centre, like we have now. I reached Sence, the club where Joe worked, but they'd already left: no one was there. I rang the bell a few times, hoping the staff would see me on the camera and open the door, but no luck.

I started to cry inside, and every single dead family member appeared in front of me, telling me to run towards the attackers. I'm not sure if I was hallucinating or if I was just reliving the war when they were dying in front of me. Osman, Nijaz, Hašim, Junuz, Atif, all my family members were saying, 'Mirsad, run into them and break them, you cannot go backwards – there is a trap.' These people, among many others who died during the war, were everything for me when I was growing up. They always knew what was best for me. I always carry them with me in my heart, and if I ever get in a difficult situation, they appear in my thoughts and help me, telling me what to do. I know it sounds strange, but it is real to me. It also happens if I have a PTSD episode or flashback. I start jumping around, attacking everyone around me. Then I go into a fighting survival mode, where the different family members appear to me.

I had no choice now – I turned and ran straight at these guys, calling out for Steve, praying he would hear me. It felt like running into a solid brick wall. By now, I was thinking, I've left my clothes by the taxi rank, plenty of evidence for the police to catch these guys if they kill me. Then, suddenly, I heard a voice saying, 'Mirsad is in trouble!'

The attackers turned to see who was shouting behind them. In that split second, as I was running, I elbowed one of the guys, and he hit the floor. In front of me, there was a little army of homeless guys with bottles in their hands.

'Don't worry, Mirsad,' said Steve, 'we've got you!'

As soon as he said that, my Northerner blood boiled again and I ran straight into the attackers. I don't know where I got that energy from, but I felt sheer power running through me. They were drunk and breathless from running after me. I went for the biggest guy first, the one who had pissed on me. I punched him in his jaw, and he collapsed, then Steve and his lads started throwing bottles at them. Realising they were outnumbered and likely to get a hiding, they quickly ran off.

I hugged Steve and the guys – they had put themselves on the line to help me that night.

Every single family member appeared in my head, then disappeared, like they had said their final goodbyes.

I think Steve and his friends must have told the whole of Birmingham what happened that night! Joe and the supervisor called me the following day, as they had all heard about the incident and wanted to know what had happened. I didn't want to go over the whole story again, I just wanted to carry on with my job, but I did tell them I was going to find that taxi driver and deal with him.

I went over to Steve and the guys and said, 'How can I thank you?'

'Well, look, Mirsad,' they said, 'we had to give up our half-empty bottles to save your arse that night.'

I laughed. 'Don't worry,' I said, 'I'll sort you out.'

The next week, I brought them all Šljivovica, the strong Bosnian plum brandy. They spoke about how good that drink was for a very long time and I gave it to them a few more times.

Sadly, Steve passed away recently, a young man on the streets of Birmingham. I found out so much about homeless people by talking to him and his friends, and one thing for sure is that they don't live long. They are exposed to such bad weather conditions and many of them have mental health issues or drug and alcohol problems, but they all have their own story to tell.

The taxi driver appeared again a couple of months later and I said that he would be better off if he drove away like he did that night. Otherwise, I couldn't guarantee his safety. He sped straight off and I never saw him again after that.

After my close shave that night, the security company told me that I could bring another guy on board, so I got my friend Sadri, a half-Albanian and half-Bosnian guy, to join me. We were doing a really good job and we never had any problems, but the company used to move us about a lot and my next base was at a hotel on Broad Street. I must admit that was very tough, but after what I went through working on the taxi rank in the cold weather, it didn't seem so bad.

Next, I was asked to work at Gatecrasher, the biggest nightclub in Birmingham, which had six different venues within the club, playing different music. We had loads of different incidents, but I was always looked after there because my old school friend, Big Avy, was the head doorman.

I was in charge of the VIP area and I loved it. I could see the main dance floor from where I was working, so I could help people when they needed it.

One day, a football player turned up, and everyone was making a big fuss of him. The manager said, 'Make sure this guy is happy – he plays for Aston Villa and he spends a lot of money here.'

'No problem,' I said. But as the night went on, he became more and more demanding. He was drinking heavily with about ten of his mates and spending a lot of money. He took off his clothes and shoes and threw them downstairs on to the main dance floor. He took his shirt off, bragging that it was worth a lot of money but it didn't mean anything to him. Somehow, I managed to stop all of that nonsense and calm him down, but he still wanted attention, like he was someone really famous. My policy is to treat people equally, no matter who they are, how much money they might have and what they do, so I didn't want to treat him any differently.

He soon started picking on me. As I was letting people in and out, he brought five girls in. We normally didn't allow people to bring their friends in, as we were restricted with numbers in the VIP area, so I told him they had to leave. He took a bundle of fifty-pound notes from his pocket and asked me, 'How much money do you want?'

'I don't need money from you,' I said. 'I get paid for doing my job.'

'You get paid fifty pounds a night,' he said, and threw a fifty-pound note at me.

'That is very disrespectful,' I said. 'Please don't do it again.'

He threw another fifty at me. 'Is that enough?'

I picked up both of the notes and tried to put them back in his pocket, but he refused to take them. So I ripped them up in front of him. 'I don't need your money and don't throw your money on me again,' I said. 'I find that very disrespectful and I don't really care how much money you've got.'

He got angry and shouted to his friends that I'd ripped up his money and he wanted it back. I told the lads what had happened and said if they wanted to take it further, they should complain to my boss.

'No,' they said. 'You call the boss here!'

I called Big Avy on the walkie-talkie, but they were already dealing with something more serious. This situation was starting to escalate, and I called for backup again, but no one turned up. Suddenly, one of the guy's mates went for me, so I punched him and he fell down the stairs. Another guy tried to wrestle me and I kicked him to the floor; as he fell down he spilled his drink on his face and he couldn't see. I had to get some backup, so I climbed on top of the bar and pointed a pen laser at one of the security guards who was on the main dance floor. He ran over and he was like a bulldozer; he swept everyone in front of him and the two of us threw them all down the stairs. When the other security guys turned up, they tried to escort them outside but the football player and his mates decided to smash the front doors on their way out. Fortunately, it was all caught on the security camera, and their football club disciplined the players with heavy fines. At least I showed the guy who had the problem with me he can't buy everyone with his money.

After that, I got my brother Jasmin to do a few shifts at Gatecrasher, because Big Avy was short on staff. I made sure he was working near me, so I could always keep an eye on him. One night, when I looked down the stairs, I couldn't see him. All of a sudden I saw people running in what we called the tunnel, a little corridor that was the main entrance to the dance floor, from the other venues in the club. Immediately, I knew there was something wrong. I called Jasmin on the walkie-talkie and there was no answer. I ran into the tunnel, pushing past everyone to see what was going on. Again I heard the voices in my head: 'Your brother is in trouble!' When I got through the crowd, I saw a big rugby player had Jasmin pinned against the wall and was strangling him. He was attacking my little brother and I lost it. I cracked him over the head with a water bottle that I had in my back pocket, and when he dropped Jasmin, oh my God, that was only the beginning! I was crying, punching and kicking this guy to the ground before I threw him down the stairs. The guy was so scared, he pissed himself, and when the security guys at reception picked him up, the smell was so bad that they pushed him straight outside. None of these guys had ever seen the angry side of me, and I think they were shocked at how quickly I had turned into an angry animal. But people don't realise what it means to lose very close family in a war. Once this has happened to you, if you think your family are being threatened, you will do anything to protect them; you are even prepared to kill in order to save your beloved family.

I was soon moved on again, this time to a club called Botanist, where I was working on my own most of the time. The staff loved me there – I always helped out with picking up empty bottles and I managed to win their hearts. But I realised I needed to take a lighter approach to the customers. I thought this was a perfect opportunity to earn respect and show a different side of me.

Most nights I worked alone, but over the weekends I had other guys with me. This was the most enjoyable venue that I worked in, but I always remembered what Joe had said to me: 'Mirsad, never get too confident in this job, because if people see that in you they will try to bring you down.' That was exactly what happened there. The manager – Julian – was really nice to me and always helped me whenever I had any problems. This job was a promotion for me, and I was chosen to do it because they knew I could deal with homeless people and they were having a lot of problem with them at that time: they were attacking people in front of the venue, which was putting the customers off. So I used my skills to win them over first and find out their problems, then I tried to help them. I knew how to deal with them in a professional manner. It did take me time, but I felt privileged and proud that I had achieved what I set out to do.

One of the people that I met there was bodybuilder Dorian Yates's son Lewis. He ran Temple Gym, underneath the club, and any time I had any problems, they were quick to jump in and help out.

One day, a man in his fifties turned up really drunk with another skinny young man. I was working alone and I was called to deal with something inside the venue. When I returned to the front door, these two guys were in the front lobby, smoking. I said to them politely, 'Lads, this is a no-smoking area.'

'You don't know who you're talking to,' the skinny young man said. 'This is Jimmy, the Albanian guy who runs this area.'

'Mate, I'm not really interested who your friend Jimmy is, or who runs what. All I said was this is a no-smoking area. If you want to finish your cigarettes, please go outside, and then you're welcome to come back in.'

Now, Jimmy got angry: 'Who do you think you're talking to?' he said.

The atmosphere changed instantly; I could feel the tension in the air but I stood my ground.

'Well, I was talking to your friend earlier and now I guess I'm talking to you,' I said.

That was the end of the conversation, and Jimmy started throwing punches like we were in a ring. I knew I had to get him outside, where there was CCTV: if this guy tried to stab me, at least I would have evidence. As I tried to draw him outside, Jimmy missed the step and lost his balance. Straight away, I punched him and he stumbled, then I pushed him out the door. The young lad who was with him was running around me, excited, like he was fighting. He was raging with anger, kicking and punching, but I knew I'd won: I'd got him and his friend outside all by myself without any bruises or scars. The rest of my job was to make sure they didn't get back in. Three steps above them, it was very hard for them to hit me. As soon as they came near, I was able to kick and push them away from the door. They were also extremely drunk, so I was winning all the way. They wouldn't give up, though. Jimmy was shouting, 'I'll stab you! You won't come out alive!' and they were banging on the metal gate so hard that it was distracting the other customers.

I knew my way out would be through the back where my car was parked, but I still wanted to show these guys who was in charge of the venue. The staff called the police and Jimmy and his friend were arrested. They were still shouting threats at me as they were taken away.

Julian told the police he would give them the CCTV evidence, which showed the men threatening me. He also said that they had attacked me first and he was prepared to be a witness. I made a statement saying that I had punched Jimmy in self-defence, because he had attacked me and threatened to stab me.

The staff were very pleased with how I handled the situation but from that night on, there were always two guys manning the door.

I stayed there for two years and I had a great time, but this was the last venue that I worked at because now I wanted to pursue my teaching career.

18

Coming Full Circle

In 2004, I was about to begin my teacher training, when I heard about a local community project that was to be staged at the Midlands Arts Centre. The producers approached the Bosnian community in the UK to see if they could suggest any Bosnian actors who could play a principal role in the piece called *Unearth*. It was a highly successful theatrical event, involving professional actors, a full orchestra, a choir and a community cast of hundreds. Actors, musicians and singers all came together to portray the tragic events of the Bosnian War, including the 1995 Srebrenica genocide. The writer Peter Cann offered me the role of the Bosnian interpreter, which was an ideal part for me. Peter had done lots of research on the Bosnian War, including visiting the morgue in Tuzla, along with Graeme Rose and Steve Johnstone, both of whom later became my acting mentors.

Greg Hobbs, who was cast in the play as Arkan, the Serbian paramilitary warlord, subsequently became a highly influential mentor and friend. He was an inspiration to me as I watched him research and develop his character. When he played Arkan, most of the Bosnian people who saw it wanted to kill him. I mean that as a testament to his acting talent – he truly brought Arkan back to life. My cousin from Coventry, Nedžad, could barely watch Greg's performance, such was the intensity of the character. After the performance, Nedžad told Greg that he would only talk to him once he'd taken off his costume – a Serbian uniform. A small Bosnian community from Birmingham came every night to see this epic drama, seeing their common and recent tragic past played out in front of them.

Greg spent a huge amount of time researching Bosnia, the culture and the history of the country, and of course the war. He has visited Bosnia numerous times with me, and he even learned a significant amount of the language.

After witnessing Greg's performance, I was inspired to continue to pursue my dream of acting, and I was encouraged by the positive reviews I received for my role. All the local newspapers had pictures of me playing the Serbian interpreter during the war. Apparently, I was so convincing that they thought I was the real interpreter that I portrayed in the play. It had also been a great opportunity to gain some fresh acting experience and to be able to bring that to the school kids I would be teaching drama to.

I had come back to Moseley School to do my graduate teacher-training programme, and I received a very warm welcome from all the teachers who used to teach me. Everybody was very impressed with my achievements. Most of my old teachers were still there and they congratulated me on my success, telling me what an asset I was to them. Some of the local newspapers were interested in writing an article about me: 'A refugee with no word of English to a successful teacher'. And I must admit it's a very flattering story – but that wasn't important to me, I just wanted to give something back to Moseley School. The school walls were plastered with newspaper articles about me, and soon I became an inspirational figure in the school, especially for the kids from Afghanistan and other different ethnic backgrounds.

From the start, I threw myself into the programme. I got involved in everything and accepted all the help and advice the teachers offered, and I will always be grateful to them for looking after me. I attended Mr Thacker's teacher-training sessions, 'How to Become a Successful Teacher', as he was an advanced schoolteacher and I wanted to be the best I could be. Mrs Hatton became my mentor and Mr Manda my supervisor for delivering PE lessons. Mr Ling helped me with personal, social, health education (PSHE) and citizenship classes. I took over Mr Hebdon's lunchtime weight-training club, and Mr Hebdon stuck a picture of me on the wall from when I was only sixteen, flexing my muscles and showing off, and that helped inspire a lot of the kids to start weight training during lunchtime and after school.

I certainly had my hands full teaching all those different subjects: drama, performing arts, expressive arts, PSHE, citizenship and PE, though of course I never minded working hard. For the first two years, I was studying to be a teacher as well as delivering lessons in all of those subjects, and I divided my time between Moseley and Small Heath School.

I developed a good strategy with Mrs Linda Lovenbury at

Small Heath. A very experienced advanced skills teacher, she was also one of the best drama teachers that I have ever met in my life. She coordinated my teacher-training programme and always made sure that I was on top of the game with my paperwork – she always wanted me to be the best and to stand out among the other teachers. Linda was very strict and she reminded me of my dad in everything she did. When my assessment day came, I was shining like a little star and I came out with great results. I made them all proud, especially my old school teachers and Linda.

I qualified as a teacher in the first year and passed my practical the following year. Now, I had a tough decision to make: I had to pick which school I would work at permanently. It was very hard because I liked both schools, but I had made a promise to myself that I would give something back to Moseley School, so I had to honour that promise. Small Heath School found it so hard to accept my decision to leave them that in the end I made a compromise and agreed to continue working at both schools; I taught at Moseley School for three days a week and at Small Heath School on the other two days. I enjoyed learning about different cultural values and needs. Each school had its own ethos and I had to adapt my methodology to the different work.

After another year of working at both schools, I decided I wanted to try and get back into acting, but I also wanted to carry on teaching part-time. Teaching would give me the flexibility to pursue acting opportunities, while also providing me with a steady income. At this stage, Greg Hobbs did everything he could to promote me. He put a lot of effort and commitment into helping me realise my potential as an actor, suggesting me for various parts linked to the Bosnian War. He is also an accomplished writer, with many short and feature-length film scripts about the Bosnian War (*Arkan, Love Through 9mm, Bargain, Mister Ballistic, Return to Terrorgrad*) to his credit, and he wrote various parts for me. As a result of his efforts, this little shy character found himself in front of the camera, acting and realising that I was now on my true path. He was my role model, my idol, and one of the reasons I decided to return to acting full-time later on.

But now, once again, I had to decide between the two schools, and it was clear to me that the Moseley School kids needed more help to get better grades – Small Heath had a passing ratio of 58 per cent A–C, while Moseley had only 33 per cent. I would be able to make a much bigger difference working there.

Linda Lovenbury and Mr Slough, the head of school, were both very disappointed that I was leaving Small Heath School. I was also sad to leave – I had made lots of friends there and they helped make me a good teacher. But my loyalties lay with Moseley School and they were glad I was staying with them.

Mr Peck, in particular, appreciated me being there, as I had a special way of dealing with naughty children. I knew what it felt like to not be listened to. I realised these kids may have been like me – not naughty, just not able to fit in – so I talked to them calmly, in a soft voice, and I learned to pinpoint their needs instantly. I would question them about what they wanted to achieve in life. Then I would break down for them the basic skills and good values they would need to achieve their aims. Behaviour would always be top of the list, followed by listening to the teachers and meeting their expectations.

They all had different needs, but they had bad behaviour in common. I always started by talking about my own problems as a pupil at that school and how I had managed to deal with them. At the end, I would try to inspire them by telling them what I have achieved in life and that all my success started from Moseley School. It had given me the tools to thrive as a teacher in an environment where I felt safe and happy.

It seems strange to think that in this environment things could go wrong, but the situation changed abruptly. The school came under new management and a new head was appointed. Austerity quickly became the norm, and all the teachers were under increasing pressure to deliver quality education under difficult conditions. Morale was extremely low throughout the whole school, and many teachers chose to leave.

Every aspect of my teaching was placed under scrutiny, and it began to erode my hard-won self-confidence. The atmosphere began to affect me badly. It reawakened memories of all my past troubles in Bosnia, and the torment of my early days at the school. I could not believe it was happening again. In a short period of time, my PTSD kicked in and I began to feel suicidal again.

The old teachers from Moseley School encouraged me to stay, but I couldn't risk my health and wellbeing. I had been considering a return to acting full-time, and the situation at the school had helped me make the final decision. Perhaps later in life I will go back to teaching, but the time felt right for me to pursue my dreams of becoming an actor.

It was 2014 by now, and while I had been at Moseley School, there had been many changes in my personal life.

19

A Love That Could Never Work

After our first visit home to Bosnia, we made regular trips back to see family and check on the gym we had set up with Edin Paratušić. Each year, for the summer holidays, we would go for six weeks, enjoying the hot weather and staying in the village with our family. One day in 2007, when I was on holiday in Kozarac, Edin asked me to cover his shift at the gym, which I was happy to do. I was chatting to the lads who were training when a young girl with long dark hair came up to me and asked if I was the owner of the gym. I said no, that I was just covering a shift – I never told anybody that it was my gym, I always said it belongs to the community and the people who live there. She extended her hand towards me. I thought she wanted a handshake so I put out my hand too, but then she opened her fist and showed me money creased up in her palm.

'I want to pay for my membership,' she said, not taking her eyes off me. She clearly had more confidence than me.

I looked her straight in the eye and took the money. It was probably the first time that I had looked at a girl like that, and my stomach flipped. I hope she is not Serbian, I thought. Before the war, we had all lived together peacefully, and didn't take much notice of ethnicity, so it is not always easy to tell just by how someone looks.

I could see the other lads looking at each other and discreetly making sexual gestures, but I pretended I hadn't noticed and carried on looking for the membership card. I asked her name and couldn't wait to hear it, in case it would give me a clue to her background. All the while I was desperately hoping that she was not a Serbian girl.

She told me her name was Marina, but she had quite a common surname and I couldn't guess anything from it. That was the end of our first conversation, and she went back to the ladies' gym, where girls normally trained.

Straight away, all the lads came up to me, laughing and teasing me.

'You're in there – she's hot and she likes you.'

'Did you see the way she looked at you?'

'She's the fittest girl in the town and everybody's after her.'

'No, not me,' I said quickly.

The lads smirked at me, but soon realised I didn't find it funny when I frowned at them and gave them the stare.

My head was full of problems; I knew I liked her, but I also needed to know if she was Serbian. I was definitely puzzled and wanted to clear my brain. Why did she come around and why did she come straight to me? I sat down and thought deeply about everything, struggling with my past, the war, torture, enemies, until my head was about to explode.

After twenty minutes, she came back in the room with a sweaty face and her hair tied back, heading towards me again. 'Sorry, can I ask you a question?' she said. 'Do you know anything about training?'

I was very hesitant to talk to her. 'Err, well, I don't know,' I said.

'Why do you work here then?'

'As I said, I'm just covering for my friend.' At this point I started blushing and I said, 'I don't want to be here.'

'Really?' she said. 'Well, since you don't train, could you give me a tip on how you stay that fit without training?'

'Well, it's in my genes,' I said quietly.

The boys had already started giggling and making silly gestures again, and I was feeling very uncomfortable. I am not confident talking to girls and I'd had no real experience at it apart from at university, but I had always treated them as friends and I never took it any further than that.

She grabbed my arm and pointed to the photos on the wall. 'How do you explain all these pictures of you that are plastered everywhere?'

I blushed and didn't answer, but then I took her arm and said, 'Come with me, I'll show you what you need to do.'

We went in the other room and I wrote her a programme to follow every day. She pointed to the body parts she wanted to work on and where she wanted to lose weight. I was very formal with her, as I didn't want to encourage any more conversation; I was aware that she kept looking at me but I ignored her attempts at eye contact.

The next day at the gym, all the lads were talking about us, and Edin said, 'So now I know you have been talking to Marina.'

'Yes,' I said. 'I did her membership and induction, and showed her how to use the equipment.'

'I did her induction two weeks ago,' he said. 'She knows how to use the equipment.'

I thought that was strange, but I just shrugged and carried on with my training.

Marina walked in the room again and started talking to Edin. I ignored her, but I was starting to get irritated with the situation, and I walked out quickly, pretending that I had to rush somewhere.

The next day, I thought I would come in early and get my workout out of the way. But again she walked straight into the room where I was training. This time it was obvious that she had put a lot of effort into looking good. I was uncomfortable but I kept myself together, pretending I was calm. She greeted me, and I nodded back. I went to the other side of the room, rushing through my workout, breathing heavily, imagining she was not there, but she followed me over and said, 'Why are you avoiding me?'

'Eh? I'm not,' I said, embarrassed and not looking at her face. 'I'm just busy doing my workout.'

I walked out quickly; I had to get away.

I missed the gym for a couple of days, but when I came back again, she was there, talking to Edin. I walked past, not even saying hello to him.

He came straight after me, saying, 'Why are you angry? Is something wrong? Are you upset with me?'

'No, no, I'm not angry,' I said. 'Why should I be angry with you?'

'I don't know.'

'I've just got a lot going on in my head at the moment. I'm very busy. I just need to get through the workout.'

'OK, if you need any help with anything, just let me know.'

I trained for only half an hour and left. It was the last day of the week and I never trained over the weekend, but on the Saturday I popped into the gym. Edin asked me if I was all right. I said yes.

'Well, for the last two weeks you haven't been yourself. You look angry and anxious, like you want to kill someone. All the gym is talking about you and they're all worried about you. You're a nice guy but something has gone wrong in your head. Even that girl Marina was asking about you.'

I moved closer to Edin and asked, 'What was she asking?'

'She just asked if you are always like that. I had to be honest with her; I said I'd never seen you like that.'

'Is she Serbian?' I asked.

'I think she is,' he said.

I walked off quickly, and went home. My mum and dad noticed my strange behaviour straight away. Dad was worried that someone had upset me at the gym, maybe one of the Serbian lads. He knew if they had, I would retaliate. My dad went to the gym to ask Edin if I was all right.

'He's all right,' he said. 'You don't need to be worried about him here.'

One day, I sat down outside, thinking about my grandmother and granddad. I got a piece of paper and I started writing poetry about them. All the negative thinking had got in my head and I wanted to get away from all of it.

I missed the gym for the whole of the next week, visiting my different family members in Bosnia, but then I was called in again to cover for Edin, who wanted to take a holiday at the Croatian seaside.

There she was again, the same girl in the same outfit said the same thing: 'Can I pay for my membership again?'

I dealt with her paperwork and then I started training. Again the lads started teasing me about Marina, while she was still in the room.

'You like her, don't you?'

'You'd go out with her if you had the chance – I know I would!'

I shrugged and carried on training. Marina came up to me in front of the lads and pointed to the back of her arm, saying, 'I have a bit of pain here. Do you know what to do or which exercises to do to get rid of it?'

I just shrugged and walked off.

She wouldn't give up, though, and the following day, she said, 'I know all about you.'

'What do you mean?' I said. 'You don't have a clue about me.'

'Yes, I do,' she said, smiling at me.

For the first time, after all these weeks, I let my guard down, and we started to talk properly. She told me that she had been very close to her granddad, who had just passed away. She was struggling to get over it and her friend had suggested she go to the gym to try to clear her head and help her move on. We spoke for a couple of hours and I realised we had a lot in common. It was just a natural, spontaneous conversation about our lives and where we were from.

She lived in the same place as my aunt, and I knew that Croats and Bosnians lived together peacefully in that village, and there were very few Serbs there. 'My aunt has many friends where you live,' I said, 'and they are all Croats.'

'Well, I am half and half,' she said.

I assumed she meant she was half-Croat and half-Muslim, but I was confused when she said, 'My dad is married to a Muslim woman.'

I didn't feel comfortable asking her straight out if she was Serbian. I wasn't sure where this was going with us, and Marina was pushing things much harder than I was ready for, but I knew in my head I could get away with seeing a half-Muslim and half-Croat woman, but not half-Serbian, half-Muslim. After what we went through with the Serbs, my parents and my family would never forgive me. But I wanted to get to know this girl better, and I thought, even if she was half-Serbian, half-Muslim, I would be able to persuade them.

We carried on chatting until late at night and it was time to go home. For the first time in three weeks, I felt relaxed instead of tense, but I knew this would be a difficult relationship.

Part of me was thinking that I needed to give the Serbs a chance and this girl might be the perfect opportunity. But I had very little experience with girls; I usually acted as their protector and advised them how to deal with boys. Marina had been brought up around boys and already knew how to deal with them, and I liked that about her. She became my training partner at the gym, which I found fascinating as I always saw bodybuilding as such a macho sport. We would train until late at night then I would take her home. We were good friends and we developed a strong relationship in a very short period of time.

Her cousin started training at the gym too, and told me

all about Marina; they had grown up together and were very close. That just added to our friendship and it couldn't be better. He explained they were raised around Muslim people and never had any problems with them. In fact, he had only positive things to say about Muslims and he seemed to know more about Islam than some of the Muslim people I knew. Marina had the same story and I loved that. I was beginning to think I could forgive the Serbs for what they had done to us, but still, I was not sure about her full identity.

I asked people about her name, and they all said that Marina could be a Croat as well as a Serb name. I was still too embarrassed to ask her, and at the time we were just friends anyway.

As we got closer, things began to get complicated. There were so many things that I started questioning about her and I wanted to find out everything about her. I always felt she was holding something back, but I had chosen to ignore it up to now.

My summer holidays were coming to an end. Marina said she would miss me, but I told her I would be back again the following year. She said that was too long to wait. Now I began to realise she wanted more than a friendship. I was prepared for that, of course, but how would I explain it to my parents if she was Serbian? Part of me was thinking Marina told me that she was half-Croat, which would not cause me that much grief with my family, but I was not sure.

My brother Jasmin was the first person to meet Marina in the gym and he thought she was OK, and asked if we were going out together. I told him we were just friends, but he smiled as if he didn't really believe me. I tried to explain my problem with her background, and how difficult it was, not knowing if she was Serbian. Jasmin suggested we go to Zlaja's cafeteria for a coffee, and invite her along with us. I didn't really go to nightclubs, and Jasmin knew Zlaja's was my favourite place.

That night after training, I asked her if she would like to meet my brother, and we went down to the café, which was just underneath our gym in the shopping centre. She was very pleasant to Jasmin and he gave me his silent approval. He was happy I had made a friend, and knew how worried Mum and Dad had been that I could never seem to find anybody.

Jasmin was ten years younger than me, but he always had my back; he is a very humble, intelligent young man. My sister Meliha always supported me too, particularly at school, but I was more reserved towards her and never wanted to show her any weakness. Instead, I wanted to be her protector because she didn't have older siblings, just two younger brothers.

Confiding in Jasmin made things a bit better for me; letting him know where I might be heading with this girl helped me examine my own feelings for her.

After meeting Jasmin, Marina started pressing me about our relationship and she wanted some security before I went back to England. It was too much, too fast for me. My family always comes first and I value their opinion, and I needed time to think before making any commitment to a relationship. I said I was going home and would come back again before the summer.

I always spend the last three days of our holiday in Sarajevo, and I met my friend Mirsad there. I told him about Marina, but he just laughed and said, 'Tom is in love!' – an old Bosnian expression meaning a male cat is in love. I hadn't really expected anything else though, as he always just said typical bloke things.

I came back to Kozarac as I wanted to see Marina before I left, and we went out to Kozara National Park for a picnic. It was very romantic, but I held myself back, like we were friends. She'd made some cakes, which we ate, and we spoke about everyday things and had a nice afternoon.

I went to the gym in the evening to say goodbye to the lads and they were still teasing me about my girlfriend. Before I left, Marina turned up to train, and she said she had something to give me. She handed me a passport photo of herself and I put it in my pocket. That night I felt worse than ever about the situation, because I was concerned about this girl falling in love with me. She was ten years younger than me and seemed very naive. I got frustrated and agitated, and told her I was no good for her and that we should go our separate ways.

'I know what your problem is,' she said. 'You suffer PTSD.'

We were alone in the ladies' gym and I started crying. Nobody in Bosnia knew that I suffered with PTSD, but she had sussed me out.

'It's OK,' she said, 'don't be embarrassed. I suffer with it too, since my granddad passed away. You can trust me, you can tell me everything.'

So I told her everything about my past. I laid my head on her lap and we both talked and cried all night. Marina listened to me better than anybody else in my life. She told me all about her life; how she missed her granddad and, when she met me, how she felt the same as when she had her granddad around.

All too soon, it was morning and time to go back to the UK. I silently sneaked into my bedroom and pretended I'd been there all night.

I was fond of Marina and she felt like the woman that I needed in my life, but I was scared to find out who she really was. I decided to take my time and not to rush into anything stupid. At that time, I was doing well, enjoying teaching and heading in the right direction with my life.

Back in England, I often looked at her picture and was developing deeper feelings for her. When I turned the picture over, I saw writing on the other side, but I didn't recognise the language so I texted her to ask and she was happy to hear from me. She said, 'It's written in Italian and I want you to find out what it means.'

I phoned my Italian friend and he told me it means 'I love you'. I told her I knew what it meant now, and from that day we were texting each other constantly and our relationship was developing.

In November, I went back to Bosnia to see her. She wanted me to meet her brother. He was a farmer and he was very nice to me. The next day, I met her mother, and she was nice to me too. 'I know all about you and who you are,' she said. 'I don't have a problem with you, as long as both of you are happy with each other.'

I hadn't expected that so I was surprised. Most Serbian mothers would never tolerate their daughter marrying a *Balije*.

When we left, I asked about her father. I wondered if he hadn't shown up because he had a problem with me as I was a different religion. She said her dad was married to another woman and they lived in Germany.

At the gym, they all now knew that we were going out with each other. Edin said to me, 'You've fallen for her, haven't you?'

I kept quiet.

'Yes, you have! I can see that. My friend, I know how strong you are, but I want you to know a lot of these girls here in Bosnia are very poor and they would do anything to get out of this country. Don't fall into that trap.'

I didn't say anything, and just continued with my training for a little while. Then I went straight to Marina, and it felt like she was always waiting for me by her window, no matter what time of day I went to see her.

As I was getting out of my car, I could see the guys from next door, where her cousin lived, giving me dirty looks. I greeted Marina and her mother and asked her to come out with me. As we sat in the car, the guys were still staring at me. I was starting to get annoyed, so I asked her what their problem was. She was good at calming me down, and held my hand and said, 'They don't know you and that is quite normal behaviour in Bosnia. You're going out with me and they're just being protective. It is a different culture here and you lived most of your life outside of this country in the UK.'

'That is not how my parents behave with my sister's boyfriend,' I said.

'Look, I haven't got a father figure in my household and my uncles are just making sure that I am looked after and not messed about.'

'Well, why don't I meet them as well then?' I turned off the engine and I could still see them in my mirror, looking at me.

'Mirsad, it's too early for that – we've just started going

out with each other. I don't really care about them, the most important thing is that you've met my mother and my brother.'

I was happy enough with that, so we continued with our day out. The rest of the day was pleasant, and we enjoyed the magnificent scenery of Bosnia in autumn. I hadn't seen that beautiful scenery since I was thirteen.

We went to the Hotel Mrakovica at the top of the hill and had a serious conversation for the first time about our differences and our problems.

'Marina, I want to know about your mother and father.'

'Well, my dad is a Croat and before the war he married my mother, who was from Serbia. They had my brother and me and after the war, my father found a Muslim woman who lived in Germany and he left us to go and live with her. That's why I was very close to my granddad, as I didn't have my father around while I was growing up. I struggled when my granddad passed away, but since I have met you I am happy now again.'

I felt really sorry for her and she felt very sorry for me too. It seemed that was what we had most in common in this relationship.

'Marina, you're taking all of this too seriously and pushing things too quickly,' I said. 'I need time and you know you're my first proper girlfriend. I have a lot to digest and deal with from the past.'

'I know all about you, your life before, your cruel past during the war, your problems and your family,' she said quietly.

'Marina, you don't have a clue about my family and their loss during the war. You were a little girl, you were only three when the war broke out.'

'Listen,' she said, 'I would like to meet your parents.'

I didn't say anything; I just nodded my head. I needed time to think and didn't want to see her for a couple of days, until I went to the gym. I saw her cousin first and I wanted to ask him some questions. 'I was at your house the other day,' I said to him, 'and I saw your family.'

'Yes, I know,' he said. 'My father told me that he saw you picking Marina up.'

'Well, your father was staring at me like I was his biggest enemy.'

'I don't know how to say this, but the war has separated us a lot.'

'What do you mean, mate?' I said. 'Come here.' I brought him to the window in the gym, where you can see the whole town. 'Look around you, my friend, all of these buildings are destroyed. Who the fuck do you think has destroyed them? Not Muslims, not Croats, but Serbs. How dare you guys tell us that you are angry with us! We have all the reasons in the world to be angry with you guys and we are not! We are still more forgiving, loving and caring.'

Marina walked through the door and I was furious; it was the first time she had seen me angry and we all froze. My PTSD was at its worst. She acted as though she hadn't heard anything.

The next day I was due to return home, but I was still angry. We didn't speak, just said goodbye to each other, pretending everything was OK.

At home, my parents knew something must have happened in Bosnia, and they were concerned about my wellbeing. While I was away, Jasmin had told my family all about Marina and me. My mum didn't get involved and she never said a word to me about Marina. She was quiet, but she had lost two brothers during the war, so her silence told me that she was upset. But, as always, she just wanted me to be happy.

I kept in touch with Marina, and we were texting each other like nothing had happened. I told her I just needed time and space to deal with my PTSD. She was concerned about my health and always said to me, 'Don't do anything stupid.' I had confided in her about the suicidal thoughts I'd had in the past and she seemed genuinely concerned about my wellbeing, and that's what kept our relationship going.

In the spring of 2008, my dad suggested that the two of us should go to Bosnia, and he was happy to meet Marina. We decided to drive and on the way, he told me many stories about our history and the people we used to live with. In particular, I asked him about Marina's granddad and he said he was a very nice guy: he was the most respected man in their village. Our granddad knew him as well, as he got on with Muslim people and they did a lot of business together. At least that made me happy, but my dad stressed how complicated things can get in mixed-religion marriages, such as when the kids are born, how you're going to name them and whether you will send them to the mosque or the church. I didn't say much, I just listened – it was one of the nicest trips with my dad that I will always remember.

Bosnia is beautiful in spring when it's the beginning of everything; the fields are green, trees start to grow and flowers bloom. I went to see Marina and she was happy to see me. I arranged for her to meet my dad at the gym. Dad told her exactly what he had told me in the car. He also said she had more advantages than any other girls, because she came from the same village, Kozarac. She was very happy to hear that. My dad didn't really have anything negative to say about her, and thought she was very intelligent. I was pleased to hear him say that, but it also reminded me of what Edin had said about the girls from Bosnia. The rest of my family knew about Marina, but they didn't want to get involved.

Marina and I grew closer and our relationship seemed to be heading in the right direction. We started going out everywhere together, and nobody could tell that we had different backgrounds.

Back in England, I was looking forward to my summer holidays to see Marina again for the fourth time. Just in that one year, it felt that we had seen each other a lot. In the summer, all my family went back to Bosnia, and we spent six weeks together. I was happy to see Marina again and I found her the same as when I first met her. Her smile and everything about her was the same.

I was visiting relatives with my family a lot – in the summer we always spend a lot of time calling on our families that we haven't seen for ages. I visited my auntie who lived near the gym and afterwards thought I would just pop in and see the lads – I was in a very good mood and just wanted to catch up with them. I saw Marina's cousin training at the gym and he obviously wanted to talk to me about something. Straight away, I could see that he wasn't himself and I asked him if he was OK. He said he needed to talk to me, but then clammed up. I asked if it was about Marina, and he said yes.

We found an empty room in the gym and he started talking about his family. In particular, he spoke about his father, who is Marina's uncle, and how strongly he was against me going out with her.

'Mate, I don't really care what your father thinks about me,' I said.

As I walked off, he grabbed me by the shoulder and said, 'Mirsad, you're a nice guy and you don't deserve this. I have something to show you.'

I turned to face him. He took his phone out of his pocket and showed me a picture of a girl. I glanced at it and said, 'Yes, that's a girl, so what?'

I thought perhaps he wanted to introduce me to another girl.

He handed me the phone and said, 'Look closer.'

I took a closer look, and couldn't believe my eyes: there was Marina with some other girls, holding a Republica Serbia (Republika Srpska zastava) flag and she was wearing the Serbian Nationalist Party uniform. There was a thunderstorm in my body and I started sweating, holding the phone until my hands started shaking. I sat down in shock.

'Mirsad, are you OK? Do you need any water or anything?'

I shook my head. 'Mate, just leave me alone.'

He took back his phone, but before he walked away, he told me she regularly attended Serbian Nationalist Party meetings.

The next day, I phoned Marina and confronted her. 'How do you explain that picture?' I asked angrily.

'What picture?'

'I have seen the picture of you on your cousin's phone!'

She was silent, and I eventually put the phone down.

She phoned me many times after that and I never answered. Through the few text messages that we exchanged, I made it clear that I had ended our relationship in that last phone call.

She texted me: 'These people were only my Serbian friends and I attended those gatherings with them before I met you.'

I replied: 'OK, but you wore the same clothes as them, which makes you the same as them. If you were not like them, you wouldn't wear the same clothes as them.'

And for me that was the end of it. The people in the picture had the same flag as those responsible for the many atrocities committed all across Bosnia during the war. People who are part of that National Serbian Party share the same beliefs of killing my people. They tortured me and nearly killed me, and wiped out most of my family. In the end, I realised that I had lost my trust in Marina, and I couldn't live with that.

So I packed my bags and bought myself a ticket back home to the UK. I knew the best thing for me at the time was to leave her: I had lost trust in Serbian people again and no one would be able to restore it.

This latest setback convinced me that I would be surrounded with bad feelings and emotions all my life. I could feel myself becoming cynical and negative again, and I couldn't pull myself out of it. One morning, I woke up after dreaming about my granddad and how he always told me never to give up. He used to say, 'You must keep the flow, shake the tree and carry on.'

Granddad's advice always helped me, and I got up and said to myself, 'I must give myself another chance, there must be someone out there for me.' And that someone would turn up when I least expected it.

20

From First Love
to Real Love

Back home in Birmingham, I had tried to put my experiences with Marina behind me, but it wasn't easy. One day, I went to the gym to shake off my stress and I bumped into my training partner, world weightlifting champion Kamran Majid. He is also a lawyer and one of my most intelligent friends, and he always gave me the best advice in everything. 'You look a little bit stressed out,' he said. 'What's wrong with you?'

I told him what had happened and he said, 'You are a very strong person, you will get over it like you did before. I believe in you and I am convinced that you can put yourself together again.'

We went to get some food and another friend, Ibrar Hussain, joined us. We used to train together at the Birmingham Sports Centre. I felt so much better being around positive people again. People that cared about me and wished the best for me.

'What is Bosnia like now after the war?' Kamran asked.

'It's OK,' I said, 'a lot more peaceful than during the war.'

'Why don't we go for a week, all three of us?' he said. 'I have travelled and competed all over the world, but I have never been to that side of the world.'

Great, I'm up for that, I thought, just to get myself out of that miserable mood and negativity. I told my parents that Kamran wanted to come over during the summer holidays later that year and they said he was very welcome. We started to plan our trip; I wanted to take them all across Bosnia, and as we had our cars there, it wouldn't be a problem.

Summer soon came around and I was happy to accompany my good friends to my home country. We got a plane to Croatia, where my friend Mirsad picked us up. They loved the scenery and warm weather. We started having fun, and I was proud to show them around my village: where I was born and where I grew up before the war. We spent a couple of days in Kozarac and they loved seeing the Solak Gym.

Then we started exploring Bosnia. We went through lots of different cities, Banja Luka, Doboj, Travnik and Zenica, until we arrived in Sarajevo. We had the best time there, and the lads loved looking at the old buildings and experiencing the multicultural community. As we sat down outside, drinking coffee and people watching, Kamran said, 'These ladies are the most beautiful in the world!'

We were all laughing and joking, as lads do when they see good-looking ladies. Then Ibrar said he wanted to go and find an Internet café, so he could get in touch with his family.

We arrived at the National Theatre, where I thought we would find one. It was the Sarajevo Film Festival, so it was very busy, and then we saw a tent housing computers. They looked like Apple promotional laptops, and we quickly sat down at the computers to log on. A woman started walking towards us. I turned around to look at her, then I nodded to Kamran and said, 'This is my lady, I will marry her.' Those were the exact words that I used that day.

We said a few more things to each other about her, assuming she couldn't understand us. I looked at her again and there was a heatwave coming from my legs straight to my face. I was red and excited, and my heart was racing. I said, 'They don't understand Bosnian.'

'I gathered that,' she said in Bosnian. 'How can I help you?'

'We just want to use these computers to go on the Internet.'

'These computers are new, just for people to test and check them out.'

I interpreted for the lads, who said, 'No problem, we'll pay.'

'You can't pay,' she said. 'They are free.'

'Can we just use them for ten minutes and we will be done?'

She agreed, and I turned back to the guys, a smile spread wide across my face. I was barely able to talk.

'What's wrong with you?' Kamran asked.

'Nothing,' I said. 'I'm just excited to use this new Apple machine.'

'Shut up!' he said, smiling. 'Your fingers are shaking – you can't even use the keyboard. You're excited about that good-looking girl with the long black hair!'

'Well, you're probably right,' I said, blushing slightly. 'I don't really need to use the Internet.'

I turned around, looking at her, trying to get her attention. She came over and by the time she reached me, my body was shaking, even my lips.

'Why are you shaking?' she asked.

'I'm cold,' I said.

'Cold? It's forty degrees out here!'

The lads didn't understand what we were saying, but they had worked out that I was embarrassed, and they started laughing.

'Do you need help to log in?' she asked.

'Yes, please,' I said.

'I thought you didn't need a computer,' Kamran said, still smiling at me.

When she leaned over, her clothes were touching my elbow. Everything negative came out of my body and I was flooded with those warm emotions.

Kamran nudged me, enjoying teasing me. 'I bet you're not cold anymore!' he said.

Then the woman answered him in English: 'He was not cold in the first place – he was just embarrassed.'

We looked at each other and all said, 'You speak English?'

'Of course I do. I understood all the comments that you have made.'

Now I couldn't speak at all, English or Bosnian.

'Come on, Mirsad,' Ibrar said, 'I thought you were our interpreter.'

I couldn't wait to get out of that tent, to get some fresh air and to start breathing normally again. The lads were talking to her, asking her name.

'My name is Lejla, and I'm studying law.'

'I'm also a lawyer,' Kamran said.

She smiled and said she wanted to find out more about that profession. Lejla went to make us all coffee, and while she was gone I whispered to Kamran, 'Get her number for me – tell her you can talk more about law.'

He smiled at me again. 'You need to ask for the number yourself, mate!'

I looked at her while she handed me a cup of coffee, brushing her hand as I took it. All my problems dissolved like they had never existed.

'Perhaps we could see you here again?' I said.

She smiled and turned to go, but I couldn't resist running up to her and asking for her number.

'Sorry, no. I don't give numbers out.'

As I walked back, the lads were smirking at me, knowing that I'd failed. 'It's all your fault, Kamran,' I said. 'You should have asked her!'

I had to see Lejla again, but the following morning we were due to leave Sarajevo to head towards Mostar. Kamran had heard so much about the magnificent city of Mostar with the old bridge built by the Ottoman Empire and the beautiful Neretva River, with its green water. He had researched so much about the place that he knew more than me, and one of the main reasons he came to Bosnia was to see that bridge. How could I stop him going just so I could stay another day in Sarajevo to get Lejla's number? I couldn't, it would be unfair, and these guys had come so far to see everything over here.

But I just had to get her number. I left the lads at the hotel, pretending I wasn't feeling well and needed some fresh air, then I ran back to the theatre to see if I could catch Lejla again. I was so happy when I saw a girl with the same long hair, but when she turned around it wasn't her. I asked her where Lejla was, but she said she had gone home. I ran back to the hotel as quickly as I could, so the lads wouldn't know where I'd been. They were at the hotel swimming pool when I got back, sweating from running. I told them I was too ill to drive the next day. They wanted to take me to the hospital, but I persuaded them that I just needed some rest.

The next morning, I got up about eight and ran back to the theatre to try to see Lejla. She still wasn't there, and the woman I spoke to said she had phoned in sick.

'What about tomorrow?' I was getting desperate.

'Sorry, I don't know,' she said, and understandably wouldn't give me Lejla's number.

I ran back to the hotel, where the lads were having breakfast. I was still sweating and they were getting concerned about me, but I said I just needed to lie down. I felt very guilty when they asked if I wanted to go and look for Lejla. If only they knew!

By the afternoon, I was still lying down, pretending that I had a temperature and that I was ill. I was driving the car so they couldn't go anywhere without me.

The following morning, I ran to the same place again and finally, Lejla was there! I looked at her and her beauty blinded me. I couldn't see anything around me, just her, her long black hair, brown eyes and tall, slim body. Marina went completely out of my head at that moment, and I saw the whole world in this girl.

She smiled and said, 'You guys are still here?'

'Yes,' I said. 'I didn't feel well, so we didn't move.'

'Where are your friends?'

'They're at the hotel.'

'Why are you here?'

'I need to use the Internet.'

'There is Internet at the hotel.'

I blushed. 'Well, this computer is better and faster.'

She smiled and asked me if I wanted a coffee. When she came back, I hadn't even logged in.

'I thought you were going to use the computer,' she said.

'Well, I am in a bit of a rush.'

I wanted to say something, but I couldn't find the words, and stood there blushing. She leaned across me to switch on the laptop and my heart started racing again.

'Here you are, you can use it now.'

'Well, you know I have to go now, I am in a rush.'

'I thought you wanted a computer.'

'Yes, but I've run out of time, so I have to go now.' I got up and started to walk off, then I turned back to face her. 'Do you have a mobile?'

'Yes.'

'I forgot mine – can I call my friend Kamran to tell him where I am?'

'I haven't got any credit.'

'Oh, well, OK.' Blushing again, I asked her outright, 'Can I have your number?'

She said yes.

My hands were shaking, but somehow I managed to write it down. I said, 'I have to go now – the lads are waiting for me.'

I hugged her, wanting to kiss her, but she didn't let me. I kept turning around to look at her as I walked away; I had only just met her and I didn't want to leave her side.

I came running into the hotel, where the lads were waiting for me. As soon as I saw them, I started smiling and showed them the phone number. The lads were annoyed with me. They said, 'You've done us over; you delayed us all and messed up our holiday, all because of some girl you don't even know.'

'Yes, you're right,' I said. 'I'm very sorry, I like that girl.'

'We only have two more days before we leave Bosnia,' Kamran said crossly.

'I will drive non-stop and I will get you to Mostar.'

We left immediately and I drove as fast as I could to make sure they got the most out of their last two days. Kamran loved the scenery around Mostar Bridge once we finally got there.

I texted Lejla and she texted me back. I asked her lots of questions, wanting to know everything about her. She was from Tuzla, and worked in Sarajevo part-time during the summer holidays. Most of her family was of loyal Communist stock with those long-held values, and mixed marriages between Croats, Serbs and Muslims were accepted readily in that area.

Before the war, it was rumoured that all the Serbs in towns had received blue envelopes that secretly advised them to leave, just before it all kicked off and their town was attacked. Many of them moved out and fled with all their belongings, but some of them stayed, mostly people in mixed marriages, as they believed that only Tuzla could offer that multicultural lifestyle.

When the war broke out, Lejla was only three. Her dad fought during the war, while she was hidden in the cellar of their flat.

I asked her if I could see her before I left and she said she would be in Tuzla. When I looked at the map, I realised we would have to go back the way we came and make a huge circle just so I could say hi to her. And when we finished our visit to Mostar, I did exactly that. I was driving and drinking Red Bull like water for about four hours, until we arrived at Tuzla.

I parked in the car park of the Hotel Tuzla and the lads asked me what was going on. I said I was tired and hungry and I couldn't go any further until I had a rest and something to eat. We went into the hotel, and just as we sat down, Lejla arrived.

'Mirsad, you've tricked us again!' they shouted, but they didn't seem to mind. They could see how happy we both were.

It was a very quick visit and then we had to say goodbye to her.

For the rest of the trip, the lads kept teasing me about falling in love with the girl that I didn't even know, but I didn't mind – I knew it was true.

We had to drive all the way to Croatia now without stopping. I'd been driving for a long time and I was so tired, I almost fell asleep behind the wheel as we drove through the hilly mountains of Bosnia. At one point early in the morning, the car was going so slowly that Kamran thought I had dozed off. It was a very memorable trip going back home with my friends and certainly the happiest holiday for me.

Out of the blue this lady had appeared in my life and now she would always be with me.

I knew Lejla had a boyfriend in Austria, who came from the same town as her, and her family was very keen on him. He was tall and handsome, but I guess she had fallen for my cheeky smile and odd sense of humour.

When I got home, we kept in touch and I kept taking short trips to Bosnia, just to see Lejla for a couple of days. I would turn up unexpectedly and call her to come out. I was trying to be romantic and I put a lot of effort into the relationship. She wouldn't believe that I was in her town, until I called her to meet me and gave her a bunch of flowers.

I had fallen in love with Lejla and on one trip I decided to ask her to marry me. I took her out to a beautiful hill with a view of her whole town. I parked the car and I couldn't wait to ask her, when she interrupted me and said she had something very important to tell me. I was devastated when she said, 'I have decided to go back to my Austrian boyfriend.'

I choked back the tears and told her all about Marina and said I didn't have much luck in life, especially with girls, and she was only my second serious girlfriend. I told her I couldn't live without her, and I think she realised how deeply I felt about her. Just like my granddad had done with my grandmother, I had finally won her heart, and soon after that we got engaged.

She arranged for me to meet her mum and dad, but at the beginning they did not approve of me. All of her family seemed to think I didn't deserve her. Eventually, they realised what was best for her, especially once they found out about Northerners' values.

My life became happy again and I knew from the moment I saw her that this lady was definitely for me.

In the summer, while we were on our annual holiday to Bosnia, I told my brother that I wanted to bring Lejla to meet our family. Her home was a four-hour drive from our town, so I got up at four in the morning, and set off to pick her up.

Lejla's dad told me to make sure I brought her back the same day – they really didn't want her to go so far away from her family. But I had won Lejla's little heart and gave my word that no one would ever hurt her.

When we arrived back in Kozarac, the first person who greeted Lejla was my grandmother, Hasnija. She was so pleased and emotional to see me with a girlfriend that she was crying. She blessed Lejla with words and called her our angel, the new member of our family. My grandmother has always had a spiritual touch, and seems to have a gift of predicting the future, like she said that I would be an actor when I was only eleven. My mum and dad didn't even know that I had met someone and that I had a girlfriend, so when my brother Jasmin said that I wanted to bring my girlfriend around they went out to buy food to welcome her, and didn't get back in time to meet her that day. My favourite auntie, Asima who lives next door, came around to meet Lejla. My auntie and the rest of my family gave our relationship their seal of approval, and I was a happy chap.

After my mum and dad met Lejla, I was very proud to introduce her to the rest of my family and my friends from the gym. Our relationship grew stronger and there were no complications. Both of our families were happy for us and we grew together as a couple, as though we had known each other for years.

We were married in Bosnia in 2010, and I invited all my friends from the UK, including Peter, Barry and Mark from the college and sports centre, as well as Luke Brown and his dad, Joe. We had 440 guests share our wedding day. My granddad Ramo gave his word at his first meeting with Lejla's father that she would always be there with us under our protection and no one would ever touch her under our roof.

Lejla was still at university when we got married, and I was happy to wait the two years until she completed her law degree in 2012, before she came to England. That was her wish and her father had spent a lot of money on her education, so it would have been a shame to leave her degree course without graduating.

In 2013, we received our best gift in life, our little daughter, Jasmina Solaković. Since having my own child, I have learned how to give her everything and protect her from evil. Jasmina is now five and she is full of life. She loves people and she loves the world. That is exactly how my wife and I wanted her to be. We now have another child on the way. We will pass on our dearly-held values and always teach our children about their past and culture, just as it was taught to us, and it will give them the best foundation to be the best they can in all they do.

I was feeling happier and more at peace than I had for many years, but there was still the odd unexpected bump in the road, and I would struggle to get over the next one that came my way.

21

End of an Era

Things had been going really well for me. I couldn't have been happier with my family life, and I was still enjoying working at the sports centre and had great friends there. Sadly, it was not to last. I was devastated to hear that the sports centre was going to be knocked down and the land that belongs to the college sold.

Siham, my friend from college, was the first person to tell me what was happening. At first, I didn't believe her. We worked together at the college while I was running the weekend sports facilities there, and we had as much fun there as at the sports centre. Siham was one of those people that everyone liked – she was always happy, full of life and full of hope. But on this occasion, she had to break the bad news to me as gently as she could, as she knew how my life had changed for the better there.

It was very sad seeing my friends panicking about how

they would cope without their jobs and losing such a valuable sports centre that had brought us all together. It devastated me – the sports centre was where my life in the UK changed; it was where I made lifelong friends, who gave me confidence and boosted my self-esteem; it was where I really started to feel that the UK was my home. Now I felt as I had done when I was leaving my home during the war in Bosnia when we were ethnically cleansed. I looked at the sad eyes of Peter and Barry, who gave me everything from the age of eighteen until I was thirty-six, and we had lost it all. It felt like someone had stripped me of all my clothes and I was in danger of losing all my hard-won confidence. I would have to start all over again, but I didn't know if I had the energy anymore.

I still never fully believed the centre would close. We signed different petitions organised by Peter's wife, Monica Lee, but none of them worked. It looked like the decision had already been made by the time we heard about it. Apparently, our sports centre was moving to Alexander Stadium, where they were extending their multimillion-pound complex for the use of the Olympics. It was a done deal and there was nothing that we could do.

It seemed to me that the only way that I could save the set-up we had at the sports centre would be to replicate it somewhere. And the only place that I could do that at the time was in Bosnia, as everything was much cheaper there. I told Peter and Barry that I would like to have whatever fitness equipment was left when the centre closed to take it to Kozarac and expand the weights room we had set up there into a proper fitness centre. They loved the idea and said they would help in any way they could.

After the council had taken everything they wanted, I organised the transport to Bosnia for everything that they were going to scrap. The kids in Bosnia would be very grateful for it and it softened the blow of the centre closing – at least the equipment would do some good. I even took the old signs from the gym to remind me of the good times.

The week before the centre closed, we started to clear out all our personal belongings, and anything else we wanted that was destined for the skip. Everything had some sentimental value for us – old picture frames, trophies, even old tables and chairs, etc. It was a hard and emotional time for all the old staff that had spent half of their lives at the centre. I still see many of the friends I made during the course of my seventeen years at the centre and we remain good friends.

I consoled myself with the thought of the new gym in Bosnia and building something good there. I was glad that I was able to save at least some of the old machines that I had used to build my body and give them to the future generation in Bosnia.

As always, my dad was on board and he backed me financially as well.

Once we had installed all the equipment, and completed all the work, we occupied the whole top floor of the shopping centre. We officially registered the fitness centre and in 2014, we opened as a recognised sports gym. We are now one of the most prestigious fitness centres in Bosnia and offer a whole range of facilities, including a state-of-the-art weights room, resistance machines, a kickboxing room offering a wide range of martial arts, including karate, kickboxing, MMA (Mixed Martial Arts) and boxing, and a ladies' fitness suite.

All our equipment is imported from the UK and regularly maintained and upgraded. We are always looking at different ways to provide the best service for our customers: we have a variety of customers of all ages and with different needs, and we try to satisfy everybody's expectations.

The centre offers a variety of different self-defence and martial arts programmes, and we try to encourage the kids from the streets to keep fit and channel their energy and frustrations into sport. Edin Paratušić, who is one of our expert coaches, specialises in different martial arts. He used to live in the UK and he has brought all of his experience and knowledge back home to Bosnia.

We provide facilities for all levels of athletes to participate in different exercises to develop their muscular frames according to their sports. We also encourage young and old to keep fit in their leisure time. Through sport, we want to bring people together and share good basic values in life. Our aim is to celebrate each other's differences and learn to value each other through sport. We strongly believe that sport can unite people from different cultural and religious backgrounds. Our mission statement is to involve everybody to live a healthy lifestyle with healthy minds.

Over the course of thirteen years, we have dedicated time and effort to grow the centre into an internationally known organisation and we welcome visitors from all over the world, mainly Bosnian people from the Diaspora during the holiday season.

The gym has been registered as a charitable organisation, and we try to make the facilities accessible to all – it is free for kids under sixteen and disadvantaged families.

Together we have achieved so much with the young people and the local community, which is what we set out to do.

For me personally, the new fitness centre also helped me to deal with the closure of the Birmingham Sports Centre. It was not just a job to me – I felt I belonged there. It had been such an important part of my life for so long, and I would struggle to come to terms with it.

22

Meeting Big Joe and Iron Mike Tyson

The closure of the sports centre had hit me very hard. My life had revolved around it for so many years; my body clock was attuned to the shifts and workouts I did there, and the routine and exercise had helped me control the symptoms of my PTSD and kept me on an even keel. The loss of my job at the centre had also coincided with the big decision to leave the teaching career I loved to return to acting full-time. But it had been more than a few years since I had left drama school, and I was also now a husband and father, and if I wanted to be successful and fulfil my lifelong ambition, I had to be positive and make it happen.

Over the years, I had made many good friends who had seen my potential, and had encouraged and inspired me to pursue my dream. One such friend was Greg Hobbs, who I had met on the production of *Unearth* in 2004. I strongly believe that I never gave up acting because of this guy. Greg has played many different parts, predominantly villains, gangsters, military types and general tough guys. He trained me, coaching me and demonstrating how he develops a role.

Taking the role in *Unearth* had also confirmed my belief that you can learn or gain something from every role or opportunity you are offered and every new person you meet, as long as you are open to them. While I was still teaching, this mindset had helped me overcome my natural shyness, and led me to make another inspirational friend who helped change my life.

One night, I was in Zaffs, my local takeaway, talking over my plans with my friend Bob. He knew how passionate I was about acting and was very encouraging. He said to me, 'Don't waste your talent and don't lose your inspiration and hope in something that you love a lot.' He showed me a flyer. 'Do you know who Joe Egan is?'

I took the paper from my friend and read it. It was an autograph card signed by Joe Egan, and there was a picture of Mike Tyson and Joe, with the caption: 'The strongest white man on the planet'.

Bob told me Joe was a former boxer who lived locally, and he had turned to acting late in life. He said, 'Joe's a very nice guy. He came round yesterday and left me this card. There's a number on the back – phone him and tell him that you're my friend.'

I was in two minds about doing that, as I was naturally a very shy person, especially not knowing this guy. It took me a couple of weeks to convince myself to make that important phone call. When I finally called, I discovered that the number belonged to Joe's agent. I politely asked if I could speak with Joe and he asked what it was about. It was difficult to explain to the agent that I just wanted to meet Joe, so I said I would call back. I phoned a couple more times, and the last time I asked if he could pass on my number for Joe to call me back. I left it at that and didn't really think that I'd hear back from Joe.

Then, out of the blue, he rang me. His voice was polite but loud, and full of energy and enthusiasm. 'Is this Mirsad? This is Joe Egan here, I am just returning your call.'

I was thrilled, not believing my luck. I told him I'd heard good things about him from Bob in the local takeaway. It was a rather short conversation, but I told Joe that I was also an actor and I would like to meet him. We arranged a meeting for the following week in a local Subway.

When he turned up, straight away I could see why Mike Tyson called him the strongest white man on the planet: he was a great lump of a man! He was wearing shorts and his legs looked like tree trunks. He was tall, but also a huge man. In Bosnia, big men are considered wealthy and happy, as they always have a lot of money to feed themselves and their families. Joe certainly had that quality. The way we greeted each other felt like we were family, almost like those family members that you know you have, but have never met. It also made me think of how much I missed my family and how good it felt to have family around me. I was living in a big city and there was no one for me to lean on anymore. I had never connected so well or so quickly with anybody like I had with Joe. He has this spark of energy and enthusiasm that feels like he can electrocute you with it. I immediately felt I could trust him and open up to him.

Joe seemed to be interested in my experience during the war, and he listened to me for a couple of hours, captivated by my story, interrupting me occasionally to ask a question about the war. We seemed to develop a dialogue very quickly, and we were soon talking about anything and everything. I hadn't felt that happy in a very long time. It gave me the lift that I needed to build my confidence back up again. From that day our friendship started.

I came home feeling blessed and overwhelmed with positive feeling and energy. My parents couldn't believe how happy I was, and they were excited about my meeting with Joe. I'd told my dad that Joe was Mike Tyson's sparring partner and he couldn't wait to hear the whole story, quizzing me until I'd told him everything Joe had said about Iron Mike.

Soon after, I introduced Joe to my dad and he wanted to know all about Tyson from Joe himself. Joe was very open and patient, answering all my dad's questions.

'When Tyson threw punches at you, did it hurt?' my dad asked.

'At times I wouldn't be able to smile or cry, not even wink!' said Joe. 'That's how damaged my face was.'

'Was Tyson bigger than you, Joe?'

'He was a lot smaller, but he was very muscular at his peak.'

'Who was the strongest opponent against Iron Mike at his peak?'

'No one – he was the best in his prime.'

'What's he like as a person to talk to?'

'Tyson is a human being with a heart, a very knowledgeable man about his history and geography. He has a special love for the pigeons and he has a lot of them.'

My dad interrupted, saying, 'Oh my God, we all love pigeons in Bosnia and we have a lot of people that breed pigeons! Mike would love Bosnia. Everyone knows who Tyson is in Bosnia, especially older people, my generation born after 1955. Do you think Tyson would ever visit Bosnia?'

Joe shrugged his shoulders and said, 'I don't know – we can ask him.'

My dad is a genuine gentleman like Joe. He has always been a people person, who embraces people with love, regardless of who they are or what they believe in, as long as they return love and care in the same way to him. Dad always suffered with heart problems and he was born with a hole in his heart. He had an operation in Belgrade, Serbia, and he always had a special connection with that city. My dad believed that Serbia saved his life and that he owed them so much, prolonging his life from childhood to a mature man. That is the type of man he is, he finds it difficult to hate anyone.

Joe and my dad got on so well their conversation went on for hours. Dad seemed to have a never-ending list of questions for Joe, which he happily answered, but after a couple of hours, I said, 'Come on, Dad, now you're tiring Joe out, more than Tyson in the ring.'

Joe smiled and said, 'No, no, Mr Solaković – nothing would tire me out more than Tyson in the ring!'

Joe had one last story for my dad before he left that day: 'When I retired from boxing I wanted to pursue my acting career. One of my first acting roles was stage fighting. The stage fighters and stage coordinators were so gentle with me while we were rehearsing scenes and they kept stopping and asking me if it hurt. I said, "Nothing hurts as much as Iron Mike, and, for the amount of money you're paying me, you can hit me and kick me as much as you like!"'

We all laughed and I will never forget that day and how happy Big Joe made my dad.

'Mr Solaković, one day I will introduce you to Mike,' he told my dad.

Dad was very happy, but he didn't really believe it would happen.

Meeting Joe was a true blessing for me and helped me overcome my PTSD and war scars. He was a great person to be around and seemed to create happiness and adventure whatever he was doing. My true happiness started here.

The next day, I was fortunate enough to meet another Joe Egan, Joe's father. He was another pleasant man, and with his true Irish values and family around him constantly, it reminded me of Bosnian families and our values. Joe's father was a tall, skinny guy with many wrinkles on his face, which reminded me of my grandfather. I listened to him talk for hours about his life, sport, kids, living abroad and all sorts of things. He was a lovely man to talk to. He must have had quite a journey in his life raising a big family in Ireland and then coming over here to England and starting all over again. He spoke about his family and children with pride and dignity for everything that they have achieved in life. He was also very proud of Joe and his achievements in boxing and acting.

I believe everything happens for a reason and we all complete different journeys in life. Some with more luck, some with none at all. But we all have something to draw from our experiences, and we can use them to reflect and change our lives for the better when we can. Looking back at my life, I was left with lots of scars: mental, as well as physical. Bearing all of that in mind, I was convinced that I could do something good and positive in this world that perhaps one day might at least inspire younger generations.

A little while later, I received a phone call from Joe asking me if I was interested in meeting Mike Tyson. I was absolutely thrilled, jumping up and down in my living room and so excited that my wife Lejla thought I had suffered another one of my emotional breakdowns. I couldn't believe my luck that I would be standing in front of one of the biggest boxing legends in the world. I phoned my dad first, of course; unfortunately, he was in Bosnia at the time, and so he couldn't make it, so I asked Joe if I could take my brother Jasmin. As always, he said of course. Then I phoned my relatives, telling them I would be meeting Iron Mike. They couldn't believe it at first, thinking I was pulling their leg, until the day they saw the pictures of me with Mike Tyson on Facebook.

I was very excited about meeting such a well-known celebrity, but I was also very nervous about how to present myself, my nation and my country, because I knew he would ask me about the Bosnian War and what it was like in Bosnia now. Joe prepared me by telling me a lot about Mike, so I knew what I would be talking about.

The event was in Liverpool, and Jasmin and I spent the journey there talking about all sorts of things like: How big is Mike? How tall is he? Is he still strong and powerful? Does he still have a most powerful punch? Is he a nice, gentle person or just vicious, the way they describe him in the ring? All of these questions were burning inside us to ask him.

There had been quite a lot of negative press towards the end of Tyson's career, and some of those issues had concerned me in the past, making me wonder if he might be a very difficult person to get on with.

When we arrived at the event, it was packed with people, and there were lots of celebrities from everywhere. It was the first time I had attended such a prestigious event, and we were feeling a little shy and out of place until we discovered that Joe was already there. All of a sudden, I heard Joe's voice calling me: 'Mirsad, Mirsad! Come and meet Mike Tyson!'

My brother is easy-going and he was certainly more relaxed than me, but as soon as we heard that, we almost sprinted from one end of the room to the other to say hello to a man that we had only ever seen on our TV screens. My brother reached him first and Mike was very kind towards Jasmin. I came after my brother, giving Tyson a firm handshake and establishing eye contact.

'Hello, Mr Bosnia,' he said.

It seemed to me that Joe had already told him so much about Bosnia and me that he actually called us over before his event started to say hello to us. I was happy to learn how different he was from the media stories, a person with a big, kind heart and a good character.

'How is your family?' he asked straight away.

'Well, we lost a lot of family members during the war, but the ones that are with us are fine,' I said. 'They all know that I am here with you today and they are sending their blessings and love to you.'

'How is Bosnia now?'

'Considering what the country and people went through during that bloody war, the situation now is much better.'

'I remember watching the news with my family about

Bosnia in 1992. It was a horrible and bloody war, but the world stood by and did nothing about it, until towards the end of the war, then America stopped it. You must have lost a lot of your family members during the war and that must be very difficult for you to talk about.'

'Well, it is not easy to live without very close family members, especially abroad in a different country surrounded with different people. But life goes on and we have to carry on without those people that we were used to. Now I have made new friends like Joe and many more who keep us going and they ignite light in our hearts.'

'Well, I am glad that you came out of it alive with your close family and that you have found sanctuary in the UK. I have learned from Bosnian people in America what they had to go through in the war and how difficult it was. I fully sympathise with you guys and I feel your pain for your loss and being without your families that you have lost during the war. I can tell you this from my own experience: people that have never been through pain will never be able to understand your pain.'

I heard that phrase for the first time in my life and I started using it myself. Whenever I come across negative thoughts and emotions, I always hear Mike Tyson's words and they help to calm me down. In the past when I got disappointed or angry with people, I was never able to see their emotional side. Now I was able to recognise that and deal with those issues considerately and constructively. I always believed that you can learn something from everyone you meet, but I was very impressed with what Mike had to say to me, especially about empathy. Towards the end of our conversation, I felt so easy and relaxed talking to him, like I had known him for years. I told everybody that I met Mike Tyson and what a kind and genuine person he was towards my brother and me. I couldn't be more grateful to Joe for organising it for us.

But that was only the beginning of our friendship with Mike Tyson. A few years later, in 2015, there was a big fight in Las Vegas between Manny Pacquiao and Floyd Mayweather, and Joe asked me if I would like to go. I couldn't believe it – I grew up in a family of boxing fans, and this would be the opportunity of a lifetime for me to see the fight live in Las Vegas. It would also be my first visit to the US, something that I had dreamed about for most of my life. My friend Kumel, who is also a big fan of boxing, thought it would be the best way to celebrate his fortieth birthday that month in Las Vegas with his friends. I was up for that and Joe said he would arrange for Mike Tyson to meet us there. It was almost like three dreams rolled into one for me to see such a historic fight, to go to America for the first time and to meet my idol once again. When I went to see my parents, I didn't know where to start telling them about the opportunities that Joe Egan had created for me. My wife was also very pleased for me.

I was so excited in the weeks leading up to the trip that I could hardly wait. When it was time to go, I was quite emotional thinking about my life – the war, how we landed in the UK and started a new life here. I was also thinking about when I was young and wanted to leave the UK to start my acting career in the US. I had never left Europe without my parents or my family so that journey was special for me. All of these feelings and emotions were a little overwhelming, but they couldn't dampen my excitement.

My friends were travelling separately, and it was a long

and exhausting journey – from Birmingham to Amsterdam, then to LA, then on to Las Vegas – which lasted for fifteen hours, the longest journey that I had ever travelled on a plane. When I got off the plane in LA, it was everything that I always dreamed about America. It was spring and the weather couldn't have been better; massive buildings, huge cars and big, wide streets. Everything was big, even the people were bigger than the average European. I had been warned about the American police and their zero-tolerance policy to crime, as well as not going out late at night alone. It was an incredible feeling, stepping out of the airport and walking around the busy streets of America, surrounded by people everywhere. I hardly knew where to begin with my adventure.

What impressed me most about America was that Americans seemed to spend their weekends with their families. Usually people go camping or travelling away from their homes. I loved that idea. In fact, I loved everything about America, apart from the gun laws, although, of course, I knew they had problems with crime there, as there are drugs and guns everywhere.

Once I took the final flight to Las Vegas, I entered the fairyland in a desert, where someone had built an entire city in the middle of that desert. There was an incredible view from the plane, with skyscrapers, buildings with huge, outdoor swimming pools, magnificent architecture and theme parks. There are buildings replicated from every part of the world, from India to the Emirates, London to Paris and the rest of the world in between. I could feel the heat in my body and my heart was racing with excitement.

As I got off the plane, I saw gambling machines everywhere

– from the airport to every hotel and even service stations. I was the first person to arrive out of our group at the hotel, and found the people there very friendly and helpful. They would explain something a couple of times without any hesitation or difficulty.

Kumel and our other friends arrived shortly after me and our adventure started from there.

Kumel was responsible for communicating with Tyson's team and arranging the tickets to watch the fight. For me, it wasn't just about the boxing match but America itself, and everything that makes it unique. I had always put a lot of effort into exploring my European values and learning about my culture and my people, now I wanted to explore America and do the same. Everything about America that I had heard from the relatives and friends who lived there seemed to be true. The scenery was out of this world, especially at night, with all the lighting on the buildings and streetlights of downtown. It took me a couple of days to get my head around everything that went on in this city. But this was just the beginning; the real adventure started when Joe made a few phone calls to people that he knew in Vegas to look after us. We started exploring the city and very soon we were hardly sleeping, not wanting to waste a minute; we just kept going, using every opportunity to have fun and enjoy ourselves.

Once our tickets were arranged, we went to see the press conference, which was a good build-up before the big fight. For the first time I was standing in front of the MGM Grand Garden Arena. A huge building, the biggest that I had ever seen in my life, it was almost unbelievable, very hard to describe.

One of the first people that we met in Las Vegas was James

Tillis, a great guy with a huge smile, who chatted to us all about Vegas and his life as a boxer. We arranged to meet up with him at the Caesars Palace Hotel reception, where we had a short conversation about his boxing career, his fight with Mike Tyson in 1986, and his life now. I was very happy and privileged that James signed a copy of my first poem in my poetry book to encourage me to continue with my writing.

Our next meeting would be with Mike Tyson himself at his boxing memorabilia shop. That was the most exciting day for me to meet Tyson again and see if he remembered me. I took the Bosnian flag to remind him where I am from and to see if he would hold our flag out of respect. Of course he did, and he was happy to do so. He also signed my boxing glove and we had a brief catch-up. It was a busy day for him, so we were pushed for time and had to move pretty quickly, but I managed to tell him about my ideas for my first poetry book about the Bosnian War. He encouraged me and supported my idea, and that meeting inspired me to continue with my writing.

The day of the fight was one of the most exciting days for me. There were thousands and thousands of people queuing up, all desperate to get in and see one of the biggest fights in history. It was an unforgettable day and it reminded me of my childhood in Bosnia, watching Mike Tyson's fights in front of the little telly with my family who are no longer around. For me and the friends around me it was a dream come true. Tyson and I were supporting Pacquiao, while Kumel and his relative Dr Navraj Kular were supporting Mayweather. Unfortunately, Pacquiao lost the fight on points, but he gave Mayweather a run for his money and that made us happy.

Our party continued in Las Vegas until we got back on

the plane. We set ourselves targets for the next three days to have the bare minimum of sleep to make sure that we saw everything, but in the end we ran out of time. One of my most enjoyable and memorable days was visiting a state where predominantly Native Americans lived. Just outside the city, it was a tourist attraction, where you can buy everything from souvenirs to the clothes worn by Native Americans. I bought all the souvenirs linked to the cowboy and Indian films my dad had watched growing up in Bosnia. From what I experienced, they were humble, simple and mellow people. They were happy to answer any questions about their history, culture and heritage, and I found it all very educational. I connected Native American history to Bosnian history and found out that we have a lot in common.

On my last day in Las Vegas, at about 8am, as I was packing my bags, I got a call from reception to say that there was a family downstairs who wanted to see me. I couldn't imagine who it could be, but I got dressed quickly and went downstairs. In the foyer, I found a whole Native American family standing in front of me, greeting me with their religious ritual and playing their instruments. I cried like a little baby – I hardly knew these people and they wanted me to meet their family and say goodbye to me. I had left them my business card and told them where I was staying, so it was easy for them to find me. Atohi, the main chief of the family, gave me his flute and said, 'This is your gift from my family to keep our spiritual connection while we are alive.'

I was very touched, and when I got home, I gave it to my daughter Jasmina, who was two at the time, and it is her favourite toy. She is always producing different sounds with it and she will never take it out of the house, which always reminds me of the Native American family. I don't remember all of their names but I remember one boy was called Catori, and they told me it means 'spirit'. I loved their spiritual connection and those memories will always stick in my head. I had a brigade badge on a chain from Nova Travnička Diverzantska Izviđaička Brigada (New Travnik Scout Special Brigade) belonging to my cousin Nijaz, who died as a hero in the war, and I gave it to Chief Atohi. Native Americans love receiving gifts and it is a big part of their culture. Using hand gestures, he instructed me to put it around his neck straight away, and said, 'With all my heart, I will treasure this until I stop breathing and when my heart stops –' he pointed at his son Catori '– he will wear it around his neck and he will also follow the chain, passing it on to his son.'

I thought that was incredible, how they value their history and culture. I had another souvenir like that, a military award with a lily on it from my family member who died in the war, and I will treasure that for the rest of my life. I believe that Chief Atohi will tell many of the tourists about his present from the Bosnian guy who was caught up in the war as a child. I wonder if one day I will be able to take my family there, and trace those people through my souvenir present. I am sure I will, and only time will tell.

As I was coming back on the plane, my poetry was born and I wrote lots of poems that were in my first book, which was published in 2017.

At home, I sat down with Joe Egan and I told him in detail how my life had changed since I met him and during that trip to Las Vegas. Joe was happy for me that I had changed my course in life and that I had found mental stability and happiness. He said, 'The next person that I want you to meet is Frank Bruno, who is a friend of mine.'

What I love about Joe is that he has this magnetic power of drawing people and an audience around him. He always said to me, 'Mirsad, my friends are your friends, my family is your family.' That was exactly what I needed, as I was missing half of my family since the war. He told me, 'Frank also suffered some mental problems that are in some ways similar to yours. That might be a good healing process for you to meet someone like Frank. He has achieved so much despite all of his problems and obstacles that he had to overcome in life.'

I met Frank Bruno at a dinner event at the Village Hotel in Walsall. He is a big, tall guy and had a great smile on his face. Joe introduced us and he welcomed me warmly. Frank probably doesn't even remember me; he must have met thousands of other fans in his life and these brief meetings are probably not very important to him. But I was touched that he spared that moment to listen to Joe about my story and he embraced it with all of his heart.

When I met Frank, I brought along the same poem that James Tillis had signed and I asked Frank if he would sign it too. Without any hesitation, he briefly scanned and signed it.

Now at the time that probably didn't mean much to Frank, but for me it was another life-changing moment. I wanted to play the game right, and I thought, if I get people to accept my writing, I will feel obliged to continue with it. Anyone who has read my poetry book has said, 'This is full of emotions and inner thought,' which is exactly what I wanted to achieve.

* * *

I met many new friends through Joe, and they opened new opportunities for me. He introduced me to Jason Ash, a local guy from Walsall, who had his own film production company. I played a character called Dragan in his trailer for the film *Dockyard*. I quickly noticed that all of Joe's friends were very driven people; they had already achieved so much and all had strong goals in life. I was the same – I was very proud of what I had achieved already, and these new friends gave me the confidence to push myself even further. I realised in Joe I had someone very strong, who would back me all the way to achieve my goals.

My first appearance with Joe was in a pilot for a TV series based on the reality-TV series *The Only Way Is Essex*. It was filmed in London in a private manor house with a swimming pool, and there were lots of celebrities there, including Brian Belo, who won *Big Brother* in 2007. It was my first experience on such a glamorous film set.

I had gone along with Joe to help him with the driving, and somehow he managed to get me a part playing a paparazzo. The actor scheduled for the role hadn't turned up on time, and Joe told the director that I was a fully qualified actor and would be happy to do it. I already had a professional camera around my neck to take photos of Joe behind the scenes. I was thrilled to be on a set after such a long time, and there was always something new to learn behind the scenes and in front of the camera. I never felt more appreciated than when I was performing. It was my lucky day, and I wanted to prove myself and demonstrate my acting skills. I rehearsed my few lines and delivered them in front of the camera, and people seemed to be very impressed with me. I thanked Joe and told him I could do with a few more parts like this to get myself back on my feet with acting.

Joe had seen how dedicated and passionate I was about acting and was more than happy to help me reach my goals. His next appearance was in a film called *What's the Score*, a comedy about celebrities playing football against retired Premier League footballers, and he made sure that I had a little part. I played a substitute goalkeeper who manages to let in thirteen goals in the first half of the game – I was never good at football so it was the perfect role for me to play! Among many celebrities and actors there I met John Alford, John Altman, Calum Best, Jonny Blair, Jeff Brazier, Craig Brown, Terry Marsh, Ian Wright and Fabien Barthez.

Alex Reid and Frank Bruno were also there, and I had a long chat with both of them. They are extraordinary chaps with huge personalities. I spoke in length about my home country and the war. Alex already knew a little bit about Bosnia but he wanted to learn more from me. That was my most enjoyable day on the set.

I was called for another day of filming without Joe as he had to be somewhere else. I had begun to realise that the way someone introduces you to people affects how they embrace you and respect you, but then it is up to you to make the most of the opportunity. I had enjoyed a great start to my career and with such good people behind me to push me further and further, I knew I was on the way to achieving my goals.

23

Restoring Family Pride

In 2013, I fulfilled my promise to Suada when I met Arnold Schwarzenegger at an event in Leeds and showed him the letter of condolence he had sent the family after Fikret's death. Once again, I had Joe Egan to thank as he knew the promoter putting on 'An Evening With Arnold Schwarzenegger' and had arranged the meeting. Arnold repeated what Suada had told me, that he didn't hear about the death of his friend until the next year when he visited American troops in Bosnia in 1993. While we were talking, I realised that he thought that I was Džemal. I had to tell him the sad news that Džemal was killed after the war when he went back to Bosnia to compete in bodybuilding to continue his dad's dream. Our conversation stopped and there was complete silence in the room.

Before he left, Arnold asked if I wanted to have a picture with him. 'You are a young man with a lot of history,' he said. 'You must record it somewhere.'

I guess this is where I got my inspiration to put this book

together. I had lots of different stories in my head that I needed to connect and write down. Arnold's encouragement helped motivate me to write this book.

I didn't have time that day, but I also wanted to tell Arnold about the Solak Gym in Kozarac and what we wanted to achieve there: first, we had to show people that you cannot simply wipe out an entire generation and race; and, second, the gym was to get the youngsters off the streets, away from drugs and alcohol and involve them in sports, just like Fikret had done for us when we were kids. I also wanted to explain to Arnold how important it was for me to continue the tradition of bodybuilding in the area.

Somehow I felt I would meet Arnold again as he was intrigued to hear what happened to us during the war in Kozarac.

I framed the picture of Arnold and me, and hung it in the gym, which inspired lots of the local youth to join the fitness centre.

My next challenge was to take pictures of all the youth training there and to give one to Arnold. In 2016, I had the opportunity to meet my idol again and to hand him the framed picture of the Solak Gym. I was very cheeky with Arnold, testing him out, and I asked him where he had met me before; I was very touched he remembered it was in Leeds.

My life was going very well; I was a husband and a father, and I was feeling settled. But I hadn't forgotten our experiences and I wanted to find different ways to honour our past and our most successful people. So I set myself a challenge to compete in bodybuilding as an amateur – I wanted to enter one competition and retire straight away. I applied to enter

Aesthetics Amateur Bodybuilding competition in Birmingham in May 2017.

I was allowed under the special circumstances to use Fikret Hodžić's name in honour of his achievements, and I was privileged to compete under his name. Many people thought that I was being silly or that I might undermine his success. That just pushed me to train harder and achieve better results. It put me under huge pressure, but I always thrived on that. I believe that I am the only bodybuilder in the world to have done that: compete under someone else's name, qualify for the first time and then retire straight away.

It was just to prove the point to myself that I could do it. I also wanted to prove to other people that they could never kill us all – someone would always fight back for their culture and beliefs.

I started training intensively twice a day, and I was reading *Arnold Schwarzenegger Encyclopedia of Bodybuilding* again, a book I had had since I was a child. Already I had the muscles; it was just a case of shaping them to look the best on stage for the amateur competition. I had three months to transform my body into a bodybuilder's physique. The challenge was on and I announced it on all my social media. I took pictures of the progress of my body and shared them too.

People still thought it was the most ridiculous and stupid idea, but I had decided to do it and nothing would stop me. It's like anything in life: once you decide what you want to do, it's no one else's business. In no time my body was growing strong like a tree, with help from my family, and I was on my journey to beat the best. I was convinced that I could manage to get at least third place. I had all of these diet plans and intensive workouts; I also had lots of help from Suada about the best food and when to eat, which was very useful. Just as Suada had done for Fikret, my wife made all my meals and made sure that I had them on time. I followed Fikret's rigorous routines to the letter and lived his life for three months. It wasn't easy, but when you have love for someone or something, nothing in life is hard.

I was thinking about the success and then I felt it. It was like being on top of the world. As my body grew, so did my confidence. My communication improved and I had a lot more to say and even more to prove to people. I carried out exhaustive research on the Internet about how two legends – Fikret Hodžić and Arnold Schwarzenegger – trained, and I believed my hard work and determination would pay off. I was hungry for success, to claim it under the real champion's name, so I did everything to make sure that my body looked shredded in every way.

In the weeks leading up to the competition, I bombarded social media with posts about the importance of the event and everyone contributed in a different way to encourage me to get the best results. I think Suada was probably the happiest person when I took on the challenge and she gave me wonderful support. People respected me for the courage and energy that I put into this challenge. My own people already believed I was the winner just for taking part, but that was not important to me. The only thing that mattered for me was to participate in the competition and bring the name of the champion back on stage one more time and honour his success.

I invited all of my Bosnian friends from the community and all the Northerners from the UK, and they all wanted to support me as much as they could. It was a spectacular event attended by some well-known people, including Joe Egan, Alex Reid, Colin Burt Vidler, Greg Hobbs, Jason Ash, and too many more to name. As always, I had the best support that anyone could hope for from my family, and they cooked lots of food for all my friends who came to the event.

Unfortunately, I didn't win, but the most important thing was that I took part in the competition under Fikret's name and honoured him that day. I did achieve third place, and the pictures gave me the glory that I needed. I posted them on social media, so everyone could see my tribute to Fikret and that was the biggest part of my success. That was all that mattered to me on that day. Suada was living in Bosnia so did not attend but she gave me her blessing and full support. She was very proud of me and she knew just how much dedication, courage and discipline I had needed to get the results.

I came out of the competition with a huge smile on my face and even bigger respect from my friends, my family and Bosnians worldwide for taking on such a challenge. There was another achievement under my belt, which just boosted my confidence and gave me the willpower to keep the bodybuilding community going in Bosnia.

Epilogue

In my life I always think about what would happen if I had to go through all of this again. Part of me thinks I would not be able to make it again and deep inside, I am convinced that we are all humans and deal with different situations in a different way. I do get a lot of flashbacks, day and night, and I still feel those attacks. They are still deep inside me, stored in my heart with all the feelings attached to them.

To hold that pain for the rest of my life, it's harder than anything that I have been through, but as a grown man at least it all made sense. But it has taken most of my life to find the answer and settle my thoughts, and I guess the answer lies with my granddad, deep inside his soul, somewhere far away from this world and the war. He left the legacy for our family of what it means to be a true Northerner with a smile and no glimpse of fear, just like Sefo Solak and those boys. I guess it takes us back to the beginning of the book and how we were taught to survive with honour against the cowardly invaders who wanted to wipe us out.

I still try to remember and hold on to some of the good experiences in my life to give something back to those who deserve it the most. As human beings, we can never know what challenges we might face, and it is up to us how we deal with those situations and how we come out of it. I went through terrible times, along with my family, but I survived, kept my values and started my life again. Now, how do I forgive those with no remorse? I tried to go over those feelings again and perhaps forgive all the Serbs who had attacked and killed my family, and were responsible for some of the most violent acts of war in living memory. I have failed in that, because I could not forgive.

All I can do is try to meet some more good people and attach them to my soul. Former boxer Joe Egan is certainly one of those people who I will always remember, because he came and helped me when I felt at my lowest. I believe that the people around you make who you are.

In 2014, Bosnia had the worst floods in its history, and many people lost their homes for the second time. Joe wanted to help the people most affected by the floods, and said to me, 'Among your friends, actors and the Bosnian community, whatever you can raise to help the flood victims, I will match with my own money and we will go and hand it out.'

It was a very nice gesture for people in Bosnia in need. This is where I started learning from Joe about building bridges and how your generosity affects others. He comes from a big traditional Irish family with very strong values. For us

Bosnians, Bosnia will always be our motherland and the place where we will go back and celebrate our success with our people who struggle there. I will always sacrifice everything in life to try to be an example of a good person.

Joe's family was very pleased for him to visit Bosnia, especially his mother Anne Egan and his sister Constance, who lives in America. I told him about Medjugorje in Bosnia and how lots of Irish people visit there every year. Joe's mother already knew about it and she was very happy for him to visit the holy place. Medjugorje is a town that has been an unofficial place of Catholic pilgrimage since the Virgin Mary reportedly appeared on Apparition Hill in 1981. There is a Queen of Peace statue marking the site of the first apparition and one in front of St James' Church. Liquid has been said to drip from the Risen Christ statue near the church. A concrete cross tops Cross Mountain to the south.

For our arrival in Bosnia, I asked the lads from the gym to display the big banner with Joe's picture to welcome him to our village. I was so proud when I saw how warm and welcoming local people were towards him. It was a special occasion and everyone in the village felt happy to participate. Joe made a speech about his past, his boxing career, acting career and how he met me. He told my people how much I had achieved since I came to the UK and what a genuine hard-working person I am. I felt honoured and proud in front of all my community in Bosnia. As a child during the war, I had lived through atrocities and torture, now I was back home and we were celebrating my success as well. Many Serbs attended that evening and they fully supported the event. It made me a good ambassador for my people and my country.

I feel I have reached and touched many people's hearts in Bosnia after the war. I wanted to spread peace all over Bosnia and teach its people different values in life through success and sport. My humanitarian work means much to me and it is good that people want to be part of that venture too.

I have brought many British values to Bosnia and I always try to share them among normal everyday people who are struggling for existence and survival. I share my common values with different faiths and different cultures. I want everyone in Bosnia to feel as one; to tolerate, respect and celebrate our differences as one nation, one country: Bosnia and Herzegovina.

For me and Lejla, life goes on; we have found happiness that we never thought we could, because of my past. If it wasn't for her, I would never have got this far and this book would never have found its place. I would have been just another boy from the war, far away from his home in Bosnia, only defined by his past and what happened to him there. But our family legacy lives on, because I am still that little boy who was there: 'The Boy Who Said Nothing to the Evil Invaders Who are No Longer There'.

The Krajina still live there without me and those who brought me up there, but this story will find its way to the people and the world and to those true Northerners who are still out there.

'You say what you do and you do what you say and there is no other way.'

Mirsad Solaković:
selected poems

'Aged thirteen, Mirsad's idyllic pastoral multi-ethnic childhood in northern Bosnia was torn apart overnight by the unspeakable brutality and confusion of internecine civil war. Beaten, starving and suffering from post-traumatic stress disorder, he and his close-knit family endured an epic and terrifying flight to safety. Offered refugee status in Britain, the Solaković family settled in Birmingham. For young Mirsad and his family the horrors of Bosnia from which they had escaped were nothing compared to the persecution, squalor and deprivation they encountered in Britain's second city. This account of how a young lad who found himself in a strange and violent country maintained his smile, integrity and honour against all the odds by strengthening his body with weight-lifting and never backing down from a bully's challenge, is a revelation and an inspiration. The poet Robert Graves once said that good English prose is largely a moral thing. Mirsad Solaković honest and unemotional account of a trial overcome by sheer integrity lends weight to Graves' thesis.'

Jeremy Clarke, *The Spectator*

SMALL FIRST-GRADER

The words are knitted, born and raised
and they rise high to the sky.
They fly, fly day and night
and reach shiny stars.

'Go son!' says the mother
'Recite stanzas and rhymes!
Show that little glow
which dances in your heart!'

On the benches tots are sitting
princes and princesses,
they are waiting for the bell to ring,
so they can go home.

After first day in school my
heart is beating fast, my soul is singing,
first-grader is hurrying home
to lay in his grandma's lap with a song.

UNCLE

My uncle left with his head turned
away
from his doorstep.
He parted from his wife and children
and the most beloved little pet
the cuddly puppy
who had always been beside him.

Sorrow has remained, misery has remained,
no one has ever found a single trace.
Only the last words
of my uncle have remained:
'My *children, this is no good,*
they are plotting against our lives in secret.
Give me a glass of water
to clear my soul
which the enemy has not taken away yet.'

He emptied the glass of cold water
and left down the curved path
to eternal tranquillity.

THE BOY WHO SAID NOTHING
(Part I)

Silence is only till the crucial moment,
as when two joints meet,
which are far from one another
many long days and years,
many green hills and floral meadows;
or when, before the decisive battle
in the early dawn, armies merge,
columns fill big valleys
and flags rise decisively towards the sky;
or when it thunders and flashes
and suddenly the hill moves
river cuts new bed
and changes its course.

THE BOY WHO SAID NOTHING

It happens in that moment
when there is no more anger in the body,
so it says loudly and clearly why it is suffering and
wants to respond to injustice with spite.

It happened to me on the judgment day,
when destiny knocked on the door to interupt my
childhood,
and in one mere moment,
the boy grew up,
The boy became a mature man.
The boy was now the guardian of the family.
The boy standing at the edge of an abyss,
in front of him wild beasts
were growling threateningly
while the circle around him was constricting.

'Tell us!
tell us the secret!'
with a knife in a hand, the brute, a monster,
a barbarian is shouting
and threatening to cut the boy's veins.
The parents have lost their breath.
They are being shaken by fear,
trauma has become an open wound
which remains until the Day of Judgment.
The boy's tears dried up
His scream died out
The sun was extinguished
The whole universe
Disappeared in a black hole in a single moment.

The boy did not say one word.
He looked defiantly into the eyes of the beast
while he was being put through infernal torture
throughout long days and endless nights.
He had given his father a vow of silence
when he was telling him in the quiet night
that the dogs of war might come to the door
and you need not be scared,
because their hate cannot harm you.
'My dear son, be happy and live for my sake.
Keep the secret deep inside yourself
and do not tell them under any threat
what you know, for they know not what is in your
head.
Do not tell them anything about me.
Just keep quiet – your silence will distract them.
The secret must stay inside you.
My dear son, be happy and live for my sake,
maybe it means that they threaten to kill you,
But your silence will only distract them...
In your silence you will find the peace,
which glows eternally as the flame of life.
My son; my words might be big or small,
might be worthy or maybe without any hope,
but in the right moment
they will give you support and hope
which will help you to win the decisive battle.'

The boy said nothing,
he did not reveal the secret to the monsters

even though they engraved on his chest a
bitter wound with a sharp knife.

Watching his family in shock
Without a word he said:
'My mother, don't worry!
No, it is not my blood which is flowing!
That is their shame flowing
down my chest
and drawing these beasts to Hell
where they shall eternally be tortured!
The joy of sun is waiting for us
after this gloomy night.
Don't worry my dear mother,
just peacefully close your eyes
and wait to be woken by the
magic song of the birds!'

SREBRENICA – 8,372...

Srebrenica – my incomprehensible grief...

Eight thousand three hundred and seventy-two
Violently extinguished human lives
horrible genocide
executing civilians
executing kids and old men
executing men and women
executing innocent people

because of their faith
because of their names
because of their surnames
because of something which is not their own choice,
but which destiny determined for a man.

Eight thousand three hundred and seventy-two
– lapidary inscripts in Potočari
where white gravestones are standing
side by side
mute witnesses of crime,
reminder to the people,
to the Balkans, to Europe and to the world
about our civilisation and about mankind.
Eight thousand three hundred and seventy-two sad stories
of which we know only some
and because of which our blood freezes in our veins.
Sad tear of Srebrenica,
you have dropped on the soul of the world
and touched many human hearts.
After twenty years
the search is still under way
for perished innocent victims
of monstrous genocide
and for the butchers of my people
there is no refuge either in a dream or in reality,
because there is no oblivion:
Man, do not forget Srebrenica,
so evil will never repeat itself
Not ever and to nobody.

The Boy Who Said Nothing

Man, don't forget Ramo[1]
who was forced by the villains
to call his son Nermin to death!
Ramo and also Nermin were cruelly killed.

But why?
What did they do wrong?
Echoes of the creepy voice resonate through
Srebrenica
through the Balkans, through Europe and through
the world,
and will resonate until the Day of Judgment
as a reminder to people.

Oh, my world
where is your conscience and where is your soul?
Don't you remember
that justice is implacable?

Srebrenica – my incomprehensible grief...

[1]*This was not Granddad Ramo, but a father of the same name from Srebenica,*
where 8,372 Muslim men and boys were massacred

MYSTERIOUS RIVERBANKS

History flows through the current of the river
Starenica of Kozarac. Murky and fast
it meanders between mountains of Krajina[2]
through the field where Grmeč[3] and Kozara[3] meet
and where it calms down as a ladybird
calms its strong wings and a gurgle of water spills
over the greenery where from time to time birds'
magical singing can be heard.

Meandering river remembers numerous events
that have shaped the course of history.
The clear water remembers conquerors and
also defenders.

Murky water remembers
heroes – and also cowards
fast water remembers
horsemen – and also tanks
wise water remembers
firelocks[4] – and also howitzers.

Starenica was waded by commanders
and also by audacious armies.
The river is still healing from its wounds
inflicted not only by fire and steel, but also by
dead civilians and warriors which it carried.

THE BOY WHO SAID NOTHING

There are still the old and mysterious water mills
on the river of Kozarac. To witness centuries past
and how once upon a time
the mighty river milled white flour
and fed the people of Krajina.

The banks of Starenica
remember harsh years
at the begining of the nineties.
They remember the dark twentieth century
when exchanges of gunfire were held from both
sides of the riverbank,
they remember the exchanges which destroyed the
walls and roofs of
houses and homes, inhabited by both animals and humans.
Only scorched land remained, ashes and rubble,
covered with corpses which interrupted
children's games.

The Rika river remembers everything;
it sings epic melodies with waves and waterfalls.
It lures dreamy trackers into stopping by, even if
just for a moment, to hear mysterious
and untold stories,
stories which are hiding beneath demolished walls.
Stories which are napping in old stumps, which are
walking in meadows with a cricket's symphony
which are echoing in waves with sparrows chirping
and pigeons cooing.

Falconers are hiding, and also falcons
with grooms are hiding and also black horses
and that secret chain connects
generations that haven't yet been born.
The truth is a glorious testament of a victory
which prevails even in the darkest of night
and cannot be turned off.
Meandering river remembers
and the memories revive.

[2] *Region in Bosnia and Herzegovina*

[3] *Mountains in Bosnia and Herzegovina*

[4] *A firelock is an early form of musket, in which the priming is ignited by sparks*

RACISM

My veins were pumping blood like a waterfall, my heart had
an earthquake and my words came out like a lava from
a volcano...
Who are you calling that, what did you say, what did I do to
you...

You mentioned me in something that you are differentiating
my; race, religion, nationality and my way of living...

I always thought that we live in a sophisticated world full
of laws that we follow in democracy, freedom of speech and
tolerance. I thought that we are freely able to express our
differences to enrich our society, community and country...

My dictionary hasn't got enough space, enough memory
to store that horrible word, so therefore I erase it from my
memory for ever...

My message for all of those children is that whoever still have
them in their heads, they should erase them and tattoo the new
words in their heads with; love, peace and care for the rest of
the race...

SPLENDOUR OF TRUTH

Everything that we saw,
heard and knew
we can't see now and we don't want to know.
What happened – we knew,
but we don't want to know now.

Evil has repeated itself again
and we fear that it will happen again,
but it is all because we fear to tell the truth.

The truth is sometimes harder to tell
than to experience.

Why one nation must go through a path of
suffering, while the rest of the world turned a blind eye?

WORDS OF A HERO
(dedicated to Osman Solaković)

In defiant Bosnia, in the bitter Krajina,
the hero and the flower are speaking
Osman is talking with the lily
beside Sana river – where the meadow is green
and the hero's words are echoing
through days and years
through living memory.

Osman is a symbol of our majesty,
our past, present and future.
The beats of his brave heart empower us and
comfort us in our dreams.
He gave us a crucial grain of hope
to stay there – on our own
and defend our pride,
our majesty...
My Osman,
we don't have you any more,
but this verse will always warm us
and will open new horizons to us.
You were that firm stone of ours
that didn't want to give up Bosnia,
for our bitter Krajina.
You didn't leave even a shred hope to your
Enemy.
That is our man from Krajina.

THE BOY WHO SAID NOTHING

Osman's message goes on, he never surrenders,
his strength, this his heartbeat
which binds us and makes us all stronger.

Through time
the words of our Osman echo:
'People, don't give up what is ours!
Have hope in the barricades of Kozarac
that are going to defend our doorsteps!
Foes are dreaming to take them from us
our children and our mothers.
The justice is only in the hands
of one hero!
Don't give up Bosnia for my sake!
Don't give up our homeland for my sake!
I'm lying there – in a meadow in Krajina
upon which golden lilies
bloom.'

Osman's words echo
and emerald Una[5] carries them down Krajina
and they echo through Bosnia
through days and years
like a sun of hope
like a message of wisdom
and like a warning:
for the dead
and for the living
and for those – not yet born:
bitter people from Krajina

and proud
Bosnians and Herzegovinians!

HERO NIJAZ – BOSNIAN DRAGON

Kozarac heedfully keeps memories
of fierce and courageous fighters
Nijaz is scent – which captivatingly lasts.
Nijaz is the golden lily – of Kozarac.

He left everything he had
with sadness, he left his warm home and
gave everything for the homeland.
He was defending freedom and liberty.

Hero is going towards home
with a heavy foreboding in his heart:
'Wait, dad – I'm close by,
once again l long to see your eyes!'

But his dad left without farewell,
so his wish remained unfulfilled
with a gun in his hand he went to fight in the trenches.
He became a living target when the battle started.

Nijaz defended his land with his comrades.
He gave hope and safety to his people.

THE BOY WHO SAID NOTHING

He manned front lines throughout his homeland.
In Nijaz's heart – there lies a true Bosnian dragon.

'Let's go foward – assault!'
– golden lilies are going to attack
to liberate a beloved homeland
from our enemies.

That shameful aggressor
is strong while attacking unarmed civilians
while torturing the weak in concentration camps.
But when ghazis enter the battlefield
suddenly they don't want to fight.
They run away – they leave their weapons.
We took back our beloved Bosnia.

The golden lily fell in battle
while he was attacking bravely
to accomplish his great dream
to make Kozarac free again.

TOMAŠICA NEVER AGAIN

The earth swore to the sky
that nothing inside it
will stay hidden
and will sooner or later be revealed.

The wind rose and started to blow
dogs, wolves and sheep wonder
what moans drearily?
On a hill which is called Tomašica[6]
in a small grove
a forest moans and branches shake
leaves fall to emphasise the sorrow.

A landowner watches his land,
listens to the painful and sad voices
that are creepily echoing down the meadow
until the early dawn...
The earth cries
the innocent buried bodies cry,
but locals live there normally
without realising the extent
of unseen atrocities.

Lifeless skeletons are lying all around
they will not leave the place
until human souls find
eternal tranquillity
in the grave,
in the graveyard,
not thrown in a pit,
a shameful mass grave
where skeletons are intermingled
where bones are mixed
where skulls are shattered.

THE BOY WHO SAID NOTHING

Terrible crimes happened so quickly
so quietly,
that no one could even think
how much evil
is hidden beneath that fatal hill.

Tomašica – torment of Bosnia,
Europe and the world!
Tomašica – your name
shall be written with black ink
in the memory of civilisation
and a river of tears cannot wash away
the pain which bears your name
Tomašica – abyss of torment!

On a barren lea,
not even donkeys graze there, nor horses,
nor cows nor sheep,
not even one tree grows there any more.
What is here there?
What happened here?
Why are those leas and hills eerily deserted?
What kind of a disaster came upon that place,
That neither grass nor snow will cover it now.
There is no tranquillity for animals or for
people, until the secret that hides beneath the
bosom of tragic Tomašica is revealed
from that spacious black hollow
where cries died and horror froze.

The old villager spoke out;
he could not take that horror with him to the grave –
the hole is too small,
the coffin is too narrow to contain all that torment
and horror.

The earth opens beneath the sky.
A mass grave opens
vainly hidden terrible truths
are revealed
to remind us
not to forget
so Bosnia and Herzegovina remembers
and Europe remembers
and also the civilised world,
and that horrible crimes upon innocent people
are never and nowhere repeated:
Tomašica – never again!

⁶Tomašica is a village in the Prijedor municipality of Bosnia and Herzegovina where experts excavated what is believed to be the largest mass grave from the war in the 1990s

HOMELAND MEMORIES

Written by my sister, Meliha Solaković-Hadzovic

Memories are something
that hurt a lot,

The Boy Who Said Nothing

happy childhood and
school days with friends together we had wonderful
adventures!

Every rock and stone
of my land,
means more to me than
the whole of England!

No one knows my sorrow, my pain,
but my wounded heart that misses my country so much!

If I just could once more
see the garden where I grew,
even Medo won't be there to welcome me home, no,
that brave dog doesn't live, no not any more,

Nor old flowers blossom as before,
now even the sun doesn't shine there, no not any more!

THANK YOU, HOMELAND

With safe steps I walk
I carry my homeland in my heart
The love inside me is stronger
than all the challenges of life.

Thank you my father!
Thank you my mother!

Thank you my my grandfather!
Thank you my grandmother!

I am grateful to you, Krajina!
I am grateful to you, Bosnia and Herzegovina!
Because in my heart there is no
place for hate.

I WAS BORN AGAIN

Acceptance was a way forward to resolve
the conflict through the cultural norm
and allow the new life to be born
amongst the people that I don't know.

I was always scared of losing the bad days as well as
good days,
because those days taught me a lot about life.
People and the kids from different ethnic backgrounds.
Who are we to judge. We don't judge,
but our parents judge,
because they might have different values attached to their little
lives.
The sport doesn't judge, but it makes us superficial and better
than others, why?
Because we learn from our values to respect and treasure
others like in a karate film
Miyagi and his passion for the sport. For me it was more than
that,

as I run out of options looking for acceptance,
until the bodybuilding was born from the family member that
we all know.

BEATING THE BULLIES

When I stood out from a little boy showing those muscles
glowing, all the kids wanted to know who I was. Where I
came from it didn't really matter any more. For me it meant
I am accepted, now I know how to bring my Northerner
values alive and teach them more.

The boy didn't say a word, but the silent treatment gave them
the truth and my own way forward to deal with the past.

The smile allowed the freedom and hid the fear even a little bit
more. For Roy it was a challenge and for me it was a way of
survival. Uvin my coach knew and has seen the shadow in the
background of a shy boy coming alive and speaking out.

For Peter the lion doesn't need to make a noise as he is in the
safe cage with the rest of those the same who cannot find their
way.
For Barry the smile brought tears, but he sold it for the true
values of the business when his bosses came and for the little
Northerner who lost his way, he knew one day he will come
out of his cage and eat his prey.

All my friends knew who the little boy was there and how the life revealed itself from a little way. For me the acceptance was the way to the throne, who didn't want no more trouble from them all.

REFUGEE

Refugee – we came here for a reason with no meaning to take anybody's land or a way of living.

Nobody sees that in us, we all became threats like those evil invaders.

Even us kids who could not foresee what will happen to us in the future.

Our parents were stuck in their own way of thinking there is no other way.

Let's earn a bit of money on the farm and let's get the hell out of here, but where? The war is still raging in our motherland where they all struggled to survive there.

Where do we belong now? We can't even fit here amongst a civilised nation in Western Europe. No one wants us anywhere, where do we belong again? 'We are stuck again like a lion in a cage.'

Why did they bring us to die here? Take us where we belong,
at least there we would die because of the war?

Even our kids cannot survive here on this little island where
they cannot find their way.

LIFE IS A JOURNEY
(dedicated to Mark Summers R.I.P)

Mark will always live in our hearts!
He has left marks in all our hearts and he will always live in
our hearts. He was a big strong man that we all still have a lot
to learn from, even when he is gone. In our memories
his words will whisper to our hearts and tell us his stories one
by one, day and night, week by week, month by month and
year by year, it will never stop...
Then we will reveal all of those connections and hard work he
has put in us; to get us where we are today.
He has told me; his last words: 'Mirsad, life is a journey and it
always has to come to the end. I have reached the end and I've
got what I got. Now, you need to stay and carry on and make
the most out of life.' Those words are embroidered in my heart
forever and my soul will recite them every so often, whilst the
big man is resting somewhere above us high in the sky!
My thoughts are with you and all of your family on this very
sad day, where we lost someone very close to us and in
our hearts!

LUKE SMITHERD

Very strong, full of emotions to be drawn, I love the flow!
This is where it all started from you, my old friend who always
used to care!
The old uni days as a young boy, you helped me to stay there.
I always remember who was there, when I struggled all the
way!
I will store it in my soul and let the emotions dissolve!
Until the day I die I have found a real friend, someone who
always cares!
That is Luke Smitherd who will always be there!

LOVE THE WORLD, LOVE THE PEOPLE WHO SMILE

Think good about the people and people will always think
good about you.
Emily is one good example.
British people have given us Bosnians a second chance to
rebuild our lives again and hope for a better world that we can
embrace and find good people in the world to trust and love
again...
Perhaps we can all learn from British people and deposit our
love to our children to share our care...
I was at Coventry University amongst Emily, Susanne, Fran,
Liz, Claire, Charlene and many more to name that I loved and
cared for, because they were my girls that I always protected
and cared whilst we were out and about – late nights, good
times and beautiful girls, everything that youth brings.
I was rather a popular guy with girls with my tight top and

little muscles, that would make their day. I always had a smile,
that won young girls' hearts... Now the smile has disappeared,
but I am glad that the words have exchanged that beauty and
they smile inside my soul... It's too much to say to my friends
who cared for me so much and embraced my soul with love
and care...

I came out of war with visual and mental scars, deprived and
stripped out of my pride... The soldiers took my family away
and we never found where they were...

I only found my way to the UK, my new home where people
care...

I found my new family and settled here... They never told me
that I don't belong here, but when I go home I am foreign
there...

THE BOY WHO SAID NOTHING
(Part II)

Many years have passed.
The boy who said nothing
is walking down the streets of London
while rain is drizzling
he stops by the Thames
and remembers his Kozarac.[7]
In the waves of the big river
he hears the gurgle of his Starenica
calling him
to come to the river banks
to reveal the secrets to him,

which it has been keeping for years
which it has been hiding for decades
which it has been concealing for centuries,
because nobody understands
its songs, its rhymes
and they don't hear the voice
which tells us the stories.

Many years later,
to the boy who kept the secret
that was hiding in his heart,
a secret was revealed.
It was levitating in the universe
and made him realise that there are
men and non-men that exist in the world.
Some have souls and others don't.
The love opens horizons
and hate blinds,
there is no happiness in the misery of others
and that sometimes man is deceived by his own eyes,
because beneath the skin of lambs wolves are hiding
and in that moment a boy becomes a man,
and that from the Thames, Kozarac can speak.

[7] *a town in north-western Bosnia and Herzegovina*

KOZARAC – THE PRETTIEST SMALL TOWN IN THE WORLD

My Kozarac – is my pride!
Joy for our souls – for our hearts!
Source of happiness – for my homeland!
– My Kozarac – is my pride!

My dear people of Kozarac
they are sweet and kind
and they always wish well for everyone
– My dear people of Kozarac.

They always carry their town in their hearts
wherever they stand, wherever they walk
wherever they fly, wherever they sail
– they carry their town in their thoughts and hearts.

They remember their dear youth
captivating blossom and ripe fruit
welcoming eyes and warm smiles
– they remember their dear youth

*

In a small, but big, town,
in Kozarac my mother gave birth to me,
mother gave a birth to a fierce man from Krajina
– in a small, but big town.

As soon as I got up on my feet
I was running far through meadows, the
stars were calling me
– as soon as I got up on my feet.

*

Hate struck Kozarac
suddenly – unprovoked by anything
people are led to death camps
– hate struck Kozarac.

Hate struck Kozarac,
The war, akin to a tsunami, destroyed everything
not a single brick was left
– hate struck Kozarac.

The hate that blinds reason
descended on the streets of Kozarac
and struck down both grandson and old man
– the hate that blinds reason.

The hate that blinds reason
was brought by ghostly dogs of war
they pushed Kozarac through the doors of Hell
– with the hate that blinds reason.

What must not be forgotten
is the painful look of the man from Manjača
with his ribs protruding through his skin, he was
the camp prisoner of Omarska
– it must not be forgotten.

THE BOY WHO SAID NOTHING

What must not be forgotten
is the barbed wire around Keraterm,
Trnopolje and Omarska[8] camps
cruel shooting of the innocents
on the rocks of Korićanske Stijene[9]
– it must not be forgotten.

Remembrance is Bosnian testament
Remembering missing persons
who are being searched for by relatives
whose souls are still without peace
– remembrance is Bosnian testament.

*

In a remote world a desire is burning.
The expelled returned to their birthplace
to build again paradise in it
– in a remote world desire is burning.

They built our Kozarac from scratch
In their soul they have the vow of peace
hardworking hands astonished the whole world
– they built our Kozarac from scratch

Full of optimism and love
people of Kozarac are dreaming while touring the
planet, dreaming
of the prettiest little town in the world
– full of optimism and love.

Mesmerising glitz of Hollywood
adorns Kozarac in everyone's dream
in summer or cold winter
– mesmerising glitz of Hollywood.

The old tower of Kozarac remains, built from
mighty walls, it has stood by the road since
ancient times
– the old tower of Kozarac.

It witnessed ancient times and
reminds us of glorious battles
captains and daring rebels
– it witnessed ancient times.

Cannons were striking with fire
from the fortified tower of Krajina
when empires clashed
– cannons were striking with fire.

Black horses were rushing
into the distance across the fields whilst
heroic hearts were rising up to the heights
– while black horses were rushing.

To be raised from the ground
that is the destiny of Kozarac
whenever new age comes
– to be razed to the ground.

The Boy Who Said Nothing

The tower of Kozarac remembers well
who Omer-pasha Latas was
and how a bad reputation followed him
– the tower of Kozarac remembers well.

It remembers also May of '92
when it was besieged by the beasts
who were seeking reasons for crime in their religion
– it remembers also May of '92.

But hate did not defeat love, even though
innocent people perished,
because people of Kozarac are survivors.
– but hate didn't defeat love.

[8] concentration camps

[9] mass grave in the mountainous area of Korićanske Stijene

SO EVIL WILL NEVER BE REPEATED

We remember coffin to coffin
we remember gravestone to gravestone
we remember, so it cannot be forgotten
– so evil will never be repeated.

We remember death camps
we remember barbed wire,
we remember children and fathers
we remember necks cut,
we remember mutilated faces

we remember murderers' laughter,
we remember guards of death
we remember walls of blood,
we remember tortures of the innocents
we remember piles of shot people,
we remember mass graves
we remember courtrooms of The Hague,
we remember genocide deniers
we remember big mouths without shame,
we remember names in stone
we remember crime in time.

We remember coffin to coffin
we remember gravestone to gravestone
we remember so it can not be forgotten
– so evil will never repeat itself.

LIFE

Life becomes a memory box, empty with no more hope!
Memories are all we have for those that we loved the most.
God takes them away from us at their best.
Sometimes we wonder why we came across them, then again
nothing lasts forever!

Nothing really matters any more, what we did and where we
went.
We go away from this earth, like we never been here. 'All we
leave here is our family tree.'

We always face the same questions. Why do we come here and
what is our purpose here?
Maybe we come here to love our children and to love one
another.
To raise our children and to share each other's good will. All
we have is our children to live here, after we disappear.

Let's bring those words together and let's hope together for a
better day tomorrow!
Our children will be born again tomorrow with a hope to
unite us all together.

We always come with the same words, why are we here and
what is the purpose of being here?
We come here to live with one another, without our children,
we wouldn't have known each other.

Without our children what would be our purpose of being
here? Without our children, there would be no one here to
hear us.

It would be just an empty box without anybody to hold it
here, once we disappear...
'This life leaves us with an empty box, full of memories, for
our kids to hear us.'

MY DEAR BOSNIANS

My dear Bosnians,
You have always been my biggest strength
and my biggest support,
which leads me toward success
and supports my good deeds.

True support is a power
which is always dear
which gives a zest for life,
fills our souls with a wish
that a man lives for love and freedom.

As a child I started on that small road;
I directed my ideas at those small moments
Which have now become exciting big moments.

School is an experience which develops the honour and
humanity
which establish morals for a developed society.
We always were, and we will always be
on a road which leads to honour.

My favourite moments are there by my house,
on the doorstep where they love me the most.
That is my only land – joyful Bosnia!
My dear proud homeland.

ACCEPTANCE AND RESPECT

Maybe because of me, or how I looked or who I knew,
I found one culture that carried me through
and gave me the acceptance that I need.

At this time this culture was similar to mine
and it was the Jamaican culture.
I don't know what I owe to those people,
because I was different,
but our experiences conjured
mutual freedom and respect.

SUCCESS OF OUR PEOPLE

We must support our successful
people around the world,
we must exaggerate their good deeds,
protect good people
because fairness and honour are always hard to earn.

These are the people our country Bosnia needs
for whom it always yearns.

Wake up Bosnians
and evoke our hopes,
liberate our hearts
from hate, grief and misery
and fill yourselves with warmth,
love, happiness and joy.

Invest effort and knowledge into good deeds
and distance yourselves from evil and treachery.

Don't believe in those people
who don't wish good to other people,
love and respect others,
boast about success
of our hardworking people
around the globe.

Poetry, knowledge, sport
connect noble people
represent your homeland
expand your homeland
and magnify your people
one nation
Bosnians around the globe.

Our people live all over the world
and they are leaving marvellous landmarks behind them.
We should tie a dead knot for the evil and the hate
and bind our hearts with warmth and love.

LOVE THAT NEVER LASTED

Conquer the world in a different way and show the people
that you are not scared by the way you care.

The most important thing is that you learn how to take care of
the others on your way.

Then you open a new door and move to a different life where
they all care.

Perhaps the end of something else is the new beginning for the
better days.

SARAJEVO, CITY OF MINE

Sarajevo is always in my heart
And it will always be the capital city.
It always gives me a feeling of
youth and splendour, it puts a smile
on my face like a most wanted gift.
There is only one hill above *šeher*[10]
on which Bijela *tabija*[11] shines.
There is only one Miljacka, fast river,
which meanders between sharp boulders.
There is only one aromatic Bašćaršija[12]
where Sebilj,[13] full of pigeons, glows.
There is only one cold river Bosna
Which rises below mountain Igman.

I shook hands with Čengić Vila,
Otoka, Ilidža.[14]
That is my Sarajevo,
which always grows inside me,

My youthful dreams
revived
when I met happy Sarajevo ladies
who beside Miljacka[15] had flourished
and who had bestowed a first kiss upon me
on Wilson's Promenade
in the shadow of aromatic linden trees...

They say by Bey's Mosque[16]
running white water rises,
whoever drinks that cold water
he will always return to Sarajevo.
In our hearts we hold your *Vječna vatra*[17]
which warms us day and night.

*

You are the gorgeous Jerusalem of Europe
which glows in Bosnia like a diamond.
Don't give up, Sarajevo!
– the good people are depending on you.
We won't let you go!
You belong to Bosnia and Herzegovinia.
We admire you!
– the whole world is sighing.
We love you!
– you are the splendid flower of the Balkans.
Sarajevo you are my city
– you are our mother.
My dearest city
– you are our pride.

The Boy Who Said Nothing

Live long for many centuries
for our sake.

Sarajevo, we dream of you
you are our inspiration,
you are our pride
and you have always stood by us.
When our false friends
were shelling us from the hills
we were heroically defending our Sarajevo
while divine Vijećnica[18] was burning.

Women of Sarajevo were walking behind
barricades with their heads high.
They were feeding hungry pigeons
and singing *sevdalinke* songs.[19]
The years of suffering are behind us,
when darkness fell on Bosnian soil.
Today we travel around the world
and bear yellow lilies in our hearts.
My citizens of Sarajevo
are always good men and
they always know, even in their sleep,
who supports Željo,[20] and who supports
Sarajevo.
Our fans are born,
our mighty BH Fanaticos[21]
who understand the eternal flame
of defiant love
that burns for Bosnia

and feeds our souls!
Sarajevo, you are my favourite city in the world,
I always wear your shirt with pride.

In the East, West,
North and South!
All over the world.
Sarajevo is always in my heart
and it will always be the capital city
that will always give me feelings of
youth and splendour.
It puts a kind smile on my face
like a most precious gift.

[10]*šeher is a Turkish word which means 'city' but it is still used today to express love for the city*

[11]*Bijela tabija or 'White Bastion', old fort overlooking the historic core of Sarajevo*

[12]*Sarajevo's old bazaar and the historical and cultural centre of the city*

[13]*The Sebilj is an Ottoman-style wooden fountain (sebil) in the centre of Bascarsija*

[14]*Sarajevo neighbourhoods (Čengić Vila, Ilidža, Otoka)*

[15]*River that flows through Sarajevo*

[16]*Gazi-Husrev – Bey's Mosque*

[17]*the Eternal Flame – a memorial to the military and civilian victims of the Second World War in the centre of Sarajevo*

[18]*the City Hall*

[19]*traditional genre of folk music*

[20]*a football club from Sarajevo*

[21]*the largest supporters' group in Bosnia and Herzegovina who follow Bosnian national sports teams, mostly in football, basketball, handball and sitting volleyball*

OLD MOSTAR BRIDGE

Old Bridge,
nobody has ever managed to erase its arch,
The tumultuous centuries flew across it,
the greatest military leaders from the whole world
and they have carried across countless treasures
and piles of weapons.
Old Bridge is our dearest rose.

That is our pride,
our scented rose
which connects Bosnia with Herzegovina.
They are two wings of our country
that could never run from each other.
That Old Bridge of ours binds them
connects us, strengthens us and never betrays us.

That Old Bridge awakes us in the night
to keep the old love secrets
which were born and flourished there
like young snowdrops
down by the bank of river Neretva.

Love is born again on the Old Bridge
It strengthens its weakly wings
prepares it for magical flight,
for departure into the distance
to a far away world
across its hills and high mountains,

338

carrying inside the heart a secret
which the white Old Bridge keeps
in Neretva.

They all have become part of that bridge
they all have become part of that love
and they never have enough of it.
They all used to dive from the old bridge
and became heroes of that city
from there Mirsad, dubbed Mića, jumped and the
legend of the Old Bridge was born.

Everyone knows who the old Mića was
and how many times he jumped from the old bridge
and how many trophies he won
and how he entertained young ladies
and built his youth with the Old Bridge...

Books are written about those men with brave
hearts
jumpers who were flying through the sky like
swallows
and jumping to Neretva's embrace,
that beautiful green clear water.

Old Bridge remembers well
military leaders and heroes
walking upon it
leaving legends behind them.

The Boy Who Said Nothing

Separated banks of Neretva hurt,
where the white arch once stood hurts,
it has been glittering for centuries
on it young bridge keepers were walking,
guardians of the bridge,
after whom the city got its name –

MOSTAR![22]

After ten long years
once again the glamorous bridge
emerged from the green water
and a gorgeous white arch
shone above Neretva
like a dream vision –
it reunited separated banks
it reunited east with west.

[22] *from the Bosnian word* most, *which means 'bridge'*

HAPPINESS CANNOT BE STOLEN

Happiness is a secret!
Happiness is a fairy tale!
Happiness is the most beautiful dream.
Happiness is a bird!
Happiness is a flight!
Happiness is a new, sunny day.

Happiness flashes, then disappears,
without people it has no meaning,
it grows like an invisible plant
with mysterious blossoms and scents.

With my head high I am walking down the
road, searching for a sky full of hope,
the stars are circling around me
the happiness cannot be stolen!

Happiness is hope which blooms in hearts,
grows and changes, like the world itself
Even if it leaves, a strong wind will bring it back
and it continues to follow my steps.

Happiness is a secret!
Happiness is a fairy tale!
Happiness is the most beautiful dream.
Happiness is a bird!
Happiness is a flight!
Happiness is a new, sunny day.

LOVE

Love is a beauty that we admire!
Why sometimes we are ashamed of it,
when we know it rules inside us
and opens hidden doors of emotion and power?

The Boy Who Said Nothing

It smiles sometimes to everybody
and it affects people differently.
Someone covers his eyes
someone's cheeks blush
but blood rushes
through everybody's veins equally.

Love is youth
love is a maturity
love is a secret
that man cannot divulge.

Love is a monument which glows from within
which nobody can steal
it is always there to remind us
of days full of hope:
'Love is a pleasant dream that can suprise us all,
like a rainy day in a spring.'

Love is like a box.
Sometimes it is empty, and sometimes it is full of
hope,
but it is always there inside you
all the time
from the beginning and remaining till the end.

CHILDREN

Children are the future
Children are the peace
Children are the harmony
Children will destroy the wall of hate.

Children are the wings of hope
Children are the smile of happiness
Children are the shiny stars
Children are the most beautiful flowers.

Love life
love people
Hear children's voices:
'In love is the salvation
for the whole world – for us all!'

Live together with one another
respect the freedom of others
build your home and feed
the white dove of peace.

ONE LADY, ONE LOVE, MY LEJLA.

You are better than the rest,
Love you with all my heart, until my last breath.
These are the words that always come first and I hope they
will be the last.

Only one flower blossoms in my heart and the same flower
will die in my heart.
I look at your eyes and I can only see myself; the first look will
always be the same as the last look.
The only difference is, we might look older and less attractive,
but you are always the most beautiful flower in my life.
There is no other lover that can ever replace my first flower,
That first smell spread all over my heart and sprinkled love all
over my soul.
For those words I live,
For that love I should always give,
'For that flower I could kill, but losing you I could never
forgive...'

SILENCE

I lived with the inner silence. 'It was my last wall between my
heart and my soul.' If someone damaged that inner wall, I
would be facing death. It is difficult to explain with words; I
could only reach my silence, communicate, tell myself stories
and give a reassurance that I still have a chance to embrace
this world with love and peace. I always heard the inner voices
calling out my name: 'We will come out again to get you.'
Those were the soldiers that left me lying down in a pool of
blood in front of my house, in front of my family. Every time
it happened, it felt like someone was trying to invade and take
over my body. The secret invaders are here to damage my last
wall between my heart and my soul. Every day, every week,
every year they appeared more and more and I had to fight
them in silence with no words.

Sometimes they caught me tired and without guard. That day I would get damaged the most. Whenever it happened I had to unchain my thoughts and actions and embrace the new life and new surroundings in the UK. It felt like a real chain around my body, sometimes it felt like a dream that I cannot escape from.

LIFE

Life flows like a wild water,
life flourishes like a dense forest,
life carries a laughter as well as bitter tears.
Life gives you all and then it takes it all!

Life goes – rolls happily along,
but happiness doesn't last eternally.
A blizzard buries everything in snow
shackles streams and rocks with ice.

Life is like a river,
in a moment it is clean and beautiful,
in a moment it is wild and turbid,
in a moment it threatens and
in a moment it sings.

Life is like time,
an eternal dance of good and evil.
A game of darkness and light.
In a moment it is dark and in a moment the sun

shines.
Life is like a riddle
which a meandering river,
fast and deep,
carries through endless time.

THE BIRDS ARE SINGING

The birds singing in the distance over the dark fields of this
magnificent village that has a mysterious feel about it...

The birds are singing one with another, that harmony sounds
like a symphony hall, all together producing incredible sounds.

Where are the people from this town?
This village feels like a deserted place where no one lives!

The birds are showing us the sign of life with petrified sounds
calling us all to come together and live with one another...

Will it be too late? Before we start to hate and discriminate all
about the war.

No one wants this land any more, they are all running away
like during the war.

Where are the kids that once played on these fields? Even they
have disappeared during their long childhood growing up
away from home.

Our ancestors have given away our land to birds to stretch
their wings along the fields far away from the land...

Even that has no meaning any more, because even the babies
are not born here any more...

Soon we will realise it's all gone away to people that don't
even care any more...

Our land where everything existed there once upon a time.
Now it's the only place for the birds to sing at our door.

We live to hear these birds again, as they are calling for the old
voices to return home.
'Them that used to live here once upon a time'...

LOVE EACH OTHER, LOVE THE WORLD
Why do we not love each other?
Why do we hate each other?
Why do we kill each other?
Why don't we support each other?
Why do we punish each other?

May God guide us to make people behave in a good way,
away from evil and killings.
Be the one that contributes positively in our little world!

ARNOLD SCHWARZENEGGER

We are born to love,
We are born to care,
We are born to prosper,

We come to this world with the same purpose and we go away
from this world with the same reason.

All we leave behind us is our legacy for our children to retrieve
our history.

Some of us have changed the world for better and some of us
perhaps have made different decisions.
At least our children will be able to open a new chapter and
make a new decision.

With all that knowledge they should make a better world!

'You have certainly inspired me to change the others around
me.'

CHAMPION
(dedicated to Fikret Hodžić)

Always cheerful, beloved by everyone,
a champion – our Fikro!
Full of life, smiling
An adorable person

Fifteen-time winner Mr Yugoslavia
year-to-year representing his country
on the winning pedestal
a super champion – our Fikro!

From childhood he loved
bodybuilding and with homemade weights
he trained the whole day,
the gym was a magnet to him.
Halima, his hardworking mother,
had no idea back then that she had given birth to a legend,
an inspiration to be admired by many,
that Fikro was going to be a champion
who would be remembered by the world.
Fikro would have a friend by the name of
Arnold Schwarzenegger.
But when Krajina fell into darkness
and when the world remained without hope
and when flowers remained without scent
and smiles of happiness froze
in the summer of '92,
the sun darkened by grief,
then the dogs of war began to bark
apprehensive uneasiness fell on a common folk.
Hell fire spoke out
innocent people died because of hate.
Krajina men were being persecuted by beasts,
led to death camps,
they found reasons, because of their religion,
to torture innocent people.

THE BOY WHO SAID NOTHING

Thus they came to our champion
wild beasts in human form
they deprived him of life on his doorstep
and threw accolades and medals on the fire.

But it is not possible to kill the glow in a heart.
Death isn't the end of a legend.
Krajina, Bosnia and the world are still being
Warmed by Fikro the champion – who smiles.

GRANDPA'S GULCH

In a deep gulch
where a clear stream runs
grandpa's mill rises
from trees and fernery
in a deep gulch.

There started the peaceful life
of my old grandpa,
there today, though he is gone,
all still reminds me of him
where he started his peaceful life.

Agile hands of the good old man
have arranged grooves carefully
and from wilderness have created
a captivating small paradise,
agile hands of the good old man.

Many people were admiring
how he deals with it
and also today – they are admiring
how he raised the small mill,
Many people were admiring.

And while quiet water is running
he puts some small fish
for Mirso and Meliha
to play in a stream,
while quiet water is running.

Other kids also come,
so real hubbub has been made
tweets of birds are echoing
and there is no end of happiness
when other kids come.

Many years have passed
my grandpa is around no more,
but the mill is still grinding,
because papa is protecting its beams
and many years have passed.

THE BOY WHO SAID NOTHING
(Part III)

The boy who said nothing
testified with silence:
about the end and the beginning
about the nonsense and the sense
about the day and the night
about the fear and the power
about the man and the no-man
about the life and the death
about the love and the hate
about the light and the fire
about the hope and the suffering
about the last person and the first person
about the dead person and the alive person.
and when he spoke out:
– A CHANT ECHOED –
A hymn to the man with his head held high
witness of truth for all times.